THREE FACES O

CASABLANCA, PARIS, CAIRO

Susan Ossman

DUKE UNIVERSITY PRESS

Durham & London

2002

© 2002 Duke University Press

All rights reserved

Printed in the United States of

America on acid-free paper ∞

Designed by Rebecca Giménez

Typeset in Adobe Minion by

Keystone Typesetting, Inc.

Library of Congress Cataloging-

in-Publication Data appear on the

last printed page of this book.

CONTENTS

The interviews, texts, and programs cited in this book were originally heard, read, or watched in Modern Standard, Classical, or Moroccan and Egyptian dialects of Arabic, or French. Although most of these have been translated into English, in some instances translation is so inadequate, or the word, whatever its language of origin, has become so widely used in all of these languages, that I was compelled to ask the reader to learn the term. Thus, for example, I use the feminine *parisienne* to distinguish from the English *Parisian* to reiterate the socially recognized difference between two figures that would otherwise bear the same name. A parisienne is a particular kind of woman, whereas a Parisian is an inhabitant of Paris. The Arabic *hijab*, indicating a variety of headcoverings, is similarly used liberally throughout the text. The root *hjb* indicates a sense of protection, but in common usage in Casablanca, Cairo, and Paris, the hijab (often translated as *veil*) has also become a marker of various versions of Muslim belief.

For transcriptions from Arabic, my first choice has been to adopt the versions currently used in texts, signs, or labels printed in Casablanca and Cairo. When several transcriptions appear in published works in different languages, I have chosen that closest to English usage except for names of people; in this case, I employ the transcription that the individuals in question chose in the context I evoke. Thus, for example, I write Céza Nabaraouy rather than Seza Nabaraouy, for this is how she herself signed articles in *L'Egyptienne*. I use English place-names when possible. I do not indicate emphatics. The ayn appears as "ʿ," "ġ" represents the ġapu, and "kh" indicates the sound similar to the "ch" in the German pronunciation of "Bach."

ACKNOWLEDGMENTS

This project took form from 1993 to 1996 while I was working in Rabat as the director of The Rabat center of the institut de recherche sur le Maghreb contemporain (IRMC). Further work in Cairo was made possible and pleasurable by Jean-Noël Ferrié, who kindly invited me to participate in a research program financed by the Agnelli Foundation at the Centre d'etude et de documentation économiques et juridiques. In Paris, a "Media and Society" grant from the Centre national de recherche scientifique allowed me to conduct the final phases of research. These funds allowed me to hire three research assistants, Fedwa Lamzal in Casablanca, Aïcha Chilalli in Cairo, and Małgorzata Domogała in Paris, who offered practical help and stimulating ideas on the project. I am grateful to them, and to Amazigh Kateb, who kindly allowed me to reprint his song "Ombre-elle" as well as checking my English translation.

I would especially like to thank Rabia Bekkar, Waddick Doyle, Yves Winkin, Yves and Cécile Gonzales-Quijano, Abderrahmane Lakhsassi, Catherine Lheureux, Kathleen Chevalier, Celeste Schenck, Souad Radi, Paul Rabinow, Todd Gitlin, Larbi Chouikha, Susan Miller, Susan Slyomovics and my parents, Edward and Camille Ossman, for their support throughout the research and writing process. Ken Wissoker's persistent encouragement was essential in getting me to finally write this piece, as were Mark Kuroczko's and Shana Cohen's perusals of initial versions of parts of it. James Faubion's and Deborah Kapchan's sensitive readings of the project and then of the manuscript taught me many things, some of which now appear in the pages to come. Katie Courtland's astute criticisms helped me to shape the manuscript's final form. Completion has involved many stories that perhaps only my son, Nathanaël Dorent, can tell. It has opened possibilities for moving into new worlds that only Mamoun Fandy might explain. For this, and for all that has given me the patience to reach this point, I am infinitely grateful.

Navigating the multiple worlds characteristic of our modern social landscapes is never easy. The ways we move among places and activities require making complex decisions about identity and personal integrity.
This book is about how people shape their looks and make up their faces
to move with grace through these many spaces of their lives. It focuses on
this process from the perspective of the now nearly universal institution
of the beauty salon. Salon techniques and conversations show us many
things about the diverse symmetries that different people or places set up
between social worlds that are increasingly similar worldwide. They make
us more attentive to emerging social differences and the need to develop
more precise ways of understanding processes of creation, change, and
exchange than those current in debates on globalization. We cannot, for
instance, observe local bodies dressing up in global clothes: to compre-
hend the powers that make up our faces requires a more dynamic sense
of place and a less unified sense of time than those implied by such
oppositions.

Perhaps due to their association with femininity and what is often
perceived as the superficiality of appearance, beauty salons have received
relatively little attention in the literature on modernity or modernization.
Yet, their very name echoes those of institutions that scholars as serious as
Jürgen Habermas have set at the center of theories of modernity and
explanations of democratization.[1] Coffee shops and cafés, literary and
artistic salons have been the subjects of many excellent articles and books
that have pointed out how these spaces are instrumental in forming sub-
jectivities in ways that have implications for the shape of the public
sphere. But salons, where people let down their hair or take off their

clothes, have not been a popular area of study, especially for those concerned with questions of public interest.[2] I myself began my own work in salons almost by chance. While I was living in Casablanca in the late 1980s, studying the connections of mass media to politics, I noticed that the number of salons was rapidly increasing.[3] By the early 1990s they seemed to be sprouting up in even small towns and villages in many parts of Morocco. I wrote a short article on a salon in my neighborhood in 1990, then decided to track the pictures I found there.[4] From Casablanca they led me not to some generalized global space but toward Cairo and Paris. My project became one of what I call "linked comparisons": I followed the pictures and people, styles and products I found in Casablanca to the places they came from. I explored these places in terms of the shared procedures and routines of the salon.[5]

The choice of Casablanca as the point of reference involved a deliberate decision to center my work in a place that might be seen as being on the outskirts of fashion. Casablanca is a modern city built mainly during the twentieth century. It has no pretensions to age-old cultural traditions except through those that migrants from Fez, Tetouan, Rome, or Marrakech have brought there. In Dar el baïda, the city called the white house, I talked with many people about beauty and where it comes from. In Casablanca I had my hair done, nails clipped and manicured. I listened as the city, like a look, was altered by the way that words slip from dialectal to literary Arabic, taking on yet other tints in mixes of French and Tamazight. I observed how pictures in salons changed in different neighborhoods, how versions of beauty and virtue put ideas of belonging to the test.

To develop comparisons involves setting up contrasts. The second step of the process must therefore set up some kind of initial links by following images, pictures, people, or ideas pertinent to the object of study as they move in and out of the initial site. From Casablanca, seen through its beauty salons, I moved out toward Paris and Cairo, drawn by magazines, songs, and conversations.[6] Cairo and Paris, unlike Casa, can boast of long histories as hubs of commerce, fashion, and scholarship. Their names promise urbanity and innovation, a continuous work to elaborate monuments of their own magnificence in stone, but also in lighter, more exportable materials such as film, fashion magazines, and television series. These centers have established their own styles. They, along with their nations, have come to speak single languages, and this gives us an impression of their unique consistency of culture. Alternative tongues might persist, but they have been clipped in ways unimaginable in Casablanca. In each city words of nationalism and cultural distinction focus our eyes on local color. But if we begin in Casablanca, we notice how beauties braid these in many and complex ways. We follow how beauties and ways of fashioning oneself are plaited together of strands of history and trade, exchange and exploitation joining Casablanca to Paris and to Cairo. To unravel the locks of beauty means not so much examining one by one each city's strands, but detailing the common knowledge and the turns of hand that twist the tresses to hold them together.

Projects of linking can help us to recognize alternatives to standard regions of expertise and study.[7] The wholes of the Arab world, of the francophone zone, are solidified in statistics, academic training, and daily talk. But do these divisions help us understand how people live? Their life choices and chances? The lines I drew between the cities of this study progressively served to redraw how I saw varieties of faces emerge from my research. As I moved toward Cairo and Paris to explore salons in those cities, I found that my field could not be depicted on a map or as a series of photographic clichés. Nor could the faces I described adopt the names given to them by hairdressers and clients, radio talk show hosts, or fashion magazines. I came to focus less on specific looks than particular manners of formulating judgments about them; less on what might be seen as local cultures of beauty than the kinds of salons that existed in each city, if in different proportions. Moving through the initial sites of ethnography came to require a notation more akin to choreography than to marking the timeless plane of a chart or map.[8]

Any project of linked comparisons involves several moments that are related to the time of ethnography and the diversity of ways we can come to know its various sites. To move through connections requires concentrating more on some of these than others. It often implies returning in circular moves or an endless *pas de bourré* to the same spaces rather than attempting to extend the purview of one's inquiry. This kind of two-step contrasts with the oft critiqued two-step of here to there, field to home, that even many critical approaches to anthropology involve. The ethnography I advocate does not aim to paint a total picture of a culture or a place. It does seek to give us a chance to recognize practices and emotions, ideas and powers that generalizing categories of culture, identity, and class often obscure. It involves adopting an incisive manner of engaging with couplings of places and ideas and giving full attention to the nature of links and the kinds of complicity and shared experience they involve. By working through what holds people together we come to see the mirrors that modernity holds up to our faces not as cracked or fragmented but as composed of dense crystalline glass that refracts our features in patterned rainbows. We begin to notice that light itself is an essential element in contemporary conceptions of self and society.

We often hear that all places in the world are becoming ever more alike. The way we live seems ever less tied to a specific place.[1] The way we look appears unrelated to where we live. Even family resemblances seem to be put to the test by new ways of coloring hair and eyes, submitting bodies to regimes of exercise and diet or reshaping them through plastic surgery. In Casablanca, Fatima Zohra explains, "Everyone is always asking me if I'm Italian. I've never even been to Italy—but why not? I guess it's just my style, the kind of face I have, my short hair. I'm just that general Mediterranean kind of look." Iman, from Cairo, says, "Take me, for example. Everybody always asks me the same question: Are you really Egyptian? This shows that we have gotten past this difference between nationalities. Your style is what counts."[2] In Paris, Anne tells Małgorzata, "I like to play around with different styles, but usually I like exotic ones. Like I use *khol* instead of eyeliner all of the time. I like those Indian prints too—I create a sort of distinctive style from these things—not at all the typical BCBG French image."[3]

The mass media and, increasingly, extensive nets of product distribution are often accused of promoting a particular image of beauty throughout the world. Yet, even in the way people talk about their own looks or the seasons of fashion, distinctions that draw on ideas of national or ethnic or social differences persist. Fashion might promote a specific kind of modern body, but its progressions through time thrive not on sameness but on claims to seasons marked by different looks.[4] Fatima Zohra, Iman, and Anne see themselves as disengaged from any specific national or local look. And yet they employ names of nations or regions to indicate how their faces are not simply reflections of the place where they were

World Times for Sale. The window display of this chic Casablanca men's boutique echoes the everywhere and nowhere dreams some women evoke in talking about beauty. "The time of sales" is shown on clocks from six time zones surrounding the flags of Morocco, Great Britain, and Egypt. Versace, Nogaret, Factice, and other brand names are grouped around the world times. Photograph, Susan Ossman.

born. In interviews with women and men in the three linked cities of this study, I was told that people had looks described as Chinese or Indian, and others adopted styles related to a musical genre or a specific actress or a brand name. In the urban milieux that I moved through, the work of fashion did seem to have disengaged references to the land to the extent that they became equivalent to references to labels or styles inspired by individuals.[5] One could, it seemed, look "Chinese" or "classically Chanel" while feeling perfectly Moroccan. One might even complain, like Kalthoum, that while traveling in Europe one was stigmatized for looking "North African," while insisting that her face was a true portrait of Brazilian beauty.

Much attention has been given to how images of the Orient have developed in Europe over the centuries. The groundbreaking work of Edward Said, reflexive approaches to anthropology, and a sensitivity to the voices and experiences of "others" have made us aware of the ways that women particularly have been represented in scholarship and art and Western media.[6] However, such work rarely takes into account that the very norms of representation and categorization on which stereotypes of the Orient depend are not confined to the West. Indeed, studying the history of modern forms of representation and power makes the very location of the West problematic. In moving out of the two-step approach that contrasts some West to a series of Others, I encountered pictures and practices that might be somewhat unsettling to those who see the study of representation as mainly a process of dismantling pernicious stereotypes. Ways of talking about fashions were not always so very different in the three sites of my study. Neither are the media that circulate them or the salons where they are given body. The orientalist repertoire is elaborated today in Casablanca and Cairo as well as in Paris.

NEW ORIENTALS

In the course of moving from Casablanca to Paris and Cairo I often met new oriental beauties. They appeared to me in many forms; only a few are located in the Louvre or in coffee-table books for sale at Christmas. Many of the photographs and films I encountered worked with classic images of voluptuous splendor, of supine ladies and languorous time spent in Turkish baths. Some of the people I met said that they sought a "touch" of this exoticism in their manner of styling their own looks; others said that they liked to play on orientalism's conventions in order to mock or alter prevalent ideas of what "exotic" beauty might be. To take a look at some of the features of "oriental" faces today, consider three series of photographs. The first appeared in the magazine *Pose*, published in Cyprus but oriented to a well-to-do Egyptian readership.[7] The second was published in *Femmes du Maroc*, a magazine that, although expensive by Casablancan standards, always sells out almost immediately after being printed.[8] The last series of pictures appeared in the magazine of the French Buiguine, a beauty franchise with a salon in Casablanca and in cities around the world. Unlike the other publications, it is distributed without charge to anyone who visits the salon.

Each of these images relies on themes of the Orient as described in the now voluminous literature on oriental art. Like orientalist paintings, they mix elements of various origins and rework traditional designs. But this pictorial rendering of exoticism is apparently insufficient to "explain" the stories at work here. In *Pose*, the story of *A Thousand and One Nights* is evoked at the beginning of the fashion section (Figure 5). Remember that,

Mix-and-match fashion
in *Pose*.

to stay alive, Sheherazade must entrance the sultan with a new story each
night. Apparently, each night and each story requires a new outfit. The
photograph I have chosen shows her reclining, wearing a turban, a midriff
top, trousers, and large earrings and jewelry. She is shown against a
Bedouin-style tapestry—is she in a tent? Why does she have a small *tilka*-
like dot on her forehead? These unanswered questions alert me to how
fashion produces distinct styles through hybridization and collage. They
lead me to think of the outrageous outfits of the actress and singer Nelly,
who appears regularly on Egyptian television. In her comic sketches she
sets up a saucy version of a mix-and-match fashion heaven to music. Her
short musical acts, inspired by music hall performances, are short, regularly televised, and ever-changing. Sitting at a friend's house in Cairo,
beside the television, I described one of her programs in my notes:

> *Nelly dances across the screen. She embodies a series of the possible styles a*
> *body might incorporate. In a series of scenes she is shown moving among*
> *the roles of belly dancer, punk rocker, femme fatale, and Mexican hat*
> *dancer. There is no interval. She just appears with different faces. Nelly is*

not putting on a show for people she knows—her act includes lavish backgrounds, music, and indeed, quite a lot of burlesque poking fun at the various "kinds" of people she depicts. Her performance of these types is broadcast throughout Egypt—even to people who have never consulted a tourist brochure on Mexico or attended a punk rock concert. What seems to "situate" the "real" Nelly (or the actress-Nelly) is not so much any single style as the "way she performs" any one of the scenes.

Nelly is certainly not a model of chic. In fact, people I spoke with in Cairo told me she is often called common, vulgar, and uncouth. But for this very reason it is interesting to contrast her laughing version of the belly dance with the more serious and sensuous orientalizing themes of high fashion. Nelly's music and dancing allow her to parody the themes she illustrates. Her face is brilliant with gobs of bright makeup; she smiles broadly at her audience and occasionally winks. The kinds of figures she produces are easy to read. Her performance can add new styles at any point. Its seriality and playfulness contrasts with the production of the hybridized picture of Sheherazade in *Pose*. Each sets up a distinct relationship with orientalist or other stereotypes. Can this be easily explained in terms of audience expectations or genre? Can different relationships to style be interpreted according to contrasts of mass media and popular audiences to elites and exclusive publications?

Moving to the photos of Fatine from the Moroccan magazine we can pursue these questions. Here we find an image that explicitly plays on excluding certain people and congratulating others on their cultural capital. We are given words in English to tell us something about the picture (Figures 6, 7). "My tailor is rich" becomes "My tailor is beautiful." The language plays on the phrases used to teach English in old-fashioned French textbooks. The style of caftan that is shown approximates those that almost all Moroccan women own and wear to weddings and other festive occasions. But the word play implies knowledge of French style, elite education. The clothes that the tailor has designed for Fatine to wear on the other pages of the "story" render a world of wealth behind the beauty that few women can hope to know. The oriental image is only one moment in a series of poses, showing expensive evening or afternoon attire. These alternating poses and outfits, orientalizing or not, might be seen to attract only those women who can actually purchase such costly

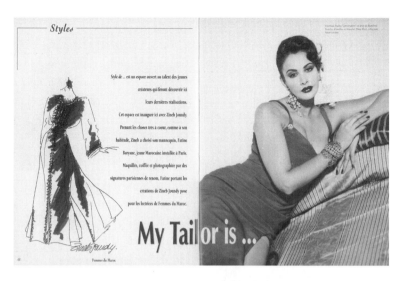

Style de ... est un espace ouvert au talent des jeunes
créateurs qui feront découvrir ici
leurs dernières réalisations.
Cet espace est inauguré ici avec Zineb Joundy.
Prenant les choses très à coeur, comme à son
habitude, Zineb a choisi son mannequin, Fatine
Baryane, jeune Marocaine installée à Paris.
Maquillée, coiffée et photographiée par des
signatures parisiennes de renom, Fatine portant les
créations de Zineb Joundy pose
pour les lectrices de Femmes du Maroc.

My Tailor is ...

...beautiful

Fatine in *Femmes du Maroc*.

clothes. However, *Femmes du Maroc* is an extremely popular magazine, and we must assume that it is read by women who may not have much money, but who understand the point about the rich tailor. For some, it might be obvious, for others, a riddle they feel smart to figure out, but there is something here that sets up a game on cross-national identities, traditions, and snobbishness that many women in Casablanca are ready to play, regardless of their financial situation. Magazines seem to play an important role in this game. When Fedwa asked Halima, who owns a beauty salon in a lower-middle-class district, where Moroccan women learned about style in order to choose their own looks, Halima said that they got their ideas "from magazines—but not everyone buys them. Even to get the information you have to have the means. There are magazines that do a lot of publicity for products, but if the woman doesn't have the means to buy [the magazines], she is uninformed." She went on to explain that women desperately needed such information; in fact, she stated, "I think that we should raise salaries so that women can allow themselves to [buy these magazines and be informed]." Access to Fatine's version of oriental splendor, according to Halima, should not be restricted to the wealthy! As we will see in later chapters, beauty salons themselves often play an important role in assuring that all women have access to images of style. In Casablanca as in Paris, franchises like Buiguine produce their own magazines that they distribute free of charge.

If the photographs from Morocco echo French textbooks, those I followed in *Buiguine* expect familiarity with poetry. Baudelaire's "L'invitation au voyage" accompanies a series of "tales" about women, and women meeting men (Figure 8). Here, the men and women have long hair and henna their hands.[9] Both sexes recline, like Fatine, but unlike in the Moroccan photograph, the clothes and the jewels are unwearable. Indeed, one could say that the point is to show off the hair of the models, because this is, after all, Buigine's business. For each poetic phrase, a new image emerges, and the authoritative voice of the poet is mimicked in its reprinting, much as the English "Beauty" seals our judgment of the Moroccan model. But who invites whom on a trip in this unisex world of randomly distributed signs of masculinity and femininity? As Sheherazade leads us through the Cairene pictures, for *Buiguine* hair is no longer braided by the gaze of male poets but given a life of its own. This life of hair unleashed is yet tangled in an array of elements drawn from a vague store of primitivist and orientalist lore.

Reading Baudelaire, like knowing phrases from French and English textbooks, might very well offer new possibilities for becoming the object of poets' desires. Changing one's attire to fit the story one tells is a fact of everyday life. The exoticism of images of oases and distant continents can be reveled in and in a sense "exploited," not only for commercial or imperialist ends, but also by those women who wish to engage with

Baudelaire's voyage in *Buiguine.*

modern spaces and who might be seen as stereotyped by them. For indeed, in the process of our dreaming about the lightness of being that is implied in the modern body, these exotic images become only partially operational as indicators of distinctions between representation and lived experience.

Those who feel they are able to engage with them participate in worlds of light that are explicitly distinguished from the "traditions" they seem to incorporate. Meanwhile, those whose bodies bear the indelible marks that these images play with are cast into the shadows. Women whose tattoos serve as approximate models for the tattooed cheeks of the Buiguine advertisement often seek only to hide or remove these marks that they had inscribed to be "like others" and that mark them as forever belonging to a certain group. Khadija Bnoussina describes how Moroccan women who have tattoos "feel disgusted [with themselves] when they look in the mirror." They regret what in their villages was considered beautiful. One woman says, "I hide my hands in the sleeves of my robe [*taksita*] when I find myself in a group of women" and "It's too bad I can't hide my whole face when I go out."[10]

To be able to make reference to these tattoos (*weshma*) not as a kind of branding that identifies one as belonging to a group or a particular man, but as a playful choice means showing a certain ignorance of the weight of such marks of possession. It implies a forgetfulness with regard to such inscriptions while reworking them in terms of exoticism and nostalgia. The space of the village, the tribe, or even the family seems irrelevant to the fashionable world of the new oriental. From Casablanca to Cairo and Paris, spaces of fashion and beauty rely on abstracting elements from their context. Iman owns a beauty salon in the Mohendissine section of Cairo. She says, "I really don't see the difference between the Egyptian and the European styles today. Because the Egyptian fashion tends to become Westernized and Egyptians select a cut that goes with their clothes. In general, we're all moving toward greater simplicity . . . there is no longer any specifically Egyptian style. Before, sure, you know I got my diploma as a hairdresser thanks to a 'pharaonic re-creation' that I found while doing research on an Egyptian hairstyle, the 'Nefertiti' cut."

To what extent does her rendition of Nefertiti differ from one that might be developed in Paris or Casablanca? Listen to Rita and Fedwa talk about fashion in Casablanca:

FEDWA: What do you think of Jeal Paul Gaultier?
RITA: I think he's an impostor. He goes to a country, and he takes something—he brings it back and sticks it in a collection. He has helped to democratize French fashion—he did collections that middle-range budgets can afford. He has three collections: pret à porter de luxe, another for young people, and a last, which is new, a unisex one. I bought some things of his in Paris at 500 francs. And even my husband got some things in the discount stores.

Gaultier is not really a creator because he takes his models in other countries. Last time he went to Turkey, he saw that the women swim in these sort of dress-bathing suits and he copied the models and put his name on it. Once he went to China. Last winter, he copied the traditional Jewish costumes.

Rita is critical of the way the designer gives new meanings to ways of dressing, but at the same time, she insists on the importance of "choosing" one's appearance. She says, "In my opinion, in our way of dressing and being we have never imitated anyone, and especially not the Europeans. The things that we can find on the market today belong to everyone and everyone can wear them. Look at the Europeans too—they imitate us—they like to wear the *jellaba* and the *guendora*. When they come to Morocco you see them painting henna on their hands."

So, in the midst of claiming choice, Rita seems also to seek to retain a special connection to specifically "Moroccan" elements that fashion uses. She follows the collectable procedures of modern fashion, yet at the same time labels Gaultier a copier. She resents that he sets his signature on things he "discovers" in the manner of naturalists who attach their own name to living creatures. Still, she buys his fashions, if at a discount shop, and she gets clothes for her husband there as well. This is not, she insists, because she copies Europeans but because she has developed her own pathway through the lures of fashion's claims, developing her own style, adapted to her self, her budget, and the fact that she is able to travel to Paris. Like Nejiba, she seems to think that not "copying" bears some relationship to the quest for personal authenticity:

NEJIBA: Fashion . . . you have to follow fashion but by personalizing it. I think that fashion runs along at a breakneck pace—we end up being manipulated. When we see magazines and stores, we feel obliged to look—it's a visual aggression set up from behind the shop window. Fashion is a good thing, because it allows people to create themselves, to be imaginative and a little crazy. I think that the designers take things left and right and they want to make us believe they're fashion-able. Today, for example, the sixties fashions have come back.

FEDWA: Does that mean there's no more creation and we are just coming back to old things?

NEJIBA: Concerning the fashion shows, I think that it's necessary to make distinctions. There are prestigious shows like those of Yves Saint Laurent or Christian Dior that have to keep up a certain image. Their collections have to be good to sell. Then there are the designers who are more marginal and *have understood the spirit of the end of this century*. For example, Jean Colonna in France, several Belgian designers like Anne de Melèstere, also some Japanese designers. Their clothes are impossible to wear because they have understood the crisis—and they've expressed it. The fabrics are not just silk or mousseline, *but also discarded material*. (Emphasis added)

Fashion sets times in motion that promise progress but confuse linear history. It relies on unwearable remainders and forays into history or exotic places to find meaning. Perhaps, more than anything, it makes us think about how the process of "en-lightening" practices and bodies that makes them part of fashion requires a certain sense of revulsion at the sight of the heaviness and stasis that we conceive as giving birth to those very forms. These become associated with anonymity, lack of personality and definition. For some people in Cairo, for instance, the hijab remains a sign of such heaviness. In a Cairo fashion show in 1996, a particular use of Walt Disney's *Snow White* provides a distinct way of telling the tale of women's unveiling:

> *In Cairo the theater is packed to see this fashion show. A series of designers are shown, each accompanied by a specific style of music and decor. One uses a "sporty" theme: we see models play volleyball. They play for a while, then walk up and down the ramps in couples, hand in hand or arms around each other. Another designer presents a series of ball gowns. In the darkened theater, parts of Walt Disney's* Snow White *are projected. We see the Wicked Stepmother watching Snow White and having the mirror tell her that she, not the queen, is the fairest of all. A Snow White model enters and shows one dress. Then, the evil stepmother arrives to give her an apple. She bites the apple and as she falls to the ground, there is no sign of the seven dwarves, but ten slim models clad in black-and-white dresses do arrive on the scene. Their faces are covered with black veils. They walk up and down the catwalk to show the dresses. Then, the handsome prince arrives. He picks up Snow White, reviving her with his touch. The ten black-and-white figures remove their veils and take a second walk down the aisle. Their faces are lit by cheerful, bright lights. In the midst, then, of a call to equally unveiled bodies lurk a series of beauty contests and poisonings, princesses and kings. Princesses suffer the eye of jealousy, but can be revived by handsome young men. The touch of the prince not only revives the beauty but unveils the distinct faces of uniform figures.*

Discarding veils, excess hair, and clothing, the process of en-lightening seems necessary to the development of fashion and the realization of the ideal of the anywhere body. But at the same time, an urge to establish a repertory of old, enclosed bodies stuck in place seems to be necessary to modern fashions. Reactions to these "remainders" sometimes provoke violent contrasts of one body to another: the open to the enclosed, light to heavy. But it can also encourage people to rework forms in new ways. If you walk through the noisy streets of Cairo or Casablanca or Paris today you will see women wearing all kinds of veils. Some are colored, others dark; some are heavy and others are lacy and sit perched, mantilla-like, atop carefully calculated curls. The hijab is one sign of belonging to the Muslim community, but this does not imply that this covering encloses a single world for women. Nor should we too readily associate removing hair or garments with liberation.

WHAT PULLS US DOWN

From my notes:

> About fifteen summers ago I was working in a Parisian office. Each day I joined thousands of other secretaries, cadres, or construction workers in the boredom of the sleepy ride to work in the train, on the metro. . . . Too crowded to read without shoving the newspaper into a neighbor's face, we watch the advertisements rush past. Electric appliances at BHV, sales at the Galleries Lafayette, and now, a young woman in a bikini offering not only static colors and forms, but even a promise over time: "Tomorrow I'll take off the top." If we can wait until then, she'll take off the top to reveal what little remains hidden by her bikini.
>
> At the office we wonder, What is this new kind of advertising? What is she selling anyway? Whatever it was, it was available to everyone. How far could this go? With subsequent days came the realization that she was actually going to do it—and at our convenience. She disrobed to the rhythm of our work schedules, and those who had long rides home on the metro got a peek at her several times in various stations. For a few days she was there—outliving by many hours the usual publicity that one is expected to comprehend through some kind of "gestalt" immediacy. One had time to contemplate and remember her, and this made her seduction so astonishingly regular, so accommodating. . . . The approach was so comfortable for casual conversation that we knew from the start that she was ours.
>
> Occasional voices cried out against our curiosity in the name of public virtue. But everyone "knew" that these were still some premodern vestiges in France! These were the same "types" who sung out for Catholic schools

and against the monokini and the miniskirt. Certainly no one we might care to speak with could hold such an opinion. The generation under thirty in an aging nation (this WE) had little new to say about the values of openness and sexiness associated with the clear marketing intelligence of French society demonstrated in this ad. While the kinds of political or ecological views expressed during 1968 had come to be associated with the babas [hippies] by the mid 1980s (although the new successes of the Greens and the fashion of having "seventies parties" by the end of the eighties have restated this judgment), appeals to sexual liberation and openness as truth also associated with changes during the 1960s have also taken root. Associated with a rejection of "traditionalist" views, the extent to which many of these apparent "liberations" continue long traditions of the placement and representation of women's (and increasingly men's) bodies is rarely made apparent.

Anyone would appreciate the skill by which the advertisers had caught on to the public imagination so regularly. A predictable striptease seemed so wonderfully adapted to a society that would soon simulate sensuality by minitel.[11] No mess, no fuss, no bother. And yet, perhaps because of the kind of mistrust for this ease, I found myself somehow uncomfortable with this promise of revelation. It reminded me of the enormous human barbecues on beaches on the Riviera, where I displayed my own prudishness by donning a one-piece maillot to the dismay of window shoppers (lèche vitrine, they say in French: window lickers). So cool, so predictable, so dull. The striptease act failed to attract more than an admiring recognition of the advertiser's skill. "Tomorrow I'll take off the bottom."

Like the girls in the Cairene fashion show unveiling, the process of uncovering ankles, then knees, then stomachs and breasts is often described in Paris as a positive move toward the liberation of women against heavy-handed patriarchy. So you see, Sylvie explained to me, it's all just for fun. A gimmick. But how was it before? I wondered. Everyone talks about things *before* the lightening began. Some people said the heavy clothes had to do with the Catholic Church. Many others simply attributed the lightening to a discarding of the heavy garments of the past. How were things "back then," I asked. Sylvie, a parisienne in her late thirties, explained that religion wasn't everything—ideas of beauty and hygiene were also a part of the change. "Let me tell you about when I took my new stepchildren to visit my grandmother Martin," she said. "We drove to the village were they live." It's a lovely region, isn't it, the Touraine?, I inquired. "Well, lovely, yes . . . but my mother sure was right to get out of there, to come to Paris!"

Anyway, we pull up here, and we have to really pound on the door since they [the grandparents] are pretty deaf. Once they let us in, it was kind of dark in there. You enter and you see everything they ever owned— it's all piled on top of each other. They never move things or get rid of them. And my grandmother calls out to Marie, my stepdaughter, "Come here, my dearie, get closer." Little Marie draws a little closer. "Bon jour grandmère," she says. Come closer, says Grandma, but Marie cannot do it. She begins to smell the acrid odor of the place, to notice how Grandma doesn't smell like most people, but that an even stronger odor emanates from Grandpa. Grandma wears her untidy hair in a bun. (Grandma has never been to the hairdresser.) Her grin is not toothless but it is very crooked. When she talks her teeth make a funny sound reminiscent of a cement mixer. Grandma did go to a dentist once, when she was eighteen, and she's used the same dentures ever since. Grandma believes that washing is bad for you, so she takes a bath only once a year, and little Marie looks away to avoid looking at the rings of dirt on her neck. She has never experienced anything like this, even though her mother has taken her traveling all over the world.

"Could this be France?" Sylvie asks. It is, she seems to be saying, and I remember her story when Christine explains how most of her own family is "still on the farm. They are nice people, but as a teenager in the late 1960s, the first time I went to their farm in the Southwest, I just couldn't believe it. They work in the fields all day, and only have one change of clothes. They hardly ever wash—just a little wipe of a washcloth over their cheeks and that's it. Like something out of another age and it's still going on."

Christine's grandfather was the first one in their family to move to the city, to attend high school and earn an engineering degree. In Sylvie's case, it was her mother who moved to the city. In these and many other instances, this move is expressed as one from stasis toward the movement of history. Places of timelessness still exist, it seems, but no one would want to actually inhabit them. Sylvie explains that her mother got a job in Paris at the post office. She attributes her own academic and professional success to the drive of her mother, who pushed her daughter to "get ahead" in her studies and to travel abroad. Something of the mother's ambition for herself and her daughter seems to spring from that initial move away from the village, that flight from the heavy spell of unmoving that is less "tradition" than a delimited space of stasis. Sylvie repeats, "My mother couldn't wait to get out of that village, out of that hole!" in a way that brings to mind a geography of stillness evoked by Abdellfetah Kilito in his recollections of going to the *hammam* with his mother in Morocco: "I myself have personally kept no memories of my first years at the hammam, in any case, no memory of young, vigorous feminine bodies. The only image that I conserve (memory? fantasy?) is that of three women of a certain age, their flabby nudity. They are standing up at the entrance of the first room; they are probably chatting, because they form a circle and look at each other. One of them is casually holding a wooden bucket, without a bottom. *They don't move from their place, they are fixed in this posture for eternity.*"[12] (italics added)

Heaviness, as expressed by such "remaining" bodies, is a condition that touches time, mobility, and strength of purpose as much as it reflects a given build. Heavy, inert bodies are often round, but even thin people can be fixed, stuck in unmoving, timeless spaces. Country and city often come to represent the contrast of heavy and dark to the light and lithe. In Casablanca, even bread comes in two varieties: the long thin white baguette is called a *parisienne*, and the robust round whole wheat bread is *beldi* (country, local). Presented as reminders and remainders of the past, heaviness is also associated both with domestic space and confinement. The "freedom" that allows one to move about the apparently universal, unfolded map of the body is indeed a world of lightness—not only of symbolic, but also of bodily lightness. Of being slim. Fedwa asks Narjat what she thinks of heavy women:

> I feel sorry for the poor women because my ideal is to be slim—just even to be able to wear jeans comfortably—any clothes, for that matter. A slim woman is lighter and more active, more expansive. She's a modern woman and she can do anything. Before, the traditional woman was fat. She too could be expansive but she was so permeated by her traditional milieu. Today a woman here can be like European

women: she can get rid of all of that religion, and tradition. She tries to live her life to the max—just like a man does. So women do a lot of things they didn't do before: go out freely at night, drink at a café, even smoke cigarettes or drink alcohol. I don't smoke or drink myself, but it's not because of religion—for me, these are unhealthy and dirty habits.

Amira Sonbol has traced the development of the lightening theme through Egyptian and Arabic literature. She describes how Bayram al-Tunsi contrasts images of "Western," foreign-looking "ladies" (*hawanim,* or should we say *belles dames?*) to the women in the traditional areas of the city in developing his stories about a naïve sheikh on his first visit to the city. She writes that he was excited by their "haunches of pyramidical size worthy of being followed, beautiful legs with flashy anklets [*khulkhal*], large heavy bosom, towering height, taut ripe body, small waist, fair color and a coy and sassy walk."[13] Hakim, a teacher in Cairo, says, "In the past the man looked for women with large hips. The woman was much more passive. Now it's the opposite—it's the man who wants to be passive. Beauty has changed as a result. Now men want a thin woman so that she can move about. A fat woman, a man thinks, will not be active. This is why we think slimness is beautiful now."

Lightness tends to be associated with equality between men and women. For many people, it is equated with the possibility of going out and leaving the home. "It used to be," says an old Casablancan woman originally from Sefrou, "those women were very afraid of the man. Today it's the man who is afraid of the woman." The man stays at home and "the women wander about the streets." Heaviness seems easily held in place, accomplished by using corsets, girdles, or encompassing architecture. The weighty figures of stability, nation, or religion are often presented as the backgrounds against which the movements of the modern lady take place. Her movements are measured with respect to pictures of remainders. The remainder may be represented as an aging woman, a French *mémé* (grandma), or the woman who "lets herself go" after getting married and having children. She may take the guise of a poor, illiterate woman (*meskeena*). But whatever picture is proposed, the point is to make us see that the en-lightened women are on the move.

To the extent that the ideal en-lightened body is one that is without qualities, possessing nothing in particular, attempts to address it as belonging to any group or tradition seem impossible. It inhabits no landscape or culture. This body is elusive because it proposes a politics of lack of content based on ideals that do have a history. But this history is a narrative of forgetfulness. From it, body and face seem to emerge as a smooth and flawless plaster of paris. This ground, like the white face of Snow White, is composed so as to allow the artist to paint on it with the subtlest colors. This ideal empty face belongs to someone who is neither rich nor poor. We know nothing of its education or family history. This body is about forgetting, loss, and transparency. The rock group Louise Attaque recently composed a hymn to this woman, the contemporary parisienne:

> Léa elle est parisienne, elle est pas presentable elle est pas jolie elle est pas moche non plus elle est pas a gauche elle est pas a droite elle est pas maladroite non plus elle est pas arrivee elle est pas terroriste elle est pas anti-terroriste elle est pas integriste elle est pas seule seule sur terre elle pas commode elle est pas comme Aude elle est pas froide elle est pas chaude pour une nuit realiste elle est pas crediteur elle est pas mechante mais qu'est ce qu'elle est chiante.

> Léa is parisienne, she isn't well groomed, she isn't pretty but she's not ugly either, she isn't on the left, she isn't on the right, she isn't clumsy either, she's not made it, she isn't a terrorist or an antiterrorist, she isn't an integrist: she isn't alone in the world, she isn't easy to get along with, she isn't like Aude, she isn't cold, she's not hot either, she's pragmatic in bed, she doesn't take loans, she isn't mean but boy is she a pain in the ass . . . she's parisienne, she's parisienne.[14]

Léa seems to share only a name with the elegant, desirable parisienne one might associate with the capital of fashion. Stripped of any glamour, bereft of any strong desire, Léa is too cool to truly be anything but "a pain in the ass." Such an image seems to require inspiration from outside of itself to have any appeal, indeed, to have any meaning whatsoever. Léa reminds me of the women Susan Bordo describes in her study of eating disorders in the United States. Bordo writes that in these pathologies, "loss of mobility, loss of voice, inability to leave the home, feeding others while starving oneself, taking up space, and whittling down the space one's body takes up—all have symbolic meaning, all have political meaning under the varying rules governing the historical construction of gender."[15] Like Léa, these women seem not to want to play the game of style. But the only way they appear to be able to do this is by adopting a politics of disappearance: becoming thin or nondescript seems the only way to both satisfy the dominant code and at the same time fail to fulfill what it purports to offer. Such approaches could be said to provide a parody of the sober, understated aesthetic of classicism in its battle against the baroque, which Philippe Perrot aptly describes: "We know the extent to which the baroque, in its arrogant affirmation of the values denounced by Protestantism—exaltation, exuberance, prodigality, extravagance, illusion—was largely repressed in favor of the order, the concision, and the measure of 'French taste.' Its reserved forms, mastered, aligned, simplified even to severe eloquence: horizontal landscape, rectilinear, geometric, rays from the center. This classicism triumphed, of course, by means of a political will to render everything readable. To render monarchical authority against the fraught turbulence of the baroque implies the restoration and respect of the 'rules of art' alongside rules of etiquette." It is "an affair of state" to hold one's body, to restrain its *bouillonnement* (boiling, seething). To discipline passions, they need to be set in a context of reason and "honesty."[16] Understanding this move toward transparency requires us to consider classicism as an expression of some of the dilemmas of democracy. For in this situation, the severity of legible lines can publicize its triumph only if it is repeatedly contrasted to the undisciplined and indecipherable. Once the flesh has been questioned, described, analyzed, and told, what remainder can offer a foil for the continuing triumph of the classic and its conversation, which has come to include all equally? The body itself seems to disappear, as linguistic oppositions become the primary focus of conversations. Léa cannot draw attention to what she has. Indeed, she *has* little that we can see. What she can do is to play on elements associated with the past or distint places as a way of valorizing the "freedom" of her own lithe looks.

En-lightenment entails the production of light images of the heavy. Once abstracted in this way, they can be put to many uses. What were remainders can themselves be lightened to act not simply as backgrounds but as ways of shading or coloring what might risk becoming too evenly ordered bodies, lightening the heaviness of hips in the process. Léa might adopt a veil as a prop, to suggest that she requires intense surveillance and decipherment to penetrate the spaces designed to enclose and confine the fleshy profligacy of baroque sensibility. She might draw on places presented as beyond the bounds of conversation in her quest to keep herself in motion. Excess and the need to keep it in check, as exemplified in references to heaviness, of hair or body, express a desire to keep the movement between the background and oneself as figure in motion. Sonbol notes that in twentieth-century Egypt, "For bourgeois writers such as 'Abdal-Qudus elegance and intelligence were very important ideals for a woman: being 'chic' was a sign of belonging to westernized classes and acquiring Western tastes. Smoking cigarettes, wearing high heels, having one's hair dressed at a beauty salon, manicuring one's fingernails and affecting a cultured speech were all superimposed on the traditional picture of an exciting, coy woman."[17] Sonbol's attention to how apparent contradictions are particularly powerful through superimposition takes on a special importance in a context where anywhere bodies like Léa's abound. For such approaches might have the effect of enforcing a coherence between model and imitation, image and a single-sided self. But they can also lead to the kind of multiplication of pictures of selves we see in portraits of heads of state, actors, or Nelly's TV performance. Modernity is not always expressed through the strictest French classicism. What Perrot calls the "exaltation, exuberance, prodigality, extravagance, illusion" of the baroque can also be reworked as modern by processes of multiplication, reproduction, and superimposition, as can those that would enforce a politics of legibility.[18] Exploring the diversity of politics involved in these different aesthetics brings up a host of questions about power, sight, and self.

STEPPING LIGHTLY

A short walk through the city might help us to pursue the ways legibility might be formed, but also overwhelmed. Imagine you live in Casablanca. You are a thirty-something professional woman. You enter a comfortable but reasonably priced beauty salon where Leila greets you and asks you to have a seat. As you wait, you pick up a copy of *Marie Claire*. You don't spend the money to buy it yourself, so you like to look at it here. As you flip through its pages it sets you on an imaginary road strewn with Cartier watches and littered with bottles to color your lips, shape your body, and curl your hair. There are several ways to move through this maze of things, words, and faces, but the surest seems to be to look for what you take to be a Parisian signpost. You might trust a name you know to guide you. You need a name you can feel at home with. You find it. A seemingly endless ribbon in black and white marked with the letters C-H-A-N-E-L leads you through the magazine. You begin to read, but then Leila calls you over to get your hair washed and decide on how to do your hair. As she trims your bangs and chats with you, you hum the love song that Samira Saïd is singing on the radio. Saïd is Moroccan but sings Egyptian style—just like you are Casablancan but wear a Chanel-inspired bob like Parisiennes of the 1920s. As you leave the salon and step out onto the sidewalk, you notice the sideways movement of your hips that the tune has made you do, rather like you'd been dancing. Your hair is dressed, neat, crisp enough to let you walk or even dance without being messed up.

You hum Saïd's love song as you approach the limit that French architects set up to trace the difference between the new and old cities. Suddenly, up ahead, just before the point on the horizon where the two parts of the city meet, the largest billboard you have ever seen interrupts the progression of your Cairene fantasy. Claudia Schiffer tells you you're "worth it." Traffic slows as drivers stare out of their cars at her. You don't know what you're worth, but it seems that L'Oreal can tell you. Claudia's gaze makes you wonder if you are indeed worth anything. Her pose seems to both incorporate and provoke the intelligence of man's eye. Her image fills the air like a perfume sample from *Marie Claire*.

Claudia is not French, but labeling her L'Oreal confuses the crisp version of Paris your own hair took on under Leila's touch. If Claudia is not from Paris, it is Paris that has set her atop the city. Her hair is painted. Her eyes too blue. L'Oreal can be purchased at any supermarket. Your hand moves to check your hair. One version of Paris confronts another as you sense how tenuous your own relationship to the CC label on your purse becomes. You begin to notice that though your pastel suit protects you from the crowd, it does so at the price of freedom of motion. Claudia's hair flows down in all directions. Its lack of form seems to mock your own version of chic refinement. Her curls conjure up cool blondeness without excluding the possibility that she is not as very cold as she looks. Bleaching and coloring hair fails to do away with our knowledge of the process that has made it. The new hair does not eliminate that other, darker, background hair that we can never see.

L'Oreal has always made hair history. It was the first company to bring reliable hair coloring to a mass market.[19] With it, you can be even more blonde than someone who is born with light hair. Indeed, a natural blonde would be unable to include two layers of hair in her self-presentation. By becoming blonde, on the other hand, you can display the change you are worth making. L'Oreal allows you to show this while at the same time permitting you to evoke a mythic, natural color past. Claudia transposes her background hair over a natural color we can no longer see. Faced with Claudia's locks, you might regret your own carefully controlled hair. You might remember Baudelaire's exquisitely exoticizing hymn to hair.

La Chevelure

Ô toison moutonnant jusque sur l'encolure!
Ô boucles! Ô parfum chargé de nonchaloir!
Extase! Pour peupler ce soir l'alcôve obscure
Des souvenirs dormant dans cette chevelure,
Je la veux agiter dans l'air comme un mouchoir!

La langoureuse Asie et la brûlante Afrique,
Tout un monde lointain, absent, presque défunt,
Vit dans tes profondeurs, fôret aromatique!
Comme d'autres esprits voguent sur la musique.
Le mien, ô mon amour! Nage sur ton parfum.

. . . .

The Head of Hair

O FLEECE, foaming to the neck!
Curls! O scent of laziness!
Ecstasy! This evening, to people the dark corners
Of memories that are sleeping in these locks,
I would wave them in the air like a handkerchief!

The languor of Asia and burning Africa,
A whole world, distant, absent, almost extinct,
Lives in the depths of your perfumed jungle,
As other souls sail along on music,
So mine, O my love, swims with your scent.[20]

. . . .

But whereas Baudelaire locates his fantasy in places that are distant and deliberately foreign, Claudia and Coco conjure up images that are both of here and there. L'Oreal beside the *medina* works versions of abandonment into visions both of the Orient and of the West. It thrusts these interdependent images toward further distinctions. Claudia's hair tells us that we need not be born into something to become it. But can anyone really "deserve" the things that L'Oreal promises? The process of lightening and labeling, of covering and yet claiming authenticity, includes both a reworking of the background body and the "rediscovery" of natural products. From nature, itself apparently unperturbed by the division of our intelligence, we might, it seems, draw new energy. Myriam Saadi, then a high school student, wrote a poem of her own about hair for the daily newspaper *L'Opinion*:

Hier, j'étais une couronne d'or
Contente, fier de mon sort.
Aujourd'hui, je perds le bonheur et le confort
Comme une farouche bête
Elle m'a mis en bouclette
Femme, j'en ai assez de cette frisette!

Chaque jour, chaque soir,
Elle assome ma mémoire
Avec ces ciseaux, et ce séchoir
Enfin, Elle m'auriole d'une façon cruelle
Avec toutes les couleurs de l'Arc-en-ciel!
Femme! Ecoutez mon conseil éternel
La vraie beauté est dans tout ce qui est naturel!

Yesterday, I was a golden crown
Content, proud of my luck

Today, I've lost my comfort and joy
Like a wild animal
She's set me in curls
Woman, I'm sick of this frizziness!

Every day, every night,
She knocks out my memory
With these scissors and this dryer
Finally, she gives me a cruel halo
Every single color of the rainbow!
Woman! Listen to my eternal advice
True Beauty is in what is natural![21]

The question remains: Is nature able to substitute for amnesia? What kinds of authenticity might emerge from such true beauty? In Casablanca, Halima explains, "Before, women here [in Morocco] used natural products, and now, when Europeans come to stay here, they use these. Even there [in Europe] the chemical products are being replaced by plants and other natural things. We too should go back to these." Halima notes that she herself uses a mixture of *produits de grande consommation* (mass-produced products) and "natural" Moroccan products she buys at the *suq* (market), and she prefers to have her facial hair removed by "the Egyptian method." An image of a display of "natural" beauty and health products from a Casablancan pharmacy gives us a vision of the degree to which plants and their properties are carefully constructed as tableaux that correspond to specific "problems" consumers might encounter. They are carefully labeled and arranged. But these properties might be as "natural" and uncontrolled as Claudia Schiffer's flowing hair.

Souad reflects this when asked what she does to be beautiful, she says, "I pay attention to what other women don't have. It can be personality—this is why when someone sees me from far away I'm different than up close. When someone sees me from far away, makeup is important. But it shouldn't be too loud, so that when he gets closer it's still natural. In my look I tend toward the wild—I leave my hair a little messy. I feel more exciting that way." In Casablanca, Dina says, "When I put on makeup, I try to reveal my fundamental self and not just to give myself an image which might not correspond to what I am—except that sometimes one wants to

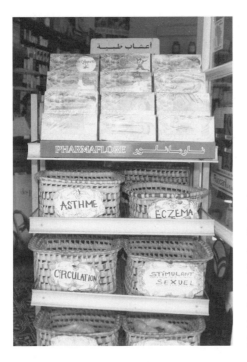

Labeling (pharmacy). Even the most "natural" products are carefully labeled in this display in a Casablancan pharmacy. However, unlike the beauty menus, this display explicitly tells us the function of each plant. Photograph, Susan Ossman.

be a little subversive and have fun. In this case, I really try to give myself another image to shock people and to *forget everything*." How might finding oneself or feeling exciting rely on messy hair and forgetfulness? How does one control and determine the placement of this moment to occasional amnesia? What are the powers that Dina might be trying to subvert or you or Claudia to reinstate? The process of forgetting is not simply one of unconscious abandonment. Forgetfulness, like memory, is supported by techniques for accomplishing it, specialists who help you learn to bridge the gap between who you were and who you are now. They produce and distribute pictures. They provide advice and instructions for how to renew yourself. They work with the ways we superimpose certain pictures and not others, submitting only certain looks to discussion.[22]

We often view our lightness as a liberation: light bears no weight and our being touched by it can no longer bring bodies or substances to bear on us. Such light might bring us warmth from the sun but no longer touch us with that of other people, or of divine grace. If the modern woman is so light as to let her wear anything, or to take it all off, her choices apparently infinite, how in fact can she choose to embody at all? Part of the dangerous aspect of this openness is precisely its apparent infinity. We cannot look behind it for some "deeper" social reality. If for some people in Casablanca, Cairo, and Paris there seem yet to be background bodies, enclosures of authenticity that we can yet liberate, fashion fails to display this move as primary. Rather, it claims its mastery by demonstrating the ability to embody a panoply of contemporary styles. By giving the impression that everything has been manipulated, reworked, undone, the sense of some primary body is perhaps not eliminated in the way we talk of our choices and our freedoms. But such talk cannot account for the ways in which these freedoms and choices are in fact limited.

Producing lightness involves adapting to techniques and norms of representation that are increasingly uniform throughout the world. These presuppose access not only to magazines, but to institutions and education that generalize particular norms. Is it true that anyone can learn these lessons of fashion? Are not some bodies more naturally endowed, certain backgrounds more promising for molding modern beauties for a world stage? To answer these questions means considering how the relationship to backgrounds has been represented, planned, or analyzed. When and how has en-lightenment come? The actress Nelly is light, but such lightness might be derided, viewed as vulgar, avoided by intelligent eyes. From what source does lightening strike, and how does this affect our motion? To answer these questions we must take note of the epic whose quests and journeys link en-lightened bodies to projects of Enlightenment and modernity. This epic relies on specific ideas of culture's link to nature, and to the kinds of liberation the en-lightened body brings with it. Against the stasis of the chubbily authentic and full-figuredly traditional "background body," the free motion of the new woman and modern man is traced. In the clearing thus created between innovative lightness and mere products of culture in context, modernity and liberty seem to take on form. "Epics of opening" recount these moves and guide us to the aperture where an incredible fluttering of potential looks from anywhere and everywhere converge.

Epics of opening have set choice at the center of beauty, power, and economy. They open a space where we can produce airy bodies with quick limbs that move with ease over vast expanses. But such epics of clearing and illumination are not the only stories that can be told about bodies and looks. At the very center of the openings and the little stories of our bodily en-lightenment that they encourage us to tell, there is evidence of a variety of spaces that constitute differences out of what initially appears the same. Studying how we actually produce beauty leads us to question the ways discourses of opening, or of modernity ignore that how we look relates to who we are and what we can do. By working through how beauties are produced in songs and beauty salons, magazines and streets, one encounters not only the remaining fleshiness of our heavy background origins but several realms where specific people and distinct ideas bring to bodies a variety of gazes, several ways of organizing our eyes' intelligence. These diverse worlds work with distinct conceptions of power, neighborliness, and virtue to braid difference into what seems similar. Background and light bodies get confused. To understand how bodies become light, and why they require heavy backgrounds, let us think about how looks are played out in ways of walking. Let us move back to the early decades of the past century and consider how moving pictures and new urban forms set feminists in Egypt and a famous French sociologist to find inspiration for understanding mimesis through the flickering images of women's movements over cinema screens, out of harems, and down big city streets.

MADEMOISELLE ANGÈLE: My poor Céleste, beauty is nothing. It doesn't interest men. What you have to have is vice. Ah! If you want to have vice . . . !

CELESTE: If you're willing to paint and powder yourself, and shave every morning, and swing your ass when you walk, well then they'll pay attention to you![1]

Marcel Pagnol's 1938 film *La Femme du Boulanger* tells the story of a middle-aged baker and his beautiful young wife, Aurélie. The couple move to a small village where the previous baker recently hanged himself. The new baker takes on the old bakery, and his bread wins popular acclaim. But it is his wife who inspires discussions about beauty, virtue, and vice among Angèle, Celeste, and other women in the village. Unlike the country women, Aurélie washes regularly. She wears lipstick and perfume. She has no children, and although we hear that she has a mother, we never see her.[2] She and her husband arrive from elsewhere with no personal reputation, only the fact that he possesses a skill the villagers need. Aurélie, on the other hand, seems to have no special skill. She seems to perform no useful task.[3] Instead, she sits behind a counter reading romance novels; she collects coins in payment for the bread her husband bakes. Her body comes to stand for luxury and gratuitous display.

Confronted with this new picture of femininity, one of the villagers notices that drawing attention to oneself requires effort and energy of a kind that is unlike that of the labor of the other villagers and peasants. Celeste calls this "having vice." To do this work you must "paint and powder yourself, and shave every morning." You must train yourself to "swing your ass when you walk." Aurélie does work: on herself.[4] But how she has learned to perform these labors remains obscure.

To learn how women like Aurélie learn to paint and powder, we might remember that one of Pagnol's contemporaries, Marcel Mauss, published his now famous essay on body techniques at about the same time as *The Baker's Wife* was first projected. It too took questions of girls' walks and the movies as its inspiration. Mauss wrote: "A sort of revelation came to me while I was in the hospital. I was ill in New York. I asked myself where I had already seen young ladies walk in the way that my nurses were. I had plenty of time to think about it. I finally realized that it was at the movies! When I returned to France I noticed, especially in Paris, the frequency of this same walk; the young girls were French but they also walked that way. In fact, the American ways of walking, thanks to the cinema, had begun to arrive in our country. This was an idea I could generalize."[5]

We do not know whether Aurélie learned to walk from the movies, but we do see her reading novels. We understand that she has not started to "swing her ass" all by herself. Do some girls have a special talent for learning to turn their books into new kinds of beauty? Do we all automatically imitate what we see at the cinema? Mauss suggests that, in France at least, all women are not equally apt to take on Hollywood in stride. Only certain "kinds" of girls are influenced by the movies, he says. Country girls might go to the pictures, but something of the city has to get into them to allow them to master the ways of walking that Mademoiselle Angèle associates with "having vice." Americans might be the apparent instigators of the process of changing girls' gaits, but Mauss does not distinguish Hollywood actresses from nurses in New York from Iowa farmgirls. What interests him, it seems, is what he already *knows*: that girls in France are not all the same.[6] There it is the parisienne who knows how to react to what she sees. It is her supple body that is eager to try out ways of walking from across the Atlantic.

So, it seems, a parisienne is not like other girls. She can gather up strands from several stories to demonstrate that she, unlike provincials, is ideally suited to moving through the modern world. She can remind us of the *grandes dames* of French literary salons. She can take on the face of the poor *grisette*, that slight figure that peopled the workhouses of the nineteenth century, scrimping and saving to appear as elegant as she could during her few hours off.[7] Whatever a woman's social position, the fashion historian Valerie Steele notes, being a parisienne sets her apart from others: "The image of 'la femme parisienne' preoccupied French artists and writers from the Romantic period through the Belle Époque. As envisioned by her contemporaries, she was more than simply a female inhabitant of Paris, but rather the symbol of a particular type of woman. Indeed, according to the *Physiology of the Parisienne*, fully five-sixths of the women in Paris were 'provincial in spirit and manners.' Conversely, there might exist 'graceful and spirited' provincials—'provided only that they do not live in the provinces.' Uzanne, however, argued that 'A woman may be Parisian by taste and instinct . . . in any town or country in the world.' "[8] A parisienne may play with complex tales reminiscent of those in Aurélie's novels. As she raises her eyebrow, we imagine her as a grisette falling into the arms of a wealthy bourgeois, or as his wife, whom he graciously allows to go to the new department stores, the Galleries Lafayette or the Nouvelles Galleries, where people of all social classes and walks of life mingle.[9] To play on imaginations the parisienne surveys herself. Her very gait integrates the unwritten rules of urbane display.[10]

The Hollywood films that changed parisienne walks did not merely replace existing Parisian images with others. Indeed, Hollywood often adopted and played on its own images of Parisian style. They augmented their meaning by the displacement of the parisienne and her male companions to the new world where they appeared as exotic, complex, sophisticatedly sexual creatures. Simultaneously, French films like *The Baker's Wife* also worked with women's walks. Although Mauss fails to mention this, we cannot easily explain why their influence would be different from that of Hollywood. We do not know where Aurélie comes from. But she does at least appear to have what it takes to call herself an urban lady. She has developed ways of walking that implicate her in connections from which others in the village are excluded. This is what singles her out. It is her singularity against a common, apparently unmoving ground of village life that draws her as the picture of the modern woman. The provincial, the rural, the uncouth: contrast with these rather than access to more movies enables parisiennes to be what they are.[11] Like a film star, the modern city girl Mauss describes and Aurélie mimics knows how to render desire visible to the watcher. She shows the movement toward what she wants and through this gesture opens up a defined space for performance. Or she seems to reflect back to the viewer his or her own versions of where she might be going. In both cases, this way of walking is assimilated to the openness of the street and the kinds of possibilities beyond landscapes presented in the movies.[12] It points toward a place which is never there, but always implied: it is a suite of endless tableaux, which allow you to display yourself, but also shows you what you can't have. The modern city of lights is organized to promote *la circulation* (traffic)—whether of buses, people, or things.[13] A spectator who is a parisienne can model herself because she walks streets that rush ahead like movies, and she is herself one of the elements that make them stream on.

Mauss's "revelation" presupposes his own ability to easily engage in a practice encouraged by the vistas of the modern city: watching girls walk. But whereas he hopes to link his observations to the depiction of the "total man," he studiously avoids any question of his own sensuous engagement in this mode of study. He proposes an image of himself in bed, gazing at his nurses. But from where has he observed these mythical parisiennes? Imagine him at the Café de l'Opera, and notice how he looks streetward, his head moving from left to right in synchrony with a host of others, as the girls stride, shimmy, stumble, or shuffle up the broad boulevard. What oriented the gaze of Mauss and his colleagues as they looked out from sidewalk cafés, their chairs turned toward the spectacle of the street? These places for potential lookers were integrated into the step of the parisienne.[14] They were shaped by the fact that girls were indeed working in hospitals or walking in the street.

Aurélie's difference is a sign of change because she introduces into the sleepy village not just makeup but new ideas about bodies and lives. She is perhaps a symbol of her husband's petit bourgeois pretentions. And yet, even if this is her role, it makes her neither useless not pecuniary. An old French children's song speaks of the female baker, who sits in the shop collecting that rare object, money: "La boulangère a des écus qui ne lui coûtent guère"—that is, she collects money that costs her hardly anything. Aurélie, on the other hand, presents herself gratuitously to the eyes of all as she sits at the counter of the bakery. When she takes a lover, he is a poor Italian shepherd who offers her no material advantage. Aurélie, as Jean-Marie Apostiledès remarks, is central to the economy of the village. When she leaves town with her lover, her husband loses his ability to knead bread and the village goes hungry. Everyone gets involved in trying to find her. Like the baker's bread, Aurélie's image moves through conversations, as her abandoned husband attempts to follow in the footsteps of his predecessor and hang himself. But the village will let neither of them go: the baker is saved and his wife returns once she finds out that her lover is married. Instead of dying, as have so many French villages in the past century, this village is reborn when the villagers admit their own desire for Aurélie and what she represents. Aurélie now belongs to everyone, and, in a sense, everyone has become she. All may now once more partake of the baker's bread.[15]

Aurélie's story presupposes a series of distinctions between commerce in things and sexuality, between city and country and virtue and vice, which had been long in the making.[16] Hers is a tale of reconciliation, of collective recognition of the disconnection of survival from the earth, and its reconnection with the kinds of desires for pictures, stories, romance, and gratuitous pleasures that Aurelie's "vice" entails. Aurelie does not labor the land, but she does work. She works on herself, and she works in the sense that she provides the key to the survival of the village.

Perhaps Mauss watched Aurélie's moves at the cinema. Pagnol's films were very popular, and the urban beauties he watched walking certainly must have viewed Aurélie's story and compared it to their own. Like the Hollywood walk that the sociologist identifies with such acuity, Aurélie's gait was projected around the world. But this world was not exactly the same one in which Mauss situates his observations. Paris, like Hollywood, was, and is, a major center for the production of films. But whereas Los Angeles was little known before the movies, the French cinema took form in the context of a preexisting image of the city as a center of art and fashion. Long before the movies, Paris had proposed looks for actresses, American debutantes, and ordinary city girls alike. But it did so with a touch that only Old World experience of empire could offer with such a mixture of self-involved "quality" and ready-to-export values. The powerful political France of the *mission civilisatrice*, like the Parisian fashion industry, was experiencing major transformations during the 1930s that would accelerate following the Second World War.[17] With the rise of American economic and political prominence, comparisons of Gallic styles and successes began to be made not only with Great Britain but also with another of what the French describe as Anglo-Saxon countries: the United States. A fear of Americanization, of its walks, of consumption habits, of language, became readily apparent.[18] And yet, we must not forget that Aurélie herself was probably unconcerned about where her lipstick came from. She might have noticed less the expansion of American influence and more that the worlds in which her novels in French, like her own image set in film, moved most easily were rather extensive at the end of the 1940s. In places where the rolled *r* of regional dialects of France, Navarre, and Algiers was gradually giving way to the *r grasaillé* of Paris, a world traced by shared films, methods of producing wine, and modes of address, sprung new patches of urbanity. Aurélie might very well have decided to follow the path of so many other Frenchwomen and move not to Paris, but to one of the new cities built by the French in Indochina, West Africa, or in Morocco. Had she moved to Casablanca she could have strolled down boulevards as wide as any in Paris. She would have been able to go to the beach any afternoon while still having access to her favorite novels, films, and beauty products. She could even have continued to purchase her makeup at Monoprix. Her apartment would probably have been more comfortable than any she could afford in Paris.

Casablanca, a rural market town turned city in the nineteenth century, became a showcase for the most avant-garde urban designs and architecture by the 1940s.[19] Women arriving there from Europe after the War might be from the provinces, like Aurélie. They would be joined by men and women from Italian, Spanish, and Portuguese villages. Parisiennes might rush past Muslim girls on their way to work as servants or Jewish matrons on their way to market. Their walks, along with the movies, magazines, and culinary practices, were part of a world that Mauss chose not to see. While he was watching girls in New York and Paris, women like Aurélie were learning new walks and trying them out on the eyes of others along the boulevards of Casa or its beaches.

If tales of learning to stroll down broad boulevards emphasized the role of the parisienne in France, moving to Casablanca makes us notice how similar contrasts of rural to urban can be quite important in different settings, yet still essential to the patterning of movement and the spatial enclosures of women's lives. The nineteenth-century Parisian bourgeoise could attend balls and eventually go out on walks, she remained stifled by her corset, an insectlike carapace that shaped her in ways that shortened her breath and constrained her ability to move. Meanwhile, her Moroccan sister wore flowing, comfortable robes. But her movement too was curtailed by thick walls or heavy head coverings. In the old and prestigious Moroccan cities of Fez, Meknes, and Tetouan, it was not the country girl but the well-off city woman who was confined in ways that many European men eroticized in tales of harems. Country women in some areas, such as the Middle Atlas and the Atlantic Plains, might move about freely and meet men at village festivals. But urban beauties had to stay put. Urban élégantes in Fez, Rabat, Marrakech, and Tetouan were not chided for their use of makeup, perfumes, and beautiful clothing. Their bodies were not transformed by waist bindings or decolletés for display to men. Instead, they were kept for the eyes of their families and their husbands. The urban lady, epitomized in the picture of the Fasi beauty, was not prevented from dancing, but her movements were circumscribed by the wall of her house, by the eyes of her men. She could visit family or go to the baths (hammam), but her movements were restricted.

However, by the time that Aurélie began using her city vice to confound an entire village in France, some women were also trying out new ways of walking in Fez and Casablanca. Their outings came to include occasional trips to the cinema. In her romanced autobiography, set in a harem in Fez, Fatima Mernissi writes about going to the movies:

> Going to the movies was a thrill, from beginning to end. Women would dress up as if they were about to parade, unveiled, through the streets. Mother would spend hours and hours putting on her make-up and curling her hair in an incredibly complicated fashion. Elsewhere, in all the four corners of the courtyard, the other women would be feverishly making themselves up, too, with children holding mirrors, and friends giving advice regarding khol, rouge, hairstyles, and jewelry. The children had to hold the hand mirrors and angle them just right to catch the rays of the sun because the mirrors embedded in the salon's walls were not of much use at all. The sunlight hardly ever reached them, except for a few hours in the summer.

She recalls how imitating the actress Camille Claudel was a favorite, if secret, pastime for young girls lulling on the broad terraces atop their homes. But she also describes its enclosures and the frustrations that women in mid-twentieth-century urban families confronted when faced with pictures, ideas, and lifestyles from afar. Mernissi represents the urban women of her mother's generation as "thirsty for liberation and change."[20] She recounts how Chama, who lived in a Fasi harem, listened to

Radio Cairo to learn of the latest news of Huda Sha'rawi and other feminists in Egypt and Turkey. Chama sees herself as a "lost butterfly." Pinned between the walls of her house, this winged spirit became burdened with the blues, the heavy *hemm*. Tradition and modernity describe the two walls between which the listless butterfly invaded by hemm is caught. A feeling of being of neither of the lively worlds incapacitates her. This incapacity is born not of naïveté but of knowledge.

Mernissi's women are in touch with international movements of ideas and images. They see and hear about Turkish, French, and Egyptian women who move differently than they do. To gauge the distance between their lives and the words they listened to on the radio, and recalling the importance of movement in stories of en-lightenment, we might read an excerpt from an article that Céza Nabaraouy wrote in 1929 for the Egyptian magazine *L'Egyptienne*. In "Le développement de la culture physique en egypte" (The development of physical fitness in Egypt), she writes, "It is wise and logical that the young girl who is called upon to become the intellectual equal of the young boy not be in a too great physical inferiority. To become active, she should possess qualities for the full development of her physical power: activity, courage, energy, independence and character. Otherwise she is condemned to remain a weak, nervous and excessively sensitive [girl] who, even if she is bright, will be more turned toward spiritual speculation than the realities of life. Her character will lack what has become in our time the particular qualities which attract success."[21]

Though Sha'rawi's voice might enter the harem and Aurélie's face be perceived at the cinema, neither formed a ground for Chama's daily experience. In the medina, even the orientalist artist could not focus his lens to show her traits. His portraits might develop Chama as a fantasy, marvelous in her captivity, enticing in ways akin to those exoticized beauties Baudelaire poeticized. But her hair is caught in some uncanny comb. She is stilled, yet moved by Egyptian radio. She knows of stories of "vice," but has no say in whether she will become a part of them. She remains in the background as children in her household attend French schools, men discuss nationalist politics, and the young girls of the family adopt new, Paris-inspired fashions. Some of the Egyptian feminists she hears about on the radio talk about her in the guise of the "Moroccan woman." For them, she stands for the backwardness of her country, at a time when they saw themselves as becoming progressively unveiled, lightened, and free. Beauty and the movement of vice require, it seems, the idea of confinement to chart their own direction.[22] But where are these backgrounds to be found? What might construct them? Could the French women who in spite of their wealth and their nation's power gained the right to vote only at the end of WWII serve as the only source of inspiration for those left "wingless"?[23]

Chama's radio suggests that we must listen to the many tongues in which opening epics are told. Already before the 1930s, the story of Aurélie was, it would seem, being repeated not only in France, but in Egypt. There, unveiling, bobbed hair, and sending girls to represent Egypt in Miss Universe contests were coming to represent progress for elite urbanites. Feminists of the 1930s and since have believed that they could have an impact on how women could be lightened and liberated.[24] For reformers in France and in Cairo, Morocco's very backwardness made it a particularly important point of departure for such an undertaking. The Cherifian realm was perceived as particularly closed, isolated, cut off from parts of the Arab world that had been colonized by the Turks and thus pushed along by the progress of the modern world. Women's confinement symbolized this broader situation. In *L'Egyptienne*, Jeanne Marques reviewed a report on Moroccan women that Tahar Essafi wrote in 1936. She noted how the city women of Morocco lived in a manner that "is quite similar to that which her sisters in Egypt of a similar status lived about thirty years ago. . . . To remedy this situation, it is necessary to educate the young girl, to get her to become conscious of her needs, of her rights, of her true duties as a human being who is free and responsible, while taking care that this be done not only by appealing to her intelligence—a very dangerous thing. But through her heart and interests. By treating her like a young sister of whom we expect a lot."[25]

Some girls from modest rural backgrounds in Egypt itself were, as Marques wrote, in the process of developing their own versions of their education and future. If we listened to Chama's radio, we might have heard not only feminists, but the voice of Umm Khalthoum, a girl of humble, rural beginnings who came to represent her nation and the Arab world. Perhaps the most famous Arab singer of all time, she was "not content to occupy the marginal position accorded female reciters of the Quran and religious singers. She learned new musical styles and practices, copied the manners of the elite of the city, and eventually replaced her father's ensemble with professional instrumental accompanists."[26] Umm Khalthoum gained renown and financial success by exporting her heavy image on light supports: records, photographs, film. She did not dance, unlike many singers who gained fame and fortune in musicals in the Azbekiyya quarter or on the silver screen. Indeed, the ways in which the lightening of bodies can be achieved are many, and at times these are most effective when they preserve a sense of their link to ideas of enclosure, of heaviness and gravity. And yet, to express this connection in terms of grounding becomes increasingly problematic. Is it a revoicing, a rewriting, a clear evolution of one body from another? The moment when a million Aurélies might confront countless, nameless villages is not easy to trace as a point in historical time. It is a recurring encounter that inspires many different stories about the process of en-lightenment. These narratives, these "epics of opening" show how we conceive of tradition, change, and possible futures.

EPICS OF OPENING

Theories of social evolution and progress did not die with the nineteenth century or early feminism. The ways of evaluating movement, however, have changed. Some women I interviewed in Casablanca made sure that I noticed that their grandmothers or mothers, like some members of the Mernissi clan, "already" carefully cut and styled their hair "back then." Family photos of upper-class weddings show the carefully lacquered hair of some Fasi and Jewish women by the 1950s and 1960s. Women and men often tell the history of moving into the same society as Aurélie, of Egyptian feminists, in terms of where women go and of how they wear their hair. Soumaya, a Casablancan university student whose grandmother, like Chama, was from Fez, explained, "I'm from a Fasi background. My grandmother already wore short skirts to go to school and her mother made her take care of herself. Sometimes I don't feel like wearing makeup, and my mother comes and says 'What's this face! You look so pale! Go clean up that face a little!' She can't stand to see me like that. And if she sees me poorly dressed she asks me to change my clothes. By repeating these kinds of things, you get into the habit of taking care of yourself.

When I wake up, she doesn't like me to hang around in my pajamas. When this is inculcated in you from the beginning, from a very young age, it becomes habit. You just start doing it."

In her accent on habit and early learning, Soumaya's explanation comes close to Mauss's definition of the role of habitus in forming bodily technique:

> I call technique an action which is *effective* and *traditional* (and you will see that in this it is no different from a magical, religious or symbolic action). It has to be *effective* and *traditional*. There is no technique and no transmission in the absence of tradition. This above all is what distinguishes man from animals: the transmission of his techniques and very probably, by their oral transmission. . . .
>
> We are dealing with techniques of the body. The body is man's first and most natural instrument. Or more accurately, not to speak of instruments, man's first and foremost technical object, and at the same time technical means, is his body.[27]

The problem is that measures of efficaciousness and the delineation of traditions are not so easy to design. Continuities in ways of handing down can form patterns profoundly shaped by the way we inscribe knowledge through language, as Mauss remarks, but also by the ways that language and looks can be recorded and stored. As Mauss's initial inspiration assumed, audiovisual media act to spread our access to new kinds of looks and ways of knowing and affect the very ideas we might have of prestige and authority and their links to certain bodies. How can we account for the ways that the voices Chama heard over the radio might have changed her gait and led her to begin to travel, perhaps, like the Aurélie I imagine, to pack her bags and move to Casablanca? When Mauss sets aside some of his initial "revelations" about films and walks, forgetting what he says to be the inspiration for his musings on bodies, something important about how we move through history is left by the wayside. He says he hopes to understand bodily techniques by focusing on tradition and on speech, but to summarize these in terms of a vague habitus tells us little about the process of teaching and transmission they require. It does not describe but assumes the places beauties go; we get glimpses of cinemas, imagine cafés. But these are so fleeting that we cannot get an idea of the very different kinds of masters and techniques that are involved in any tradition. Prestige must be related to their different goals, ideas of excellence, and modes of passing on.

Tradition is a scene of battles or of seduction, rife with conflict about who has the right to transmit what to whom, about what kinds of techniques are valued or reviled. And bodies are not just any kind of instrument. It is the musician and not her lute or trumpet or keyboard that masters technique. How women locate themselves and their families in terms of epics of opening must be taken into account in thinking about how social distinctions are reworked in terms of these stories. The name of the master or mother from whom we learn new moves often inflects how we can play on ourselves because of or in spite of access to films or fashions or nationally proclaimed traditions. Links to the process of opening that pass through families are often held up as signs of distinction, and ideas of historical precedence often play with notions of prestigious models. The models one adopts and techniques one learns are constantly being judged in attempts to delineate social groups, but also to establish how evaluations of one's virtue or vice are tied to these choices.

Lalla Khadija, an old friend in Casablanca, could be Soumaya's grandmother. She often tried to express her luck in life by telling me how her husband often invited her to the movies. Like Chama and her creator, Fatima Mernissi, Khadija was born in Fez. She married at fifteen, just after the War. With her husband, a prosperous merchant from the South, she moved to Casablanca. Initially they lived in the old medina, but gradually, the family grew too large for the cramped quarters. Just after Independence in 1956, they built a villa in a new section of town. Even today, Khadija continues to visit the old city to shop for food. She orders her jellabas from a tailor in what used to be a Jewish section of town, and buys her shoes in one of the shops in the modern city center. She likes to stroll with her daughters through that part of town and particularly enjoys trying some of the new restaurants that have opened up, serving Chinese, Korean, or French cuisines. Khadija shows me photographs of herself going out and going abroad. I see her at a wedding in a colorful caftan; in Rome, with her husband, in an expensive fur and high heels. I see her in videos of family festivities, her gold jewels shining. A widow now, she still seems to be always on the move, visiting a family member or a family she "helps" by buying schoolbooks for the children. When I go to Paris she asks me to bring her the latest beauty creams, which she learns about from fashion magazines in Arabic or French. In the early 1990s, I spent a good deal of time in Khadija's house. One day, while I was sitting in the garden, I heard loud music coming from the living room. I entered to find Fatna, a ten-year-old girl from the countryside.[28]

> The radio is blasting. Fatna sets aside her broom. She must think that I've gone out with the rest of the family. As I come down the stairs I see her tie a scarf from the sofa around her tiny hips. She moves toward the mirror, undulating her hips in figure eights, calling to her own image with her hands, which gives the impression of pulling ribbons or robes toward her, as though they were there, beyond the mirror. She sees me there as a reflection as I move toward the salon. She laughs, but keeps dancing, casting a complicitous glance at me. I get the impression that she thinks she's doing something wrong.
>
> She shimmies her shoulders and winks. Where did she learn to do that, I wonder.
>
> Khadija snickers when I ask her how Fatna learned to dance that way. "She watches those Egyptian movies on television all of the time," she says. Khadija explains that she usually doesn't hire "little maids" but that she knows Fatna's family through a network of friends. She showed up here in Casablanca one day. What was Khadija to do? The family thought they could at least teach her how to keep house and cook. It's true that Fatna seemed bright, but she could not even count to ten. How would she know if the grocery store cashier cheated her? How could she learn to make her way in the world?
>
> Khadija's daughter Badia explains that "dancing isn't all she knows about. She can't count but she sure knows about a lot of things most girls around here don't understand at her age!" As she talks, Fatna comes into the room. She turns on the radio again, and begins to dance once more. "You see!" Badia exclaims. "The little hussy! Just look at those moves she's studied—is that a sign of childhood innocence to you?"

Khadija and Badia remind me of Celeste and Angèle, except that their words on vice include explanations about how they are trying to help Fatna find a place in the modern urban world. Fatna seems to have learned many things, but she is accused of not understanding how to use her knowledge in appropriate ways. So perhaps it is not enough to know how to dance. Such techniques, if we listen to Khadija and Badia, must be accomplished in specific ways. Simple "copying" is not enough to bring one out of the "background" associated with ignorance, lack of education, and, in this case, willful immorality.

We might think back to how feminists in Egypt took an interest in their Moroccan sisters during the protectorate. How did they suggest that they be included in the outward move toward the future? Were they not aware of the dangers presented by letting "just anyone" out into the streets to see sights that might inspire them to "swing their ass"? Jeanne Marques's review of Essafi's assessment of the situation of the Moroccan woman is eulogistic: " 'La Marocaine' has a twofold interest. First of all, the author describes the situation of the woman in Morocco. On the other hand, he indicates what remains to be done to place all Muslim women on the line of modern world evolution. For, we must never forget that to speak loyally of the progress of a group whose homogeneity is composed of custom and religion it is not sufficient that one or two countries are in the avant-garde. More than international, evolutionary life is global. To achieve harmonization, it must, by vast groups, march together. *Otherwise, the remainders of the dead past block the present and obscure the future.*"[29]

This version of the march toward the future assumes that the women of Morocco are in fact unified by common customs and religion. In this, Marques's approach is consonant with Marcel Mauss's sense of technique as needing to be "effective and traditional." Remember that he insisted, "There is no technique and no transmission in the absence of tradition. This above all is what distinguishes man from animals: the transmission of his techniques and very probably, by their oral transmission."[30] For Marques, however, tradition is what, while unifying the group, must also be critically appraised. Groups of people must be "harmonized" with those of nations of the avant-garde. Perhaps "oral transmission" can develop reasoned arguments that lead all people to move as one body. Yet, how might one define the progress of the "modern" body without some reminder, some remainder that demonstrates its forward motion?[31] Today, people continue to recall remainders as Sylvie does for grandmère, who lives in the village "hole" or as Mernissi does by creating Chama and her courtyard. Often, these figures are associated with "tradition." Words that refer to such bodies as 'roubi or balady continue to link them to the countryside, wherever they might live.[32] Their practices are contrasted to those of urban ladies, whose ways of transmitting body techniques are themselves incredibly diverse. This diversity might be represented by debates concerning virtue and the proper paths for reaching the status of the modern woman, as it is when Khadija criticizes Fatna.

The problem of bringing people into the new openings in the "right way," using "tradition" as a rampart against the apparently random movement of modernity, seems to accompany en-lightening processes as they illuminate the world. Before discussing how social diversity and claims to precedence in the move toward the future are worked out, I look at one institution that might be seen as providing some link to the "homogeneous" body of tradition that Marques assumes. The hammam, often referred to in English as the "turkish bath," is sometimes seen in Morocco as a symbol of "wholeness" and, following Kilito, of the weight of the past. Indeed, it is, I argue, a site where the body is approached in its totality. But the nature of this totality produces displacements and relationships among the cities of this study that are quite different from the apparently even, grounded passing on of body techniques through discourse that writers such as Marques and Mauss imagined. The hammam, like the contrast of urban to rural, plays on but also confounds oppositions that are shared by complex geographies of bodily technique that change in unexpected ways.

REMEMBERING THE WHOLE

In the early 1800s the French feminist and Saint-Simonian Suzanne Voilquin went with her friend Clara to the hammam in Cairo. This was because: "It is the place which is the most appropriate and the best to observe the women of Cairo. We wanted to judge if their attraction justified their haste to go there. We understood that for them, these visits to the baths were a sort of Longchamps, where those favored by lady luck come to display their brilliant ornaments to the naive and curious admiration of their companions. Going to the baths is also, for these poor reclusives, a holiday. There, no more surveyors, nor masters; consequently, no more need to suffer constraint or competition."[33]

Voilquin describes how she and her friend enter the baths, which are somber and arranged in a set: three rooms, each of which is progressively hotter. The last room is very hot indeed. It has a pool in its center. Workers take care of the baths and wash and massage the bathers. They propose treatments to their elegant clients such as rubbing *rusma* over their skin to remove hair. After the bath, Voilquin and her companion move to the room where the *setti* (the ladies) chat relentlessly. There, they make themselves up with khol and dye their hands and feet with henna. They redo their thousands of braids with little pieces of gold. They build up their hairstyles from these braids. Like European ladies of the time, they also appreciate little hats, *tarbouch*, on top of their towering hairdos. They cover them with feathers, pearls, or flowers to decorate what Voilquin calls "these enormous hairstyles which are devoid of grace." She concludes by noting: "All of this interior elegance, these large pants in red cashmere, the 'ialak' (haik) or robes *à la chatelaine*, these slippers encrusted with pearls, are designed to capture the love and preference of the master. They are never seen outside. The passerby who sees these women sees these women only in a large dress without form, in veils, with a *borgal* in front of her face and with *rharba* (a big piece of black silk). Enveloped in this way, a bizarre imposition is achieved, it is fantastic but I assure you that it in no way reminds us of the idea of the odalisque."[34]

Voilquin's descriptions call attention to why movements out of enclosed environments could become so important in later feminist demands. They also call into question orientalist ideas of women in the baths. Indeed, the Frenchwoman's reason for going to the hammam was neither to reform nor to romanticize it. She simply wanted to go where women went. This motivation is unusual in discussing women in the baths even today. For whereas orientalist versions of the odalisque have been widely criticized, the location of an imaginary body of tradition one might meet in the hammam has not. How many times have I been told that to study the "real" body in the Arab world I had to abandon the beauty salon for the hammam? Many people, men and women, but especially men, assumed that an anthropologist should seek to locate the "profound," underlying body one might find in the baths.[35] Still, in evoking the centrality of this institution, such commentators rarely mention their own experiences there. Or, perhaps, they write stories about them, focusing on the moment when they, as young boys, are no longer allowed to go to the baths on women's days.

Reading such literature, we often forget that adult men also frequent the hammam.[36] The baths themselves are never closed to them, but when they begin to follow their father there, a certain en-lightening move is apparently made. The memorable bath is the one that evokes nostalgia. Abdelfattah Kilito comments, "Many men talk about the *hammam* of their early childhood as a lost paradise; they accompanied their mother into this humid, hot space, peopled by magical female bodies. And then one day it had to come to pass that they stop accompanying their mother and resign themselves to going to the *hammam* with their father to enter into the world of men, it had to happen that at about five years old they submit to a second weaning, a second separation. The maternal *hammam* is thus remembered with nostalgia and like a paradise of childish loves."[37]

In presenting the hammam as the producer of the bodies of the past, men and the assumptions of many scholars work together to comfort a certain idea of personal history in social terms. The "modern" body, which must move toward separation from the hammam, is male. Those "old" feminized bodies of the past, no matter how much they are longed for and fondly remembered, are to be set aside. They do not have a place in the world of serious things. Tradition, belief in *jnun* (genies), who love the damp world of the baths, and the time wasted in relaxation, are apparently fine for women. But for men and societies on the move, these must be carefully confined. The hammam should not be abolished, but instead, given the status of an icon of the past. Indeed, the baths and their bodies seem to crystallize ideas of tradition and desire because for men they are the very scene of separations: from femininity, from the past, from conversations unencumbered by instrumental intent. The hammam is regularly cited as one of the defining features of all Arab cities, along with the mosque and the market. Yet Omar Carlier's extensive study of the steam bath's many forms indicates that this "tradition" may be more Roman than Arab. His research suggests that, at least in Morocco, the roots of the hammam might be found in its rural, Berber form than in its urban version.[38] Still, some scholars and laypeople in the Maghreb seek to identify the baths as the site of the "real" Muslim or Arab body.

Many people I spoke with in Casablanca were surprised to learn that in Cairo, where the majority of the population is Muslim, and nearly everyone's first language is Arabic, there are only a very few functioning public baths. While in Cairo, I was warned against going to visit them; I was told that they have become dilapidated and unhygienic. They apparently no longer serve even the balady, lower-class quarters they have come to be associated with in spite of the fact that running water is a luxury for many people living in the overpopulated metropolis. This prestigious capital of the Islamic history has progressively adopted English-style bathrooms, to the surprise of many Casablancans, while the hammam remains a vital institution in that modern city. Although a few middle-class women I met in Casablanca said that they disliked the baths and preferred their shiny, modern bathrooms, most people I spoke with said that they enjoyed going to the hammam as long as it was "pleasant" and "clean."[39] I met only a couple of people who claimed they had never gone to the baths, although working people complained that they did not do so often because of lack of time. Was the persistence of this space and its techniques due to Casablanca's later development, conceived in terms of its lag behind Egypt and France on the road to new social clearings? Is it a product of the way French colonial policies carefully separated the old from the new towns, sanctifying old traditions and introducing a sense of the hammam as a rampart against bodily invasions from the North?

To some Cairenes I told of the continuing vitality of Moroccan hammams, it was obvious that this could only be another indication of that country's backwardness. A French specialist in the Middle East who visited me in Casablanca took a similar position, but extolled how the "Moroccans know how to maintain their traditions! What authenticity! You see all of these very old-fashioned things—not like in the Middle East— rather like in Yemen." Might the sleek white walls of this very modern city act as a tromp l'oeil? Might they simply conceal all manner of survivals from other times, an endless well of authenticity filled with the jewels of ancient custom? From the perspective of Cairo or Paris, one looking for the background body might try to find it here. Behind the façade of the many beauty salons and health clubs, the beaches and swimming pools, remainders must lurk. You might think you see them on the streets, taking the form of women in colorful jellabas.[40] Or you might decide to leave the city altogether in search of the true body of the place, which, as many guide books in European languages warn you, is not produced here but in the countryside and in the old cities of Fez or Marrakech. But what about the baths that dot the cityscape? What of the millions of bodies that gather in their enclosures to bathe, converse, shave, or get a massage? Might not the hammam offer some kind of total experience that is different from what bathrooms, beauty salons, or sports clubs provide?

People often go to the baths in the company of friends or family members. To prepare to go there, you must gather together the things that you will need to wash. Towels, soaps, shampoos, washcloths, razors, combs, and a mat to sit on, not to mention a change of underwear, are gathered together into a basket or a backpack. As you move through the progression of steamy spaces, you feel your skin gradually soften. You talk or dream sitting or lying down on your mat. You might massage your companions with a rough cloth covered with soap, then pour buckets of water over one another to rinse off. Or you might ask the ġsalla (washer) to "wash" and massage you. Some women shave their legs. You have to be careful as you move through the rooms to select a space to sit that is free of refuse and that allows you to rinse yourself without splashing anyone else too much.

Bathing at the hammam can be seen as a series of encounters between the body and various forms of a single element. Water is everywhere. Throughout your visit, you are engulfed in steam. You rinse off with pails of clear water and clean the floor with it when your shampoo or soap has left bubbles on the floor. While you and your friends or the gsalla might perform all manner of treatments on the body, it is impossible to select only a particular body part in the experience. You must get wet, hot, and sweaty all over. You can move to find the level of warmth you and your friends feel most comfortable with. Groups of women tend to move through the rooms together, looking for places to spread their mats close to one another in spaces on the floor, rather like groups of friends look for empty places to spread their towels on a crowded beach. Eventually, you'll wash your hair and carefully wrap it in a towel before returning to the dressing room and a cool drink or fruit. You'll want to be careful as you walk home from the baths that you are warmly dressed and that a towel is pulled tightly over your wet hair.

A visit to the baths can be compared to the setup and routines of the beauty salon. In the beauty salon, your body is not engulfed in variable intensities of a single element. Instead, you move among spaces that correspond to distinct activities. Each implies different degrees of dress or undress, visibility and light. For example, to have your hair done, you are covered with a robe and brought first to the washing area. From there, you move to a cutting area, where you are stationed in front of a mirror so that you can observe each movement of the hairdresser as he or she snips or brushes. If you are getting a facial, you'll be escorted upstairs or to a back room where there are no mirrors and you'll remove your clothing to don a special robe and lie on a covered couch. Steam can be produced by burning wood; hair dryers require electricity. Electricity warms water, wax, and massage machines, and, most important, it illuminates. Whereas hammams are dim, salons are brightly lit. Even in back rooms where women lie on couches to get massages, lights are placed so that aestheticians can evaluate the progress of their work. Whereas baths promise to deep-clean and make one feel good, the massages that most aestheticians provide are often a way of "relaxing" but also of slimming or transforming the shape of one's body.

This helps us to understand how the salon and the hammam can indeed be considered complementary, and it also draws attention to the profoundly different way the body is viewed in each space. Indeed, the body of the baths is one of continuity within a closed space. How people feel about this "whole" differs according to how this closed space is related to their own movements. In Cairo or Casablanca during the early part of the twentieth century, upper-class women's movements were carefully traced among harems and hammams, occasional festive events at the homes of friends or relatives, and perhaps visits to a saint's shrine. Poor urban women and country women had to go out of their home to work to help support their family, but they too often went to the baths to wash, chat, and relax each week after their labor. Hammams, like salons, can be a place for body treatments but also simply a place to meet and chat with friends. Omar Carlier writes of how in the hammam people are "provisionally detached, disconnected from the world and from time. Men come here to prepare themselves for ritual observations, while women come to 'densify' their talk [parole] and intensify their connection to their social group. While the bath is a special space in which biology is privileged and one submits to the law of nature, it is also par excellence the space of the social body, which is governed by culture, which is itself under the power of the laws of God."[41]

Might we see the continued vitality of the hammam in Casablanca and North Africa in general as a sign that such old-time sociabilities and bodies persist there? Casablancan women of all walks of life go to both the baths and the hair salons. In this context, what can we say about the way that the bath can "densify talk"? As the apparently global story of tearing down walls, of opening spaces up has taken hold, the relationship of the baths to the density of women's talk has taken on a new social valence. For, if some women continue to go to the baths for news and companionship, others have transformed their weekly hammam visit from a space of talk to one of therapeutic relaxation. Some are set in health clubs or in upscale resort hotels near the beach. If we consider the simple presence of the bath, we might see continuity or tradition. But the new relationships between the baths and other institutions for beauty alter its importance in the process of densification of talk. The body of the baths remains marked by continuity—but this body is constantly contrasted, cut up, remodeled by its confrontation with other versions of itself. The visit to the hammam can be seen as preparing the body for further makeup and elaboration at home. In the beauty salon, on the other hand, I both prepare the background and try to give my image form. This imaging leads us to notice a parallel between the smooth walls of the hammam and the pure bodies it prepares for later elaboration (you leave with your hair in a towel). It makes us start at how salons are timed to the radio and colored by posters. There, they give you ideas by providing you with the latest fashion magazines. Instead of directing your gaze toward the center of a circle of conversation, they set up mirrors—your picture floats for public scrutiny amidst those of Cairene singers and ads for L'Oréal.

Unlike men, women continue to frequent the same ladies' days at the hammam as in their childhood. But at least some of them will not expect to know most of the women there, as their mothers generally did. Most young girls no longer bathe nervously, knowing that they may be under observation in a potential matchmaking scheme. As the spaces of talk have changed, the hammam has in a sense become ever more a matter of creating bodies and, perhaps, of remembering how confinement schemas of the past involved other ways of talking. Today, many young professional women and men in Casablanca speak several languages; they own automobiles in which they speed across the city to go to work or pick up their children at school. Women without cars or skill in foreign languages, as in the past, often have to work to support their family. Their moves are often less varied and more limited than are those of the educated women who might live in their neighborhoods. Yet, they too progressively integrate new spaces of talk, and of listening, in the course of their daily routines.[42] The existence of alternative spaces for talk, of spaces of seeing alternatives and displacing the meaning of tradition reworks the meaning of enclosures. Still, remembering how the hammam can come to represent a personal as well as a collective past and become a subject of nostalgia, even for men who still frequent it, is important to consider what the institution itself has become. This is perhaps nowhere more the case than in places like Paris, where the steam bath has come into its own, first due to people moving there from North Africa, then because of the appeal of treating total bodies to relaxation signaled by oriental luxury.

DISPLACEMENTS

It may be difficult to find a functioning hammam in Cairo today, but it has become astoundingly easy to do so in Paris. While elegant parisiennes of the century of Enlightenment were only beginning to build *bains douches* (public bathhouses) to facilitate the washing of what until then had been a remarkably dirty population, the gradual disappearance of these public baths has been paralleled by the generalization of bathroom facilities.[43] Over the past century bathing and, eventually, washing one's hair regularly have gradually become a habit for most people in the city. Nonetheless, with increased trade and migration between Paris and her North African colonies, the hammam as introduced in France took several forms. It appeared first as the Jewish *mikveh*, then became a feature of neighborhoods where immigrants from the Maghreb took up residence. Initially, steam baths were set up to serve such "ethnic" communities, yet even these baths took diverse forms. Neighborhood baths tend to be quite rudimentary; grand orientalist interpretations of the hammam have also been built since the early twentieth century. The most famous of these "traditional" baths is surely that of the Mosque of Paris. Situated between the Jardin des Plantes and a square named after the famous orientalist Robert Montagne, their beautifully tiled rooms let us know that we are in a space carefully constructed according to a deep understanding of traditional Moroccan architecture. They are large, colorful, and beautifully lit. Although it was initially intended to serve the Muslim community of Paris, today people of many backgrounds from all over the world visit the bath and its adjacent mosque and tea room. This is no replacement for the bathroom or the beauty salon. Indeed, given the entry fee, people without the means to bathe at home cannot afford to do their washing here either. People come here to relax. They often bring friends but rarely meet people they know from their own neighborhoods.

This displacement of the hammam to Paris mirrors the immigration of the beauty salon to Morocco. It uses the same principles as baths in the Maghreb, which themselves have slightly different bathing arrangements. But these are often interpreted in ways that differ from most neighborhood establishments in North Africa.[44] For although the physical setup of the baths resembles many one might see in Casablanca, the way the services are organized is significantly different. For example, to be washed (they call it a "massage") at the Mosque of Paris hammam, you must purchase a token when you pay to enter the baths. The color of the token, which you keep with the pails and buckets you also receive at the entrance rather than bring from home, indicates how long a massage you will receive. In the manner of a beauty salon, whose prices often change for cutting long or short hair or providing one or another well-defined treatment, this hammam has learned to divide time and energy by the clock. While the whole body is engulfed in steam, the client must calculate how much she is willing to pay for a service measured in minutes. In most neighborhood baths, the "washer" simply rubs you until you are clean or until she is too tired to continue.

Baths in Casablanca rarely time their treatments, but they have developed in other ways that link them to yet other Parisian versions of the bath. In Paris, as in Casablanca, something called a hammam is increasingly included in many health clubs and hotels. These baths are often composed of a single room. Many are tiled, but some are prefabricated units with plastic walls. Often, no buckets or hoses to wash one off are provided; instead, showers to rinse off are located outside of the bath cubicle. People do not go to these baths, but rather, go to the club to exercise or the hotel to pass the weekend: the steam bath is simply one among several options for relaxing and washing up. Indeed, in such places, people rarely spend long periods of time. The bath is reduced to a site for muscular détente. The hygienic qualities of sweating, in the gym and in the bath, might be extolled. When the plastic hammam was first installed in the club I go to in central Paris it did initially provoke conversation among women trying it. Some professed to know how to use it, others sought the advice of people of North African origin or those who had lived in or visited North African locales. But then and since, the locker room has remained the "thickest" area for conversation.

Thus, even the displaced hammam continues to carry associations of whole bodies and exotic beginnings, but now the beauty salon is cited as an open place where bodies cannot but be en-lightened. In Casablanca, Hakima tells me that the practices of the "illiterate woman resemble those of the beginning of the century. Except that she wears the veil less." She goes on to say, "Even it she isn't educated, she'll still be influenced by European style. But she'll have a hard time pulling this off, since her education and background don't allow this." Education is perhaps not essential for imitation, but it does indicate a special way of enacting it. This requires particular settings for the work of self-production: "I'd say, though, that the educated woman is another woman. She goes out more and she does sports. She lives more outside of the house. She goes to the hairdresser and the aesthetician." Indeed, if we consider how sport clubs, employment outside the home, and beauty salons have proliferated in Moroccan cities of all sizes in recent years, we might assume that there are ever fewer "remainders" left without instruction in how to follow prevailing fashions.[45]

Beauty salons, unlike hammams, are lively spaces of social interaction in Paris as well as in Cairo and Casablanca. The nature of these exchanges varies, but all salons are full of conversation. Techniques for styling hair and grooming bodies, however, differ markedly, especially between Cairo and the other two cities. In Cairo, hair is generally treated with hair irons warmed over gas jets, whereas the same kind of straightening effect is obtained in Paris and Casablanca by using the handheld hair dryer. In Casablanca and Paris, one might employ Egyptian women who use sugar and wax to remove body hair for you at home, but in salons, heated wax or cold wax strips are commonly used. Similarly, the use of twisted strings to remove facial hair is difficult to find in Paris or Casablanca, but prevalent in Cairo. In each of the cities there are different ways of naming not only the spaces in a given beauty establishment, but the kinds of people one might find there. In Cairo, most hairdressers are men; in Paris and Casablanca men and women cut hair. I have never, in any of the cities, met a male aesthetician, although some masseuses, especially for men, are men. As I explain in detail later, the presence of men, and especially of diverse types of men, has an effect on the kinds of discussion women have, as does the passage between the open room where hair is styled and the back rooms where aesthetic procedures are carried out. In this regard, it is interesting that, whereas in Casablanca there are a few "aesthetic institutes" that are not connected to hair salons, in the other cities hair and aesthetic care are often offered in separate institutions.

One way that Cairene salons are increasingly specialized is not in terms of what is done where, but according to who goes where. Increasingly, salons provide special women-only rooms for women who wear the hijab. There, only female beauticians are present. Some hairdressers applaud this trend, saying that it allows women to enter a profession that has generally been reserved for men. In Cairo, although there are mainly male hairdressers, only one hair salon I visited catered to both sexes on occasion. In Paris, there is a distinction between salons that cater mainly to women and those that are unisex, even if it is not formally stated. In Casablanca, a minority of salons are mixed. Other signs of distinction in Paris include "African" salons. These provide a distinctive way of treating tightly curled hair; generally, the styles are advertised as "Afro-Antillaise-Américain."[46] One might assume that "Asian" or "North African" salons are those located in neighborhoods associated with these communities (at least, as they are perceived by general society). But, except in the case of preparing women for weddings, these salons offer the same treatments as those practiced in other Parisian salons. Indeed, most *beurettes* (women of Arab origin) or women from Casablanca or North Africa go to the same salons as women whose grandmothers were parisiennes.

Contrasting the hammam with the salon has drawn our attention to the fact that women inhabit a variety of spaces, often because these offer diverse pleasures and results. Perhaps it is important to think about how these references take form not only linguistically but in terms of bodily practices related to image building itself. Do Casablancans simply absorb models from Cairo or Paris into themselves and in so doing indicate the social group to which they belong? Or is there a more complex process of seeing, choosing, and judging going on? Are all models, like all salons, indeed "open" to all?

The past decade has seen a dramatic rise in the number of beauty schools and beauticians in Casablanca.[47] The profession has also expanded in Paris. The diffusion of the salon has been accompanied, in all three cities, by debates about the Islamic veil or the hijab. For some people, the hijab is perceived as a way of halting the rush of fashion. According to Nawal, a student in Cairo, "A woman who doesn't wear the hijab, it's certain that she will be swept away by the flood of fashion." And yet, the hijab itself is sported by models in magazines specializing in fashion for *muhajibat*.[48] The fact that more and more "background styles" seem to be becoming light and emerging as figures of "la mode" shows once again the power of the en-lightening process. We must keep in mind that even a fashion conscious *muhajiba* relies on the heavy, indistinct contours of background bodies to validate her own demonstration of making choices about what to wear.

In Casablanca the image of the ʿroubiya (country woman) is often used to comment on the process by which heavy women might be rendered light. Listen to what Bouchara has to say about some of the changes in the city: "Ever since I was married in Casablanca, I've seen how people have changed a lot. There is an incredible competition between them to appear to be the best. Then there's also been the ʿroubiya phenomenon: these girls whose parents are from the countryside pass their time imitating others. But the problem is that all of these things are not done naturally, they're not beautiful and they don't go with these people." What she means by the ʿroubiya phenomenon is precisely the process by which the broader discourse exalts the moment at which the butterfly leaves her cocoon. The ʿroubiya could not have learned her way of walking from her mother, but she might develop her mimetic capacities in ways that threaten the "natural" precedence of women from old urban families. If she learns her lessons well, a girl from the "wrong side of town" or even from the countryside might not only dress in designer clothes, but also marry into elite circles. Or she might learn a trade that allows her to pay for the best hairdressers. Even without expensive accoutrements she might be very attractive in a simple pair of jeans or jellaba. She might not care about the "old modern" ladies—or she might mock them as being reminders of a forgotten time. Saadiyya is about forty-five. She dresses in an elegant but simple jellaba and wears her henna-dyed hair to her shoulders—often pulling it back with a barette. She says, "These women of the lower classes, even if they do everything to work on their look, I don't like the results. They aren't natural. For example, I've never worn a jellaba with embroidery [*ttarz*]. While they, well, you often see them dressed that way. If I don't wear it, it's because I feel that everyone should live within his means. In my opinion, only people who have the means should follow fashion: those who don't shouldn't imitate to try to compete with the others."

These comments on the conflicts involved in bringing to sight the lower classes of Casablanca are reminiscent of those produced in Cairo and Paris with respect to Moroccan women at the dawn of the twentieth century. But they draw attention too to how en-lightening might put all bodies on a single plane and, in making them subject to the same standards of judgment, give them similar goals, bringing about new kinds of competition. What Gustave Gebauer and Christoph Wulf call "social mimesis" takes place: " 'Social Mimesis' designates the process in which rivalries arise between individuals and groups sharing the same goal of action. The approximation of individuals to each other, their becoming similar, favors the development of equivalent valuations and equivalent perceptual modes, assessments, and aspirations, while at the same time the rivals sharpen their sense of self-delimitation in regard to each other."[49] This brings to mind the strategies of some muhajibat who claim that their dress, like school uniforms, eliminates competition among women. It draws on René Girard's understanding of mimetic rivalries and also recalls Pierre Bourdieu's influential account of culture and class relations in France. For Bourdieu, taste is the expression of one's class position which suggests that these little wars are the motor behind the very creation of beauties.[50]

However, though we must keep such competitions in mind, to focus exclusively on them is to renounce understanding of why information about beauty is shared, how it circulates among people of many nations, classes, and groups. And it is to fail to notice the extent to which social spaces like beauty salons offer scenes of exchange and instruction.[51] Why it is that women like Saadiyya, while disdaining "copiers," also make a point of "educating" them? What makes it glorious to be the one to pass on models, even at the risk of creating competition for oneself? The cascade of pictures and melodies, manuals and magazines among France, Egypt, and Morocco is not sufficient to explain this. But it forces us to break out of the confines of measures of taste and types that restrict themselves to state statistics and already assumed relationships between bodies and landscapes. To explain the push to teach, to learn, to emulate is to focus on the way that openings encourage telling stories of bodies' enlightening—and these are often more powerful than the urge to have land or gain possessions. This reminds us of Aurélie's beauty and her love: neither pursuit is for profit: she is in search of something more difficult to define than money or prestige. This thing she seeks is, if we follow the film, ultimately beneficial for all. Passing on knowledge is a process that, like beauty, can be powerful beyond the ways our names adhere to land and to visible possessions. Teaching, like learning, involves a will to find one's place not simply in terms of economic or cultural capital, but in terms of meaning and interpersonal exchange. Becoming beautiful is not a process of finding one's place and giving oneself the face of it. It is, rather, an ongoing ability to move through situations gracefully. It is a study of how to attract the "right kind" of attention.

Rita, an unmarried woman in her twenties from Casablanca, reminds us that beauty itself might be seen as the capacity not simply to compete for shared goals, but also to pass among different social worlds:

FEDWA: What are the criteria of beauty in women?
RITA: To be a beautiful woman is to be elegant. You must know how to talk, know how to receive people at home, know how to talk to people of all social classes, categories, and ages. The beauty of a woman comes not from her way of holding herself, but from her savoir faire and her way of talking.
FEDWA: Do you have a model woman?
RITA: The woman I find beautiful is Lady Diana. I read a lot about her; but I wouldn't like to resemble her because she has a lot of problems with her husband. For personality I like the Egyptian actress Hana al Achrawi, and the Egyptian singer, Athar al Hakim.

Rita's explanation of beauty requires being able to move gracefully in many social worlds; her ideas about style include specific references to how the time of day and moments of life intervene in determining what is "tasteful." Nejiba too has firm ideas about these matters:

NEJIBA: I don't like clothes made out of a half meter of cloth, like the miniskirt. I don't like bright makeup. Women put on too much—married women or unmarried girls. Today a girl of fifteen wears makeup and goes to beauty salons. In my opinion makeup for young girls should be light: she should use cool and light colors; a married woman can use darker, warmer colors. But she shouldn't just wear it anywhere—for example, she can wear it at home or for a wedding, but not just to go out in the street. There are several types of makeup: makeup for the day should be light. A woman can use colors like brown, close to the color of the sun, or pink. Evening makeup can be bright—she can use colors like scarlet.

FEDWA: How did you learn about these different types of makeup?

NEJIBA: I'm not such a great lover of makeup to make this up—I heard about it on a radio program about beauty.

FEDWA: Did you try these methods?

NEJIBA: No, because I don't wear makeup a lot.

FEDWA: Do you listen to the radio program often?

NEJIBA: I followed it regularly—a program about women's beauty on Medi–1 [a radio station based in Tangiers] on Saturday and Sunday. The journalist gave advice about beauty, *she even told you how to carry your purse!*

FEDWA: Do you think that a woman should follow such advice she hears on the radio, or should she follow her own taste?

NEJIBA: A woman should take care of herself according to her own taste, but she can also take certain points from the radio shows or in magazines to complete her knowledge concerning beauty treatments. There are some women who have no taste—these programs help them to learn to be more elegant.

Nejiba's comments remind us of the importance of the mass media in the development of general norms of demeanor and appearance. But the media also provide information one might not use for oneself but to access the moves of others. Listening to these women in Casablanca, we begin to notice not simply how women sharing similar worldviews or goals interact and form boundaries with others, but how each of these worlds is in constant interaction with the other. Just as we cannot simply compare Casablancan to Parisian to Cairene ideas of beauty, we cannot always contrast the "traditional" hammam to the "modern" salon. Clearly, the hammam is not necessarily a remnant of history. Nor can the salon be unilaterally associated with the instrumentalizing forces of modern economics. Busy working women might not go to the baths each week, but they often say they would like to. And women who do go to the hammam because of limited bathroom facilities at home often also go to beauty salons to have their hair done, especially if they are young and looking for a boyfriend or husband. As we have seen, salons and steam baths can coexist in a single establishment. Today, the ultimate luxury is often defined as having the entire range of body techniques at one's disposal.

One can easily imagine going to the baths to relax, clean, and purify one's body and mind, and then moving on to the salon to select the way one will paint on the canvas that has been duly prepared. A recent hit in Paris by Gnawa Diffusion ties desire to new dreams of closure:

Ombre Elle

Je voudrais être un fauteuil
dans un salon de coiffure pour dames
pour que les fesses des belles âmes
s'écrasent contre mon orgueil

Je voudrais être un parfum
juste pour me faire sentir
et sur votre corps m'évanouir
comme une goutte entre deux seins

J'aimerais être un peigne
et caresser vos mèches
être une main fraîche
dont la moiteur me baigne

J'aimerais être la poussière
de vos ongles sous la lime
et recevoir ce souffle intime
qui m'éparpille et me perd

J'aimerais être une ceinture
et serrer votre taille

pour ne perdre aucun détail
de l'étrange cambrure

J'aimerais être une chemise
et avoir pour seul dessin
de voiler vos noirs raisins
sans sur vous avoir main mise

Je me transforme et j'abonde
Pour ne pas vous rater
Mais pour percer vos secrets
il me faudrait être un monde.
il me faudrait être un monde

Shadow Her

I want to be an easy chair
In a hair salon where femininity
Makes the bottoms of beautiful souls
Crush against my vanity

I want to be a perfume
Just to scent and anticipate
Your body where I dissipate
Like a drop of water between your breasts

I want to be a comb
To stroke your tresses
To be a cool hand
Engulfed in their damp caress

I want to fall like the dust
Of your nails under the file
Just to know that intimate gust
That scatters and loses my soul
I want to be a belt to wrap
Tight around your waist
To feel its singular curve
In my tight embrace

I want to be a blouse
And have as my only plan
To veil your black raisins
Without ever laying a hand.
I must be transformed and overflow
In order that I not let you pass by

But to penetrate your secrets
I would have to be a world
I would have to be a world.[52]

Becoming formless, taking flight, or dissolving into the dust of nails under the file is central to the way many modern men and women speak about their dreams of love and possible lives. The impossibility of becoming "a world" expresses a utopia of access through bodily becoming through dissolution. To "pierce" requires that one entity acts on another. Does this mean that to become a world that breaks through implies the existence of yet other worlds? The limits of what the singer may indeed become are traced here by the closed doors of the ladies' beauty salon. What becomes a dream space offers him the possibility of belles dames unwittingly brushing up against him.

In "Ombre Elle," the lyrics begin not by looking at the space of fantasy, but by becoming a part of its furniture. The song puts its protagonist through a series of transformations. He does not ask to become more attractive to his love by becoming stronger, more handsome, or wealthier. Instead, he wants to become a blouse, a belt, and, in the most surprising transformation, the discarded dust of his love's nails. Most of all, he wants to be a chair, so a beautiful woman might sit on him. Is this a way of pointing out that the singer can achieve such a dream only by devious means, by transforming himself into an inanimate object? That things are closer to women than are men is a frightening thought—and yet, notice how women speak about how creams, perfumes, and hairspray can be used to "catch" men.

Beauty salons draw together women, images, and seemingly endless storytelling in a single space. They offer a setting where fashions and practice can be debated and their relationship to self discussed. Women, and increasingly men, the world over meet with their hairdresser and aesthetician to select a new "look," to relax, to converse. As you enter a salon, you can expect a standard series of gestures, words, and questions that reassure the travel weary and relax those tired from weeks of household chores and boss's demands. The descent into transformation might very well be described as a ritual by which the individual is transported out of his or her daily movements, undressed, immobilized, bathed, then formed anew by contact with pictures and the hands of the specialist. These moments are observed everywhere, and they are a part of what can make words superfluous. They enchant your visit to salons that might offer new collections of images, but where you can nevertheless be comforted by the predictable nature of this generalized routine. Elaboration of the basic motions eases contacts between professionals and their clients; they reassure you as you are decomposed, ready to take on a new face.

Yet, we must keep in mind that if this process is pleasurable for many women, playing with beauties is often threatening to men. "Ombre Elle" portrays the salon as a space of femininity where men enter only at the risk of losing themselves.[53] The procedures, products, and time spent on appearance in salons seem dangerous for men—they can be used by women to entrap them, or applied to them to dilute their masculinity. If the street is the space of potential dissolution for women, the beauty salon might be perceived as a space of peril for men. For the body that the ideal salon fashions propose is one that pays no more heed to gender traits than it does to personal history or ethnic identity. In the salon, our light being's vampirelike qualities become clearer. There, we draw on background bodies to provide pictures of ourselves, our family, our nation. We turn and return to the Greeks, to the classical period of Muslim philosophy, or to the exotic predictions of soothsayers to derive sustenance. We reuse these as remainders, easily represented in our own terms. We need them to model our utopias and to demonstrate our differences. And so we imagine our present with words from diverse pasts. We look into mirrors to "remember" the brotherly ideals of citizens facing each other, eye to eye, to find their own reflection.

In the eighteenth century, the word "society" simply meant being in the presence of others. This companionship might be qualified as "polite," "brilliant," or "rough."[1] We might keep this in mind in thinking about salons, for all salons are places designed to receive society, whether as reception rooms in Middle Eastern offices and homes in Casablanca, the "salons" that different professions organize in large conventions centers in Paris, or salons where beauticians produce looks. They all thrive on exchanges between people in ways that distinguish them from the "public" arena. Yet they bring together people who need have no special ties beyond the space of interaction they define. Keeping this in mind helps us to understand how a common appellation could come to describe meetings among artists and their expositions, the saloons of the Wild West, and beauty salons.

The development of a room called a salon in the *hôtels* of seventeenth-century aristocrats and bourgeois in France was linked to changes in perception of public space. New gradations were emerging, rather like the gradual heating of the rooms of the hammam, among intimate connections, good but general company, and the broad open spaces of the public sphere. A keener sense of privacy expressed itself in architecture and in Rococo style. It was promoted by such figures as Madame de Pompadour, who, as Louis XV's mistress then advisor, "not only encouraged Louis's interest in domestic architecture, but also directed it toward the small, the precious, and the intimate."[2] The value of privacy, intimacy, and comfort was exhibited by the development of specialized spaces not only at court but in bourgeois homes. Servants now slept in their own quarters, and children were assigned their own rooms. Chambers to entertain the family and intimate friends were distinguished from the salon, where many kinds of people could be received. As Witold Rybczynski points out in his history of the idea of home, this increased specialization included a clearer demarcation of inside and out, a point that was made through attention to the details of interior decoration and the improved comfort of furniture, particularly chairs and sofas.[3]

Women played a central role in social life of the ancien régime, and many grandes dames of the aristocracy were instrumental in promoting these new ways of arranging public and private space. But this did not imply, as it might have in other contexts, that they then retreated into the "feminine" space of the intimate and the curved and padded lounge chair. Indeed, when we remember this period and recall women like Mme. de Pompadour, what often comes to mind is the way that they used the salon to bring together not just any public, but a carefully chosen society. The salons sent brilliant conversation and scintillating literary and political ideas circling around these brilliant women.[4] Salons centered a changing society and played on ideas of excellence and social status, beauty and scholarship. These were exclusive affairs. Attending a given salon indicated that one was able and willing to be associated with people of a certain social set. A certain loyalty to the hostess was necessary, as everything circled around this figure of the belle dame. Her elegance, beauty, and intelligence served to draw brilliant, passionate, or controversial people toward her. She devised the invitations and played a role in deciding who could enter the conversation. She did this in a setting that, though public, was yet a carefully decorated, individualized interior—a place that promised a comfort not available in meeting places like cafés or coffeehouses.

The literary salon of the old aristocracy would have a long life under France's various nineteenth-century monarchies and republics. In the 1890s, the institution was "exported" to Egypt by a Frenchwoman who married a wealthy Egyptian. When Eugénie Le Brun created Egypt's first literary salon for women, Huda Sha'rawi and other women who would become important public figures attended it.[5] The salon idea took hold, and by the twentieth century Mayy Ziyadah organized the first salon to "mix" men and women.[6] Such associations of men with women in society were not necessarily made in all places where the salon became a separate space within the home; in some parts of the Muslim world, for instance,

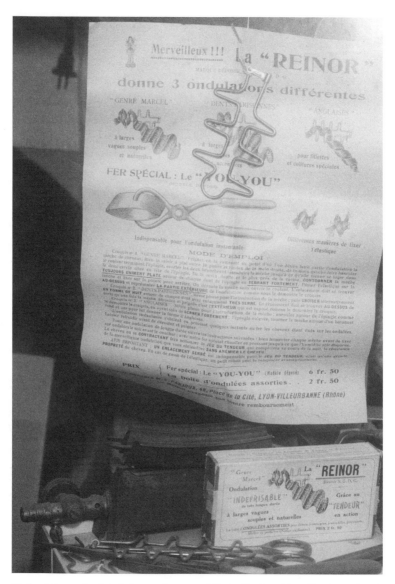

Tools of the trade. A hairdresser in central Paris displays his collection of anti-quated curling irons. He told me that he knows how to use all of these tools, some of which only went out of use with the diffusion of the handheld blow-dryer in the 1970s. In Cairo, curling irons heated over gas flames remain essential to the hairdresser's art. Photograph, Susan Ossman.

Tools of the trade. Photograph, Susan Ossman.

the domestic salon was where men and women might meet their pairs without the presence of the other sex.[7] But wherever the salon became the focus of the meeting of household and world, its ways of designating requirements for entry and its decor became important means of conveying important information about the people who offered hospitality there. This hospitality was not necessarily as regularly organized nor as centered around art and debate as the salons of literary ladies. But it did rely on a sense of progressive intimacies and the importance of reception. In some cases, as today among well-off families in Casablanca, a home might include more than one salon, each offering a decor to "fit" different kinds of society and distinct occasions. Most often, one room is decorated with long couches and round tables and called the Moroccan salon. Another is equipped with armchairs, coffee tables, and oil paintings; this is the European salon. The first is used for festivities such as naming celebrations and religious holidays; the second serves for parties and work-related events.[8]

All of these different salons have today become common in many parts of the world. Because they require the means to pay for a room separate from those in which one lives most of the time, people who cannot afford such comfort might meet their friends or colleagues in cafés, hammams, or clubs. The café is of particular interest, for, like the salon and public bath, it has appeared in different guises along the paths that define the field of this study. The café took form in Saudi Arabia around 1470, and Mecca, Cairo, and Istanbul became the centers of café society of the time. The institution later spread to include both coffee and tea houses throughout the Muslim and then the Christian world. But the *café maure* did not lead directly to contemporary café society as we think of it today. We must take a detour through the story of the café in Europe to make sense of how contemporary cafés in Egypt, but especially in the Maghreb, have profoundly reworked the space and interactions that we might observe today in these cities. As Omar Carlier writes, with colonization the "counter replaced the mat" as metropolitan forms became influential.[9] Chairs and tables filled spaces that were, like many of their Parisian counterparts, gradually opened up and turned toward the street. Old-style "Moorish" cafés continue to exist in Cairo, but the burgeoning new city of Casablanca was planned according to an aesthetic of turning outward: toward the ocean, the port, and the street. In this way, as in others, the new city on the coast of Africa did not so much "convert" old forms as offer the most avant-garde models of them to Paris and Cairo alike.[10]

In nineteenth-century Paris, the café was central to sociability outside the home. There were cafés of many sorts, and these played different roles in the lives of the well-off and the poor. In working-class cafés, as in their contemporary saloons in the United States, political or social clubs met.[11] The café thus included many of the same activities as did the bourgeois salon, but its consolidation of "society" was profoundly different. Like the salon, it was turned in on itself, away from the street, but it was nonetheless a space for which no invitation was required. In cafés, as in salons, there was a master of ceremonies. Of course, in salons, these masters were often mistresses; in cafés, although some women served drinks, owners tended to be men. The café owner earned his livelihood from the café, which was open for long hours every day. But he was different from other small businessmen. He acted as a father figure for many people, as evident in the number of bartenders who served as witness at their clients' weddings. He also had a regulating role on the nature of socializing taking place in his rooms: he acted as an intermediary with the municipal authorities.[12]

The bourgeois cafés of post-Haussmanian Paris, on the other hand, were places to display one's looks, wealth, or beautiful companion. With their large windows and open terraces they offered up the city as a moving picture.[13] These cafés produced spectacles of bourgeois opulence. They brought people to visualize emerging social distinctions and develop a new sense of "society." The working-class café offered insights into forms of sociability that might be related to the salon, but the bourgeois café shows us for what audience now light bodies were being disciplined. From its terrace we observe modern life taking form in the bodies of those who waltz alone or in groups along wide boulevards. The development of the *salon pour dames* must be related to the way girls learned to walk in front of these assemblies of eyes. All of these looks were involved in the development of a new kind of salon. The *salon pour dames* took form in response to changing lifestyles and notions of hygiene. It accompanied not only a new perception of bourgeois women "breaking out" of their intimate quarters, but also a new visibility in streets, parks, and cafés focusing on the figures of all women in unprecedented ways. The salon pour dames adopted the ideals of comfort, intimate decor, and conversation found in other salon forms. Women of "good" society could feel comfortable in these spaces. There they might catch up on the latest fashions and engage in talk with their (usually male) coiffeur in a way reminiscent of how working-class men might tell their troubles to a bartender.[14] For immigrant girls from the provinces or girls raised in "popular" (working-class) neighborhoods or by middle-class mothers who continued to pile their unwashed hair high on their heads, the importance of the salon went beyond an interest in fashion and intimate talk. It acted as a scene of instruction. It taught them new words to explain to the coiffeur how they wanted their hair done.[15] It often gave them access to publications on fashion they could not afford to purchase or, perhaps, could not read. It meant conceiving one's looks in terms of constantly evolving modes, and thinking about the picture one would make wearing these as one walked down the street. All of this research took place in the company of a specialist in a setting that, though open to all, was far from public.

In Paris the salon pour dames began to become popular in the late nineteenth century; it wasn't until after the Great War that the institution became a presence in the life of most city girls. Steven Zdatny notes that in France, "By 1921, the sector of coiffure had surpassed its pre-war population, with more than 57,000 enterprises. Through the late 1920s and 1930s the numbers continued to climb. Between 1931 and 1936 alone the population of hairdressers increased from 94,000 to over 125,000" as more women of all conditions hoped to look and walk "like the movies."[16] From the 1920s we enter the age of the "new woman"—a look that, depending on movies, fashion magazines, and political positions, had women from Paris to Cairo, New York to Shanghai bobbing their hair.[17] It is in this context, as we have seen, that well-groomed Cairene and Parisian ladies contemplated their march toward liberation and imagined ways to free their counterparts in urban Morocco.

In Casablanca, salons and French hairstyles accompanied the building of "new cities," the coming of the moving picture, and the arrival of French and southern European immigrants. At first, the Muslim and Jewish women of the medina had no use for them. The use of Western beauty products seems to have preceded the habit of salon going, but photographs collected in family albums from the 1950s show that, in at least some families, pictures seen in movies, fashion magazines, or schoolbooks were reiterated in the look of the schoolteachers, shopkeepers, and homemakers of various origins who began to inhabit the new parts of Moroccan cities. City women of some means gradually abandoned the relatively recognizable (if varied) outfits of their religious and ethnic groups to "mix" on the street or in exclusive clubs and often took up the cry for unveiling and reform of country and working women in ways reminiscent of their Egyptian and French elite predecessors.[18] So, although Cairene beauties and Parisienne femmes fatales graced Casablancan screens and might have served as models for a fortunate few during the 1940s and 1950s, only a few women had the opportunity to think about going to the salon to mimic them.[19] It was only in the 1960s and especially the 1970s that more and more city girls of all regional backgrounds began to use the salon as a meeting place and as a complement to their formal education. Indeed, with the advent of television, for instance, sources for looks required neither literacy nor fancy connections. Even in the poorest districts one began to notice how some women began to discard the scarf popularized at independence (already expressive of a move toward a "national" as opposed to an ethnic style).[20] Hassan told me how as a child in the 1960s he was startled when he saw young women in his working-class Casablanca neighborhood walking down the street wearing "hairdos." He remembers being puzzled by the new shapes of women's heads. Used to seeing girls with their hair covered, straight, or braided, he was baffled when they suddenly sprouted "cones." He recalls pondering how such changes could be wrought, and being amazed that the women never seemed to "take the hats off." The "beehive" had come to Casablanca.

COMFORT AND CONVERSATION

Today, in Moroccan, Egyptian, and French cities, small towns, and even villages, you will find a salon pour dames. The salon is judged not only in terms of the results it can promise, but in terms of the experience it creates. As a place of learning and exchange, it continues to reflect some of the characteristics of the living room and the literary salon. The interior decorating, clientele, and location of a salon provide clues to who will feel comfortable there. Decoration and ambiance are especially important for salons that draw on clientele from outside a specific neighborhood or social circle. Alex is a fifty-six-year-old hairdresser. Of Greek origin, he was born and lives in Cairo and has spent time working in the Gulf. He says: "In the salon I like to listen to nice music, to have a nice atmosphere to do good work. I'm interested in everything from the moment the client enters the salon until she leaves. I want her to be satisfied and I try to see if there's anything that she needs. Sometimes we forget this, but often a little thing is enough to make the place pleasant. A little smile from all of the workers gives a nice impression of the hairdresser to the client. This also depends on the space of the salon. In a large salon clients can stay longer and talk among themselves and feel at home. A smaller salon becomes simply functional."

For many people, simplicity is often seen as a guarantee of hygiene, as in the common use of light colors and white smocks reminiscent of medical clinics. As Malika, an employee in one such "functional" salon frequented by secretaries, schoolteachers, and sometimes anthropologists in Casablanca, points out: "The work in any salon is the same, but in a big institute of beauty you pay more than in the salon. If at the institute you pay more it is because the room is better decorated. You might have a living room–café inside the institute. But for the hairstyle . . . there is no difference between the salon and the institute. The only difference is that of price. The institute can double or triple the price compared to the salon." Toufik explains that though decor might attract people, it is how people are treated that makes them want to return. He works in a salon in a working-class area of Cairo, which, though not chic, is very popular. He says, "Each salon is understood in terms of the psychology of the person, if she feels at ease or not. Some salons are very simple but the client feels at home. In all of this it is the personnel that makes the salon pleasant, it is the interest they show for the client." Indeed, the arrangement, the dress of the workers, styles of music, and mix of magazines are often carefully attuned to what owners perceive to be their own "personality." Claudia, who owns and manages a Jacques Déssange salon in what was until recently a working-class area of Paris, points out that the salon should be very clean and the colors pastel and "natural." "This helps the clients to relax," she says. "You have to be 'soft' with the customers, take care of them and be at their disposal." The importance given to decor, to comfort, and often, to the orchestration of routine not only seems to move toward a homogenization of the process of decomposing and refashioning bodies, but does so in ways that can encourage specific kinds of discussion.

Talk is central in all kinds of salon. This observation might lead us to analyze the beauty salon as the latest development in the move out of the salon of domesticity toward a public place to receive guests, to a public arena where all were welcome. Salons often figure in the tales of "opening" that women tell to describe their increasing presence in public space. Such an interpretation seems coherent with Habermas's well-known ideas about the emergence of bourgeois society evolving a new sense of equality, of information, and of civility in such meeting places. His analysis focused on how conversation between equals shapes these spaces and ideals of democratic polities. With a keen attentiveness to how changes in English sociability, politics, and economy were intertwined during the eighteenth century, he drew attention to the development of institutions such as coffeehouses, where men of all classes could, for the first time, meet. And he connected their verbal exchanges to the expansion of news in papers, to the very idea that items of information could be conceived as discrete, quantifiable, and marketable. Habermas suggests that coffeehouses especially, but also French literary salons "encouraged a kind of social inter-course that, far from presupposing the equality of status, disregarded status altogether. They replaced the rituals of rank with a tact befitting equals." These institutions thus promoted a sense of a common set of concerns and the circulation of cultural products and information. They " ... converted cultures into a commodity (and in this fashion constituted it as a culture that could be an object of discussion to begin with) [and] established the public as in principle inclusive."[21] Such ideas might be applied to contemporary salons. However, as in many analyses in this vein, the value of exchanges seems to emerge out of these spaces to the extent to which talk leads to public, political talk and a consciousness of each man's playing a part in the constitution of civil society. The literary penchants of the French salons, for instance, are presented as less "pure" examples of how new social spaces help to open up political vistas, for at the time they involved a more veiled, artistic, roundabout way of con-fronting explicitly political concerns, given the absolutism of France before the Revolution.

Habermas developed a complex philosophy based on relating political to communicative ideals, and other scholars have pursued further histor-ical research into the epoch in which he grounds his analysis of Enlighten-ment. Don Herzog, for instance, suggests that the study of the emergence of modern public life in Britain should include research into spaces besides coffeehouses. He seeks to round out accounts like Habermas's by exploring another major eighteenth-century English institution: the barbershop. The barbershop, Herzog argues, like the café, was an arena of political transformation.[22] He details how, at the barbershop, news was shared and political debates engaged in. The barbershop, he asserts, like the café, presents men as equivalent. It is a place to come to hear the news, express one's opinion, feel a part of the new civil society. Could not the beauty salon too, which, after all, bears the name of an institution Habermas saw as central in France's "peculiar" move toward democracy and civility, act as such a forum?

We might search after the production of talk about politics or the common good in contemporary salons. As we have seen, the idea of the anywhere body seems an equalizing measure. Epics of opening fit harmoniously with the notion of a move toward a modern idea of publics and society. A friend in Casablanca did say that she sometimes went to a salon there where the beautician made a point of encouraging "intelligent debates." "The hairdresser is a political activist," she said. "It's not all about making feminine beauties, as you say. In that salon there are only intellectual things to read—newspapers and such reading materials." In Cairo, Lucy's might be presented as a likely candidate for such an embodied glimpse of an egalitarian utopia.

> In one of the old arcades in the new old city center, the salon is compact, but full of men and women. It has wood paneling, several pictures, and areas for pedicure, manicure, and waiting. The helwa (wax) for women is done upstairs. They don't do hair. On the coffee table are cards from clients and a photo of Nejib Mahfouz, who was a client. There are magazines in Arabic, German, and several other languages. A small woman with glasses and another, wearing a hijab, greet the customers and direct them to the aestheticians. Several children of employees come in with their schoolbooks. Men and women get manicures and pedicures; the man does the feet, the woman the hands. They are of all ages, and seem to know the clients well; they also know the children and talk to them. This place seems more like a "neighborhood"-style salon, but it seems people come here from other areas. The atmosphere is extremely relaxed and quite different than other salons. One gets a feeling of the

functionality of the place—it is fairly reasonable. Conversations are lively, friendly, and I immediately feel at home.

The impression of comradely exchange at Lucy's might convince us of the possibility of ideal communication situations that implicate equals in conversation aimed at the betterment of the world for all. Yet, their very particularity forces us to leave such dreams and rethink perspectives on places, public or private, developed along Habermassian lines. Many women do indeed go to the beauty salon even when they don't need to have their hair done, especially in Casablanca and Cairo. They see friends there, catch up on the latest gossip, read magazines, and even watch television. But the sense of "common concerns" varies and is rarely preoccupied with the national or international political scene in an overt way. What is held in common might be neighborhood news, a certain language, or an identification with a style of talk that excludes some women from fully participating in the conversation. Access does not guarantee meaningful involvement, and all talk is not attributed the same price in public spaces conceived as markets. Perhaps, rather than search out spaces of interaction that conform to a given idea of the polis and progress, we need to analyze how it is that certain spaces have been adopted as icons of opening epics, while others, less clear in their disentanglement of public and private, have been ignored.[23] According to Seyla Benhabib, modern philosophy's development has involved a "privatization of women's experience." She writes that, "in the philosophical tradition from Hobbes to Rawls," women have thus excluded this experience from being considered from a moral point of view: "In this tradition, the moral self reflects aspects of male experience; the 'relevant other' in this theory is never the sister but always the brother."[24]

The very constitution of what counts as serious knowledge in both philosophy and science has much to do with notions of community grounded in ideals of fraternity. The development of "intelligent eyes" in this context has been related to a move away from the consideration of the unique eye of the monarch and toward the development of a generalized eye that could see things from several points of view. This kind of intelligence was thus intimately linked to the development of an idiom that allowed for the exchange of points of view on common objects. But not all objects were of equal interest, and many kinds of people were seen as lacking the kinds of virtue that such sight required. As Steve Shapin notes in his study of the elaboration of the tenets of modern scientific method in Britain, whereas the basis of this method involves certifying the reproducibility of results, the scientific discoveries of the time were in fact evaluated as much in terms of the social status and supposed virtue of the scientist carrying them out as any real possibility of their being replicated. Although women and assistants actually carried out much of the work in the homely laboratories of the period, the light of truth fell on their work only when it was underwritten by the scientist as "Christian gentleman." "If reputation were to assist the production of true and legitimate knowledge, then an honorable man had to remain visible as the author of that knowledge."[25] A scientific community judges the work of pairs; it does so according to rules that seem indifferent to the body or the personal characteristics of the scientist and yet, to enter into the fraternity of science requires a special kind of individual. For those Shapin studied, science required a willful exclusion not only of women and men whose experience was not to be taken seriously because it is apparently too partial, particular, or bound to bodily functions or desires. The "relevant other" was therefore a member of a fraternity of like-minded men. Only those select few were trusted to produce points of view in terms that mimicked the intelligent eye associated with the quest for universal knowledge and goodness. Women and lesser men might be reasonable, they might be trustworthy in many ways, yet their eyes were not to meet those of their brothers, if for different reasons. They might be trusted with the creation of comfort that allowed men to disengage themselves from the pull of bodily needs, thus freeing themselves for serious speculation. Such disengagement was the mark of belonging to the fraternity, and to sense its importance we must be especially attentive to private parts.

Herzog's study of English barbershops leads him to maintain that their openness to all resembled not only the café but also the bordello.[26] There, all comers could receive services for a fixed fee. And yet, while a scientist as prominent as Robert Boyle was making a virtue of his sexual abstinence, those who entered the public house were evaluated in ways that might not have been so complimentary. And once inside, the comments of the women they possessed dwelled less on their sameness than on their special qualities or individual desires. Civilizing the male body included a contrast of public decorum to private, hidden vice. And thus the belle dame as mother, wife, or sister was set against the hidden charms of the painted lady. Men who could not play on these ideas of public and private might be ineligible for entrance into the civil fraternity. In the early days of the French Enlightenment, those who debated the serious affairs of the city often relied on women's salons and ideas. Yet, with the march of enlightened ideas, it seems, even this womens' work became less visible, less formative of notions of science and civility. Indeed, according to charts of progress based on measures of moving out of backgrounds, out of body- and virtue-bound existences toward a world of anywhere eyes, concern with morality, taste, or comfort were perceived as signs of femininity and of political immaturity. The exclusion of women from the public meeting of voices was, ironically, explained in terms of the very social graces that assured the success of the literary salon. The many guises of "personalism" continue to be opposed to modernity in contemporary political discourses in Casablanca, in Paris, and in Cairo.[27] In one fell swoop, too-close family relationships, economic corruption, and notions of influence are portrayed together as threats to the democratic development of society, now seen as a united body, not to mention for the correct functioning of the polis. The categorical imperative is often repeated not by professors of philosophy, but by bureaucrats who promote a sense of "individualism" as a force for democracy, and a civil society defined by its market aptitude. And this sense of "fairness" is opposed to what is often seen as the particularly feminine emotion of shame (*hshouma*) and ways of hiding, exhibiting, adjusting to the demands not so much of argument as to particular situations and how we animate relationships with specific kinds of others.

Lila Abu-Loghud explains, "The concepts of *hasham* (shame) and *'gl* (reason) are closely wedded in notions of the ideal woman. The woman who is *'agala* (reasonable, characterized by *'gl*) is well behaved: she acts properly in social life, *highly attuned to her relative position in all interactions*."[28] According to Soumaya Naamane Gessous, hshouma is both a matter of shame and guilt, but it is present in all places and all times:

> The word doesn't need to be said, *hshouma* dictates, controls, forbids, it is there behind many actions. It concerns the poor, but also the rich, men and women, the young girl—especially the young girl—the city dweller as well as the peasant; the nomad, the scholar but also the il-

literate. It is a code which one conforms to without reflection, and it legislates all situations of existence. It's what one will say that causes fear, and the discredit will not only fall on the shoulders of the guilty party, but also on those close to him and on all of those around him.

Thus, the *hshouma* of one is not the *hshouma* of the other: *hshouma* for the young girl is not the same as for the grown woman or for a man: *hshouma* for youths isn't the same as for old people, *hshouma* in the city is not like in the country.[29]

Bernard Williams echoes these remarks when he notes not only the importance of shame to ethics, but that "Shame need not be just a matter of being seen, but of being seen by an observer with a certain view." Shame, he argues, results from being seen in the wrong position; it is rooted in a fear of being caught naked. As we have seen, the very idea of nakedness varies, and shame must take on different shades in front of various others. An awareness of these diverse positions might lead us not toward an abandonment of modern ideals, but to a keener sense of possibility and the particulars of participation than simple versions of epics of opening offer us. Williams suggests that we need to reintroduce our sense of shame into how we conceive of ethical life: "It is a mistake to take that reductive step and to suppose that there are only two options: that the other in ethical thought must be an identifiable individual or a representative of the neighbors, on the one hand, or nothing at all except an echo chamber for a solitary voice. These alternatives leave out much of the substance of our actual ethical life. The internalized other is indeed abstracted and generalized and idealized, but he is potentially somebody rather than nobody, and somebody other than me. He can provide the focus of real social expectations, of how I shall live if I act in one way rather than another, of how my actions and reactions will alter my reactions to the world around me."[30]

Beauty salons, even more than barbershops, might work to produce an ideally light body. They may play on the idea that we can become anything and anyone. But even the most fleeting visit to a salon shows the extent to which they play on this "rationalization" and equivalency in terms of the kinds of internalized others Williams describes. In salons, these others are involved in the shared secrets and the "unserious" gossip of the juicy particular. They enter into the development of competencies of beauticians. They deeply affect how clients form ideas of belles dames and painted ladies, but also how they conceive distinctions of public and private. However these spaces are defined, they are formed of the eyes and ears of named and known others, whether friends or famous stars. They work together through the en-lightened body to produce beauty and distinction and sometimes a sense of sorority. Indeed, even in salons frequented by both men and women, salon talk is strongly associated with a sense of feminization and fluff.[31] That the fuzziness of salon talk spreads over even the most serious topics is what makes some people detest their comfortable spaces and claims to social skill. This talk is thick, intense. It often divulges the limits of the private and the boundaries between bodies.

If salons are open to both men and women in many locales, their talk and their attention to body care highlight how even in mixed spaces the value of serious conversation as outside their bounds is restated.[32] Most men I interviewed, chatted with, or overheard saw salons as places for "small talk." They derided such conversation as "gossip" and discussions about "beauty and products" as frivolous. Some men even express a fear of such loose words as potentially dangerous, for they imagine, some-times correctly, that salon discussion often chooses them as their subject. There seems to be a concern that talk about relations between men and women will end up introducing the girlfriend into what many men see as a relationship whose practices and problems should go unspoken. Of course in nearly all salons women do analyze and compare their experi-ences with men. And these might indeed have an effect on how they con-ceive of and work with their relationships to their husbands or fathers. This talk usually does not pretend to develop a line of action for the nation or the world in the way that café conversations often do. And so it appears to keep feminine issues enclosed, incapable of disrupting a certain sense of the "serious" business of the city. The curling and washing of hair, pe-rusing the latest styles, engaging in the changes of appearances that is the main activity of salons is perceived as futily feminine and superficial pur-suits by most men and some women.[33] These activities may include efforts to render self and style more legible. But as Gnawa Diffusion brought to our attention, for those who stand outside the door of this space, it can be a mysterious magnet for women's secrets and men's fantasies.

If the barbershop is, like the bordello, a place where all men might meet and recognize their bodily similarity, the beauty salon might be seen as the place where all kinds of women go to develop their sense of difference. There debates about bodies and virtue are not those of an anonymous fraternity but of named, known people. In and around salons the emphasis on talk evidenced in so many accounts of civility remains, but here voices are muted and augmented with references to fame and special skills. They urge us to notice how mastering techniques of bodily transformation involves salons and beauty schools and relations among colleagues.

SKILLS AND VIRTUES

Casablanca, 1992. There's a brand new salon in the neighborhood. It is located on the main street of the area, you can see it every night, and its neon lights in pastel tones present an image of a man to one side, a woman to the other. As you walk past, the entire space lights up and sparkles like a rhinestone in the night. Both the women's and the men's sides have a large plate glass window, not the discrete, covered space seen in so many of the other salons in the area. So I decide I should visit. One afternoon I go in, ask for a haircut, and wait my turn. The salon is already pretty crowded, although it's only been working for a couple of weeks. With my entrance, a heated discussion takes form among several of the women working in the salon: Who should get this new client? Foreigners are reputed to be richer than locals, a preconception that is rarely based in fact, as this is a solidly upper-middle-class neighborhood. Finally, a woman asks me to change into a robe and have my hair washed. She spends a long time massaging my scalp, and tells me I need a cream to get the tangles out of my shoulder-length hair. Once the hair is clean, she combs it out. I listen to the radio, a series of Egyptian songs. The young woman brings me to a chair to have my hair trimmed. Samia will cut my hair. She smiles and tells me what a nice color my hair is. She wonders whether I'm not Egyptian. I laugh, wondering why she thought I was Egyptian. "Well," she says, "so many of the Egyptian actresses have blonde hair and blue eyes like you; and you have kind of an accent." I tell her I'm from California, a fact that seems of no interest to her. She really loves Egypt, she says, she reads all about the actresses and singers—especially the singers, because she loves music. She's never been to Cairo, she says, but she will travel there some day.

As we talk, we both watch the mirror. She is careful not to cut off too much hair. As I'm just getting a trim, it doesn't take too long, and soon, she is taking out her brushes to begin drying my hair. One of the sizes she needs is missing, and she has to borrow one from a colleague. The other woman is not happy about this, because she obviously wanted to be the one to style "the foreigner's" hair. In these first weeks, it seems that the hairdressers are trying to lengthen the list of "their" clients, and Samia looks like she's about to win over one of the more desirable new faces.

Samia begins to dry and style my hair, mouthing the words to the song on the radio. Suddenly, the other hairdresser appears behind us in the mirror. She frowns and tells Samia, "You're doing it all wrong, look, turn it like this, the other way." She grabs the brush from Samia, who has no choice but to let go if she wants to avoid pulling my hair. The other hairdresser proceeds to take over my head, frowning and reworking the areas that Samia has already curled. Is she the manager? How can she do this? I'm wondering to myself, when she says, "I'm so sorry that she was doing that to you, but we'll fix it up. Don't worry." She begins to show Samia how to do it "correctly." Her voice sounds like an elementary school teacher correcting lessons in grammar: How could you get it wrong? she seems to exclaim with each breath. Her hands move over my head insistently, she pulls and pushes my head and hair, as if to make me feel that my hair was all pointing in just the wrong direction. Her insistent tugs seem to say You can feel how right I am—how I know how to guide your hair, whereas that other one didn't.

Finally, the ordeal is over. My hair is shorter and fuller than when I entered. As I leave, I give a tip to all of those who have treated me. The last one, I still don't know her name, is still puffing, smiling too widely at me as though to say "Look, you'll know to come to me next time?" She seems to be the manager, or one of them. She takes my money and I leave, intending not to return.

Like the steps of the ballet dancer, a beautician's skills depend on coordinating certain moves. Skill is judged by the professional's ability to reproduce specific gestures, which lead to a regular, predictable result. The beautician's knowledge is demonstrated by his or her training, diploma, and manual skill. But the professional's attraction is augmented by knowing how to employ these skills in ways that keep in mind particular faces and their relationship to sets of other eyes. We can observe this process most easily in beauty salons, but even when beauticians in Paris and Casablanca and Cairo provide services at home to avoid taxation or provide work for women who lack the certification or the means to open a "real" salon, this process is an integral aspect of their occupation.[34] One's reputation depends on gaining information about the kinds of people one routinely serves. Beauticians who cater to the rich and famous in their homes often operate salons for less illustrious, yet well-heeled clients. There, they hang photographs of "their" stars on the walls to demonstrate their links to fame. Each paying client can feel the touch of the talented hand that curled the hair of those stars.

All of those who wash and cut, curl and style hair, strip off leg hair, or pluck eyebrows must master physical gestures and ways of explaining them. Both involve extensive practice. *Webster's New World Dictionary* defines practice as "To engage in frequently or usually. To do repeatedly in order to learn or perfect." Translated into French, *repeter* adds the sense of repetition to the gestures of practice. To insist on this aspect of beauty "culture" as a set of skills one learns through imitation draws our attention to the way that hairdressing and aesthetics involve training and traditions of learning. These are passed on practically—by means of example and through repetition. One need not be a specialist to master these techniques; nonetheless, one does not simply "pick them up" in the unconscious way in which Mauss suggests that body techniques are learned. Beauty skills involve a hand-to-hand passing down of traditions and secrets. This passing on is often perceived as problematic because of the fact that these expanding professions work to "form" an increasingly large number of girls and sometimes boys. Often, these young people have not been especially successful in school, but they are savvy enough to know that in the beauty professions they might not just earn their living but perhaps one day become their own boss. Managers and beauty school operators often voice particular concern about the kinds of girls they educate and employ. One director of a Casablanca beauty school was eager to explain that she sees herself as a kind of social worker. She described most of the girls at her school as being from underprivileged backgrounds; most had not completed high school. Yet, "in today's conditions, they need to work." As Homa Hoodfar writes about Cairo, "Tailoring and hairdressing were considered by most informants as occupations suitable for women, but very few women were qualified enough to be considered skilled: top tailors and hairdressers in the neighborhoods were men. . . . The majority of these female tradespeople had turned a room of their flat into a workshop or rented a room in the neighborhood for their business. It was rare for these women to want to move out of their locality, where they were able to attend to their domestic responsibilities while they worked. At times, women would forgo the possibility of a bigger profit to work near their homes."[35]

In Paris too, beauty professions are often seen as a choice for girls and boys who lack the money or intellectual qualities to pursue advanced education. Martine explains why she became an aesthetician and her sister went into hairdressing; she attributes it to the "feminine" influence of her mother. "I enjoy working with my hands," Martine told me. "I was good at cooking, painting, and manual things and so I knew I would enjoy doing makeup and everything. My family didn't have money for me to go to the university, so I became a beautician." Malika in Casablanca said, "When I left school, I learned to sew. But I didn't like that job. I enjoyed fixing the hair of my little sisters; I spent my time braiding their hair. My father told me that if I didn't like sewing I could do something else, so I started to style hair. When my parents died and I got married, my husband wanted me to stop working but I refused since I had gotten used to my profession as a hairdresser."

Women and men who work as beauticians and aestheticians explain their choice of work in terms of pleasure, a need to earn a living, or a desire to develop their artistic skills; managers, like educators, tend to put the accent on their efforts to control the looks and movements of these apparently unruly elements. Concern for the style and looks of their employees is a major source of concern for beauty salon operators. It is relatively easy to provide a tasteful decor and pleasant setting in a salon, but because it is the relationship with the beautician and the result of his or her work that ultimately defines the "space," an often uneasy balance must be established between the kind of uniform "style" sought by the owner, and the art of the beauticians. The style of the salon extends, then, to the appearance and manner of people who work there. Monique surveys the comings and goings of her employees to get a "good idea of the kinds of people they hang around with." Halima, who owns a small salon in Casablanca, exercises strict control over the dress of her employees:

"Personally, I had an aesthetician who came to work in the hijab. I didn't accept that because the clients come to get made up and become pretty— how could she work with a scarf? In the profession of aesthetician, you must be presentable. You have to always be an example. For myself, I don't always set my hair, but I pull it back and I'm always made-up. Because when you're in the salon you must serve as an example."

The regularity of beauticians' looks are enforced by imposing uniform dress for employees. Often, this uniform matches the colors and decor of the salon itself. Managers pay careful attention to the activities of the employees in their salons as a central part of their role. The reputation of their workers might reflect back on them. They worry not only about how they look, but also how they act and with whom they associate on their lunch breaks. Their words echo a million discussions about how to turn these "poor girls" from "remainders" into efficient workers. For if processes of decomposing, examining, and reworking bodies are fairly easy to practice, the dangers of enlightenment are also on the minds of many. What happens when so many techniques for beautification, not to mention organizing competing businesses, are taught to girls from "who knows where"?

Noticing all of the arduous labor that goes into learning new practices brings us once more to think about the kinds of communities that sanction knowledge and virtues or enforce ways of walking. Indeed, to become a professional involves one in practices shared by a group of people one may never see. This shared world affects how professionals move and shape others. It inculcates habits in a way that is profoundly articulated with the ways that looks we notice or ignore can pave city streets and populate places we go. The measures of excellence that beauty instills are less like those of the habitus described by Mauss, than akin to the ways we learn to play music or master the processes of a specific cuisine. These skills take time to learn and to perfect. And they involve a more or less voluntary decision on the part of the person who practices them, defining practice as "any coherent and complex form of socially established cooperative human activity through which goods internal to that form of activity are realized in the course of trying to achieve those standards of excellence which are appropriate to, and partially definable to that form of activity, with the result that human powers to achieve excellence, and human conceptions of the ends and good involved, are systematically extended."[36] There is something about perfecting one's skills that can sharpen one's ability to learn about excellence in general. Knowledge of playing the guitar might be helpful if one wants to learn to play the sitar. Knowing how to cook French cuisine, be it *bourgeoise* or *populaire*, can, if we have mastered our art, enable us to think about food in a way that will help us to quickly assimilate the rules of Japanese or Mexican cuisine. Possibilities of acquiring specific skills are certainly limited by access to capital and level of education. But because techniques and their excellences are in constant change, a young girl "from nowhere" can truly be a threat to a comfortable, middle-aged salon owner—not simply because of a difference in social status or the possible threat of the young person's personal beauty, but because the mastery of skills itself points to potential for change. Mastery allows us to be aware of how the habits of the arts themselves offer clues to the eyes that matter in different social worlds.

To discern how the particularities of the beautician's art might teach us how to think about all manner of techniques, including ethnography, we might notice one major difference among the salons we have considered thus far.[37] Although talk is thick in all of them, the contemporary salon is unique in its plays on mirrored light. Old-time saloons often hung a mirror behind the bar for all to gaze at their mingling reflections; the beauty salon works in much more subtle ways with the central glass. It uses many prisms to illuminate faces with different combinations of rays. Are these not all a part of progress and lightening, democracy and equal rights for all? The distinct frequencies of light itself are difficult to identify if we simply notice the difference between foreground and background bodies out of context. But their rainbow colors become radiant once we set ourselves in any salon to notice what is beauty's central defining element.

MIRRORS AND REFLECTIONS

All clients, men and women, gaze at themselves in mirrors in beauty salons. But they do so at many moments, for many reasons, and in several ways. Plutarch wrote, "When you get up to leave the hairdresser's boutique, you place yourself in front of the mirror and you touch your head, examining the way in which the hair has been cut and the difference it has produced in the cut."[38] To concentrate too much on that specific moment of correspondence of reflection to desired result, that repetition of ges-

Envious eyes. When you look into the mirror you see yourself as if with another's eyes. You observe the beautician's eyes on you, and perhaps other eyes appear around your reflected image. This popular manual on jealousy and the "eye," published in Egypt, advises women on how to work with the eyes of others.

tures that reproduces an image of *copie conforme*, is perhaps to heed too naïvely the concurring discourses of men who do not wish to think of how this copying takes place over time, in front of others. Unlike the outdoor barber stalls for men that one can still find in the old medina of Casablanca, the salon does not use a handheld mirror simply to check whether the results of the haircut are adequate. Rather, the mirror participates in the entire process of elaborating a style. It intervenes to guide not only the movement of the eye, but that of the hand, not only the evaluation of the final product, but also discussions of the process that produces it. Clients catch glimpses of each other's treatments or meet each other's eyes in the mirror in the course of conversation. Words follow their glances, and these are used to bring absent, yet particular, others into the salon.

The plate glass mirror is a recent invention. Mirrors used to be forged in hammered copper or bronze and had to be handheld. The reflections they proposed were as uneven as the metals they were made of. Paintings of mirrors on ancient Egyptian implements and ancient Greek urns show women looking down into their mirrors, as if into pools of water. Like the fountain in the hammam or the mosque, itself a reminder of the river's flowing, or the surging of well water (or the *'in*: the word for eye and that for source are the same in Arabic), mirrors might reflect, but their surface revelations also signal something more. Françoise Frontisi-Ducroux and Jean-Pierre Vernant suggest that in ancient Greece, "If mirrors are reserved for women it is due to their condition being defined by closure, even reclusion, and the face to face meeting with this thing that reflects back to them their own image illustrates this closure marvelously. As for alienation, there is no risk, since the woman is other by definition. She is already an object; she is, in the tradition that sees her ancestor as Pandora, materialized at birth, by her essence and her status."[39] At the same time that mirror gazing was associated with the frivolity of such contact, it might also point toward something as deep, mysterious, and profound as the source from which the water of Narcissus' river springs. Mirrors are dangerous: they exhibit our potential for self-enclosure, for anarchy, a flight into which might be neutralized and socialized by the mediation of other eyes. For the Greek citizen passing by another, to observe oneself meant catching the eye of an equal. Friends met in public formed the ideal mirrors by which to measure oneself. Indeed, it is perhaps by focusing on the agonistic implications of this gaze of equals that anthropologists have often conceived of ancient Greece and contemporary Mediterranean societies as being dominated by a preoccupation with reputation, associated with this "superficial" reflection of self in the eye of the other. For Greek men, staring into a mirror "presents a twofold danger. Danger of becoming closed into oneself, that would be fatal for the male individual like it is for Narcissus; for his vocation is in being open to others, to those like himself, and in socialization. Danger of alienation, in assimilating a reflection made by an object, engaging him in a quasi-reification."[40]

The image of Greek men debating in the Forum has been incredibly powerful for many modern thinkers. Scholars have engaged in all kinds of research concerning the nature of these interactions and their viability as models for our own thinking. We know of the Greeks' political and philosophical debates, of their sport and amorous adventures. We now pay attention to how citizens' exchanges in the polis presuppose their status as masters of the hidden world of the *oikos*, the enclosed world of women, children, and slaves, the world of production and reproduction from which evolved our understanding of "economy." But few philosophers have been inspired to reconsider why the mirror was dangerous to political community. From what kind of envy or desire did the oikos require protection? What might enclosures have to do with how men saw one another in each other's eyes?

Even the most sophisticated versions of sight produced by Greek thinkers bear little resemblance to how we tend to think of this process today. David C. Lindberg explains that one school studying optics in the ancient world attributed sight to a kind of substance issuing from the eye to touch the thing seen, the extroversion theory. Others saw the thing observed as entering the eye through some mediating substance.[41] But both approaches involve the object of sight in some kind of mediated physical contact with the one seeing. To see the other is to share a special kind of touch with him or her. You touch with the radiant substance from your eye, or he or she enters you via the shared substance of vision. Looking at oneself in the mirror is thus an act of enclosure, not a process of enframing but a reaching out or entering of oneself. This reaching out involves not only people, but all natural objects. Avicenna, Al-Kindi, Robert Grosseteste, and Roger Bacon are only a few of the famous thinkers who played a role in developing Greek accounts of sight, leading eventually to the "modern" notion of light reflecting on the retina in the work of Kepler. The story of optics that Lindberg recounts offers us a glimpse of how the problem of the mirror is not simply a matter of reflected light, the issue of confinement not easily expressed in terms of spatial domains. Of course, it is Kepler's version of sight that "we" use to explain how we see. For us, eyes neither send out substances to touch objects nor allow shrunken things to enter them through the pupil. Today, sight as contact is definitively forgotten, or seen as a vestige of a primitive magic.[42]

It would seem that in the age of mechanical reproduction, the age of the world picture, of the domination of "empty" vistas of sight, only the heavy minds of social and cultural remainders could continue to speak of bodily radiation or being touched by the look of another. Mirrors, it seems, play a role in the disenchantment of the gaze and consequent precision of measurement and accuracy of representation. Richard Rorty writes, "Without the notion of mind as mirror, the notion of knowledge as accuracy of representation would not have suggested itself."[43] How he develops his thesis makes much of the idea of truth conceived in terms of correspondence and fidelity. These are important, of course, to stories of en-lightening and the claims of bodies being able to be "anywhere." But our glimpses into salons show us how much more complex are our ways of using mirrors and reflections. They offer us new means of understanding our common world. Neither the dangers of self-examination for men nor the power of touch have faded over the years. This is apparent to me when I notice that men, even if they do have their hair done in the growing number of mixed salons in Paris or Casablanca, have little to say about these visits. Visiting salons encourages us to think about sociability not just in terms of the intensification of conversations, but also for what it does with silence, with a quiet exclusion of some not only from talk but from ways of transforming their bodies and the shape of their day. We should remember how the en-lightened body can act as a "third," as something held in common.[44] Noticing how masculinity is challenged by this third and the bodily similarities it implies might also lead us to understand how even the "thinnest" salon talk can involve tricks on manliness.

Becoming a beautician is often perceived as a particularly appropriate thing for a young girl, but everywhere, boys who choose this profession are viewed as lacking virile qualities. Work in salons does seem to attract more gay than straight men, perhaps in part because of the stigma of this profession that works on female bodies and involves much "small" talk. Even many heterosexual beauticians feel that in the salon they must relinquish signs of manliness. In Cairo and Casablanca, a significant number of male stylists are Christians or Jews; as "lesser" men, unable to legitimately marry Muslim girls, they might also present a face that associates them with Paris, the symbolic center of fashion. How one might play on such identifications was brought home to me when I accompanied my friend Souad to see George, her hairdresser. I met his employer, a woman of Greek origin who had been raised in Cairo. Souad explained to me that George was not Orthodox, like his boss, but an Egyptian Copt. But as Souad and I talked about my research with George, he made allusions to the festivities of the Aïd al ftr, talking about his and his family's preparations for the Muslim holiday. "But aren't you Christian?" asked Souad with surprise. "Of course not!" he replied. "I'm just George here because it's better for my professional progress. My real name is Mohammed." George/Mohammed explained that people in Egypt assumed it would be more risky for a male Muslim to touch women's hair. He also intimated that people thought hairdressers weren't real men, even if they were Muslims. Perhaps his pseudonym helped him to keep things "straight" himself. To assure us of his sincerity, he talked about his wife and proudly showed us snapshots of his three children.

Many salons in Casablanca, some in Paris, and an increasing number in Cairo exclude men from their premises. But the moves toward different mixtures of male and female bodies are being made in different directions in each city. In Casablanca, most beauty salons are owned, operated, and patronized by women, but many of the upscale shops in the city centers employ male hairdressers.[45] These salons, some of which are Parisian franchises, are often perceived as closer to the centers of fashion than those located in neighborhoods, which are often characterized as closer to the center of personal concerns. Some women go to the stylish salon to get a cut, then move to the often inexpensive salon around the corner for regular washing and styling. We often find such practices in Paris, where the development of quick salons, the fast-food restaurants of the beauty world, are rapidly coming to predominate. I go into these different types of salon in more detail in the next chapter, but here, it is important to remark that these fast salons are always mixed. In Paris, neighborhood salons populated mainly by women tend to be associated with older ladies and outdated fashions, symbolized by their bubble hair dryers. In Casablanca, this is not the case, but a trend toward including more salons with less explicit boundaries between men and women is apparent. Men, it seems, are either taking over these feminine arenas of talk or, as many recent books and articles would lead us to believe, something is taking place that makes it more desirable to associate oneself with a certain version of the feminine.

As we move on toward Cairo, however, what in Casablanca seem self-evident divisions are put into question. There, male hairdressers clearly dominate all kinds of salons. This has not, however, been accompanied by the development of a mixed clientele. Although most beauty salons in Cairo employ men as hairdressers, many people see the recent "reveiling" of many women there as having brought about a change in attitudes about women's hair. Women who take the veil may indeed cease to go to the hairdresser at all, but many simply seek out salons where they will encounter only women. Dina's salon, for example, now has three separate rooms: one for hairdressing in general, one for aesthetic treatments, and another for muhajibat, that is, women who have taken the veil and who want to be touched by or take off their head coverings only in front of female, often muhajibat, hairdressers. Asmah argues that this movement toward women-only salons has actually opened up employment opportunities for women as hairdressers, a profession previously occupied mainly by men: "When I first started, I had a hard time since people are used to male hairdressers. But now, with the quality of work I do, I've succeeded in making a name for myself among the well-known salons. I've also tried to encourage women to work in my salon."

The virtue of women and making a name for oneself as a beautician seem entangled in work that excludes the kind of reflective approach to knowledge that Rorty sees as symptomatic of modern philosophy. Salons participate in trying to work the body into the even, named, and numbered sections of schedules, charts, and maps. But they also force us to look into mirrors to carry out this labor. You may show a hairdresser a photograph of the way you'd like to have your hair done. But he or she shapes this and adds to it. This extra touch is a part of what you come to the salon to get. It is the result of the specialist's skill at playing with the image as you. His or her mediation adds to the reflection to explain what you are. And this extra touch is what distinguishes competent from extraordinary hairdressers or aestheticians. Gilles, who has a salon in Casablanca, explains that he learned the "touch" while working for the celebrated Jean-Louis des Forges: "Above all what I learned there was the 'touch.' A touch consists of chatting for five to fifteen minutes with a client in order to study her style, her colors, the texture of her hair before even covering her with the robe and wetting her hair. For example, if she has a prominent nose, you should thin the hair in the back. You also have to take into consideration the proportions of her body: *la coupe garçonne* (bob) with big hips and a small bust gives a woman a look like a bottle. An older woman with hard features and long black hair can resemble a vampire. You also have to take the client's profession into consideration. A nurse who takes off her cap from a shag cut ends up looking like an egg head."[46]

Knowing how and whom to touch brings to the fore a series of questions about the relationship of sight to picture to skill. The mirror of the beauty salon draws us to think about how what looks like a move away from messy combinations of sight and touch that produce unenlightened musings on personal qualities and the shame of contact with certain specific kinds of others might not be what modernity has wrought. This makes us more aware of how one can become the special client of a given hairdresser.

Delphine is just back from vacation. She comes into the salon smiling, tan, and energetic amid the midwinter paleness of the rest of us. I sit having my hair cut, and I watch her as she greets Stéphane, the manager, and one of the women in charge of washing hair takes her coat and helps her into her white robe. I lose sight of her as she moves toward the back of the room where the sinks are. I watch as Eric trims my hair—not much new here. I've had this cut for a while and so we don't have to talk about it much. Instead, we chat about how hard the winter has been, and he tells me he's planning to take off a couple of weeks in March to go to the Caribbean. Meanwhile, Delphine reappears in the mirror beside me. The entire wall is a glass, so I can watch her every move as she is seated, and her usual hairdresser, Marc, takes his place behind her. They exchange greetings, "It's been a long time," "How have you been," and all of that, and then he starts to move his fingers through her hair. What is it you'd like? he asks. Well, probably something like I have, Delphine responds. But Marc is skeptical: It's grown out badly, he remarks; I wonder if you don't really need to get another cut. Well, you know, Delphine adds shyly, I just had it done about three weeks ago while I was on vacation in L.A. My friends from the French cultural services there rave about this one hairdresser—I can't even remember his name, but I had him do it. Marc looks ever more skeptically at Delphine's hair. He stands above her, holding her midlength locks of damp hair between his fingers as his face takes on various expressions between hopelessness and disdain. "Well, yes, they must do things differently over there," he finally concludes. (At least that guy isn't down the street but twelve thousand kilometers away, at least she can't remember his name. And after all, that L.A. look is so glossy and brash anyway, why should he feel offended? She just wanted to see herself once that way—she'll return to her normal parisienne classicism, just you wait!) Delphine looks hurt, but of course, she'd expected this kind of reaction. All her friends loved the long shag and new highlights. They made her look just a bit exotic, they prolonged her sense that she had been somewhere, gotten out of the usual routine. She'd even bought some of those flashy "outfits" they wear over there—such a funny word, sounds like you're getting a boat ready to sail. Funny how so many of the designers there are European, but the clothes don't look quite the same under the bright sun.

But what was she going to do? I wondered. Would she give in to Marc's desire to remake her as she was, or at least redesign her as his?

"Let's try what I have, but just a little shorter," she finally says. So Marc begins to snip, to comb, as Delphine watches his moves in the mirror, commenting about everyone, and by the way she'd like to have the "bangs just a little more feathered" or he should "leave the back pretty long—I need some of that length." She tries to engage Marc in conversation about his life and the neighborhood, but his look of concentration, the way his eye remains intent on her hair, reveal the extent to which he feels challenged by how "his" client so blithely put herself in the hands of another. Granted, he's not as well-known as that, he only works in an upscale fast-salon, a nicer example of the salon version of the fast food restaurant, but he pays attention to his clients. Delphine lives nearby and she always comes to see him. Like the other beauticians in the salon, he has his bevy of special clients whose color is carefully inscribed in personalized notebooks and whose cut he adapts to the lifestyle they describe to him during their sessions together.

To understand beauty and salons, we cannot simply begin with the idea that the evenly lighted, valueless worlds of modernity render us indifferent, or should make us indifferent, to the touch of fame and personal relationships. Meaning is produced in these particular relationships in ways that are not akin to the see-saw between modernity's clear-headed gaze and the warm, sensuous tug of some background body. To understand salons, their talk and looks, we have to think about the ways in which issues of value infuse bodywork, nets of sight, and ways of naming. And this implies rethinking the idea that a mirror shows us not just our self, nor a means to produce copies, but can also bring any number of other eyes before or behind or across from our own. Mirror work might be basic to the simple realization of the ego, of the self as a separate being.[47] But we should notice how we construe this ego by recalling how the mirror itself came to be placed in our way. How its changes in size, position, or frame might not alter even the contours of what we take ourselves to be.

Mirrors, if well placed, can help us get a glimpse of the others who make us what we want to be. Thus, they might help us to understand how and why the anywhere en-lightened body ekes out some place to live, some face to wear. In beauty salons, part of the process of talk and technique involves using mirrors to scrutinize the kinds of present, absent, or internalized others that matter to the kinds of beauty we will be. The art of the beautician includes the images the client verbalizes about spouse, relatives, and friends. These people have names; they belong to social worlds that the beautician must understand to be effective. But others present also take part in the production of looks. Glances and comments from the other women present sometimes play a part in making up other clients' faces according to what is known or imagined about these people. Paintings, photographs, ads too intervene in these exchanges. Glances, observations, and advice shape the way we ourselves come to look and think about ourselves.[48] And it is up to the beautician to move in sync with all of these to somehow embody the women's unique social place, to render visible who she is and where she hopes to go.

Beauticians take on the role of both seer and judge. They play before the mirror to establish their particular eyes as more farsighted than their colleagues' or competitors'. When the beautician and the client exchange glances via the mirror, they implicitly work on what is "good" for her. In front of the mirror in his Cairene salon André gives his version of mirror work: "When you see yourself in the mirror and notice that you are beautiful, this gives you a desire to live. Having a good hairstyle goes with wanting to be nicely dressed. This makes you another life, it makes you joyful. . . . God gave us beauty and we should continue to give beauty. Me, when I see a woman who is poorly arranged, I begin to draw her in my head—I imagine what has to be done to make her beautiful. I always like to learn from magazines and I also do my own creations to not simply copy these. I look at the woman's face, her style, and I talk to her a lot to get an idea of her personality and to try to give her what is best."

Look at how mirrors are set before each chair or encompass the entire room. Notice the looks of the other hairdresser-client couples around the room. Follow how the interplay of image, talk, and movement acts to create several frames: those of the mirrors that project images, those of salons, which also provide a primary closure, and those of the various areas in salons, which may or may not all revolve around the central glass.

Mirrors reflect whole worlds, each working with what seems to be a similar body in very different ways. To play with Rorty's attention to the mirror and thought, let me suggest that we think about the looking glass not simply as a metaphor but as something that actually changes how we reflect on sight and goodness and how to think. To do this, I must shift to a new movement in this research. For if we want to begin to use salons to think about how techniques and virtues, practices and ideas of excellence transform our relations to ourselves, we have to show how they participate in fashioning society.

Although salons are indeed a kind of forum, their aim is not to produce equivalences but differences. They are called on to display and rework hierarchies of all kinds. They unveil bodies according to choreographies of relative value. They open out spaces where talk is possible among many, and close off areas where only one-on-one discussions with the aesthetician can take place. Beauticians promise to assist you in determining what it is you can be. To do this they must be able to imagine where you will go and what faces of others are important to you. Beauticians must work within the salon, but also be able to imagine absent others who may be essential to your look. This is how they can help you to find the faces you might hope to become. To establish the trust needed to do this, they ask you to join your vision to theirs. Expertise, conversation, friends and families, and anonymous bodies give form to beauties that engender new distinctions. These imply several kinds of closure and offer different vistas that make sense of others' eyes. As Gebauer and Wulf write:

> While modern rational thought refers to the single isolated cognitive subject, mimesis is always concerned with a relational network of more than one person: the mimetic production of a symbolic world refers to other worlds and to their creators and draws other persons into one's own world. As is apparent in this constellation, mimesis implies the recognition of mediation between worlds and people; it does not designate a subjection to received models, but rather an acceptance of traditions and the work of predecessors. It also implies a recognition of power: the inclusion of others introduces power, if only in symbolic terms, into one's own personal worlds, into the interpretive and perspectival modes developed there. The history of mimesis is a history of disputes over the power to make symbolic worlds, that is, the power to represent the self and others and interpret the world. To this extent

mimesis possesses a political dimension and is part of the history of power relations.[49]

The idea of point of view presupposes a shared field of vision. In this shared plane we might locate not the moment of realization of the already existing ego but a formative site where the emergence of self is traced on the ground of collective sights and emotions. To share different perspectives requires that we find common ground on this clearing. This is precisely what women who rage against the 'roubiya phenomenon are trying not to do. Their attempts to foreground themselves as examples of a specific "type" are attempts to stake a claim to modernity that others seem unable to take in stride. They, unlike those others, have not so much incorporated a specific way of walking but have learned to render themselves according to changing media. The issue, then, is not whether these women claim to make a "choice" of being modern or traditional; it is a question of how they display themselves as one or the other, when, and to whom. Could we consider the idea that different "worlds" they encounter shape our looks and values differently?

Several ways of arranging abstraction to intimacy, glances to conversations appear to be at work in beauty salons. These refer to processes of opening that imply not only distinct uses of salons, but different ways of walking out of them.[50] In a roundabout way, we now return to Mauss and his marvelous intuition: walking and the movies, walkers passing points of judgment in the street—these are the faces and the bodies that must be produced in salons. We must consider their arrangement and relationships so that we can understand how beauty salons structure new distinctions. We can begin to see the extent to which issues of social difference are profoundly linked to specific arrangements of significance. From thinking about how beauties reflect diverse landscapes, we can come to see how they also shape the lay of the land by the ways they travel over it.

Moving from Casablanca to Cairo and Paris is facilitated by the common epic of opening. We can follow its development to work with time and link it to types of people and kinds of places. The pervasive tale of moving out of the background makes us constantly aware of how a single name covers a variety of looks, and this similarity is often justified by the point at which that figure is said to have emerged in the course of lightening processes. And so I wonder why it is in heaviness itself, or the way we phrase tales of its forgetting, that we tend to locate the origin of differences we observe in beauties. Many people look at the heavy body, with its pull toward the earth, toward what might be termed local or cultural or particular, to seek clues to how mirrors propose distinctive ways of shaping, clipping, or coloring our modern heads. The epics we increasingly share throughout the world encourage this kind of movement of to and fro. Yet, by moving through beauties, then into salons, I noticed how other movements might in fact upstage the interplay of heavy and light. Just as being attentive to how a common name identifies bodies that look very different raises suspicions about the way en-lightenment stories dominate our conversation, salon talk and beauticians' ways of producing beauties produce variations that are not apparent in the way we group them under a single appellation. Diversity among them might be stated according to their location, their language, or their price. But perhaps neither these nor a simple contrast of particular to general can explain the ways that different kinds of salons take form. To label a salon as typical of Casablancan or urban, Cairene or elite culture is imprecise. To recognize significant differences among salons we must explain how they play out

Halqa 'lia/Haute Coiffure, Casablanca. A hand-painted sign on a Casablanca hair salon advertises "haute coiffure." In contrast to Cairene preferences for curling irons, this image uses the "bubble" hair dryer typical of pre–blow-dryer hair salons as an icon for the trade. Photograph, Adrienne Alvord, 1989.

their routines against background bodies, but also point to each other as backgrounds against which to project their own special qualities.

Salons contribute to the tapestries that stretch between cities and mix local color. Each salon, like each city or nation, lays claim to en-lightened bodies and certain shared looks, the names and measurements of which often traverse continents with incredible ease. But the bodies they form with these looks and names are diverse in ways we might compare to a butterfly woven, embroidered, or embossed on a single bolt of cloth. A woven figure is integral to the very constitution of the fabric; a printed wing, on the other hand, might appear on one or both sides of it. Already embroidered patterns too might then be patiently stitched into it. Each procedure effects a distinct interpretation of the figure that shares a single name. Each requires a different technique. Stitching through is not the same as weaving into. But weaving, printing, and embroidering can constitute and embellish the same cloth. This diversity is not only a matter of distribution and appropriation, it is fundamentally an issue of how techniques produce distinct versions and set butterfly against butterfly. This contest is often left unnoticed when those involved in it debate origin and access as a means of demonstrating that their mode of producing the figure should serve as a model. To understand how certain bodies can pretend to lay claim to this precedence, we must avoid adopting the means of identifying beauties that enforce the common identification that serves to uphold the notion of a single model. Instead of fitting beauties into rungs on the ladder of progress or measuring their proximity to centers of fashion, it is possible to work with the kinds of society and the eyes of intelligence and shame that shape them in the precisely defined spaces of salons. We then come to understand how issues of technique, of determining excellence and eyes that can judge are essential to noticing how what looks similar is not quite the same. We can thus better understand how plays on difference contribute to the common cloth of the enlightened body.

The eyes of shame are not everywhere the same, but this can't be simply explained in terms of what a given body might seem to say. Instead of positing a body's link to the land or thinking we understand how it might represent a single identity, I began my investigations by looking into mirrors.

Imagine you are getting a haircut. You hold a picture up beside your face, telling the beautician to cut a bit more here or feather the bangs, as in the photograph. In one salon you hear the voices of several women telling you that you really ought not to have your hair cut as short as the model in the picture. In another, the beautician carefully gazes back and forth between the photo and your face and hands, concentrating on the reflection in front of him. His hands move swiftly; they seem to argue for precision. In yet another salon the stylist's languid moves seem to imply that he cares for each and every hair on your head. He converses with enthusiasm about the wave you've always hated in your hair. You think it keeps you from adopting any style you see, but he assures you that it is lovely and asks you to please put away that awful photograph—would you not rather simply look like the real you?

The central glass reflects gazes, glances, and how the hand of the coiffeur makes judgments. These in turn imply a certain touch of her hand. Noticing this led me to recognize patterns that neither stories of enlightenment nor the moves of people and images from Casablanca to Cairo, Cairo to Paris could account for. Like butterflies woven, stitched, or printed onto a single fabric, three different kinds of salons color the fabric of each of these cities all at once. Each emits particular frequencies and intensities of looks between beautician and client. Some discipline and define in terms of carefully guarded spaces. Others make sense and control bodies by reproducing measurable types that are in turn propositions about someone who takes them on might act and actually be. Still other beauty salons produce faces that claim distinction based on their relationship to special names, places, or ideals; they, like the others, are dependent on the reproductive repetition of modern media. All work to guide people in their movement through the many kinds of worlds they dance through daily. However, each produces and promotes different ways of patterning the steps of this dance. The common ground is constantly altered by these diverse arrangements.

PROXIMATE SALONS

If you are an avid reader of recent social theory, or someone who thinks that sensuous experience can be contrasted to the imagined universes opened out when you turn on your television or surf the World Wide Web, you might look for the world of face-to-face exchanges in one of the many salons in Casablanca, Cairo, or Paris that tend to attract people from the immediate neighborhood. Salons of this type are easy to get to by foot. You need not read about them in a magazine or the Yellow Pages. People who congregate in such places often know one another. These salons might be thought of as epitomizing the cozy, bodily sociability often associated with the idea of locality. Dierdre Boden and Harvey L. Motoloch write, "Co-present interaction remains, just as Georg Simmel long ago observed, the fundamental mode of human intercourse and socialization, a 'primordial site for sociality,' in Emanuel Schegloff's phrase."[1] Opposing the anonymity, abstraction, and bureaucracy of modern life, social spaces like these salons seem to express a veritable "compulsion of proximity." Close to home, close to one another, a certain warmth seems to penetrate our system-chilled bones, our *télécommande* tapping fingers.

Often, neighborhood salons have small windows or carefully drawn drapes. They bring bodies close to one another and "densify" the exchange of ideas and secrets. They seem to foster these intimacies by hiding them from public view.[2] Such protection in the process of producing beauties reminds me of the birth work of butterflies. This kind of salon, like a cocoon, is a place to nurture bodies in formation; it is also a setting in which the body to come is formed with reference to a specific landscape. But this ground is always in flux, and the density of talk in the salon, like that in cafés or the hammam, helps to constantly redraw it. The face-to-face, proximate sociabilities of cafés, salons, and living rooms are central because they involve seeing oneself through the eyes of those gathered within in terms not only of their individual sight, but of the ways the eyes of people we know work over and into spaces of sociability, no matter how concealed they are from eyes outside. Proximity is about others' eyes and the touch of a hand. It is tangled up in the very idea of the primary. It is not dialogic, but shares references to certain central figures, stories, or places.

In these salons, a glimpse in the mirror often shows a group of women congregated in a corner, chatting. If you join this group you will notice people coming in and out of the salon to deliver drinks, pay a bill, or just say hello to the beauticians. When you enter, you get a sense that their often restricted spaces offer a lengthening of time, a moment of calm respite to forget the clock. They follow the routine, like all salons, but here the most salonlike talk flows almost like the steam that permeates a hammam. Words flit from one subject to another to densify the atmosphere, but they require a special kind of knowledge to be understood. They circle around the accident that took place in front of the bakery, the marriage of a girl named Samia, or the way a soap opera character left her husband. Talk thickens as stories are passed around the circle of those present to paint a picture of people, things, or places known by all. The neighborhood salon bears a special relationship to ideas of domesticity, family, and the promotion of a man's reputation through women's looks. In Cairo, Hanem, who is a housewife, explains: "I haven't gone to very many beauty salons because ever since I was very young I got used to accompanying my mother to the salon. We went to Ġarib's right next to my house to get our hair done. I still go there myself and I find it really pleasant. It's like I feel like I'm at home. It used to be that hairstyles were difficult to do—they were complicated. . . . There were not so many beauty salons then, and women only went to them occasionally, even though the styles were hard to reproduce at home." Huda, a secretary and mother of four, tells Aïcha, "Beauty salons are often linked to family—often a whole family goes to the same one. My mother, my sisters, and I find it really nice. I don't go much

Bodyeyes. This image of a many-armed woman by an anonymous artist that I found in a Casablanca shop plays on a woman's eyes: not only does she wear a Hindu *tilka* as a third eye, but her breasts are themselves rendered as large blue eyes. This painting makes me think of the intense yet varied looks one feels and the glances one sends out as we move through the different spaces of our lives. It is as though we have several kinds of eyes we can employ at once. Tempera on wood, anonymous, author's collection, purchased 1993.

now that I'm married and wear the veil. But all women have to do their hair. Of course, now I'm veiled, but I do my hair before I put on my veil. . . . Women have to be beautiful as wives; that is what I do. Otherwise he'll go find other women. He will always try to make comparisons. He's always out—I have to work to keep him."

In Casablanca and Cairo, the "neighborhood" is often expressed as a space in which honor can be surveyed and thus, ironically, girls can circulate with relative freedom. In the neighborhood, it is assumed, people know each other's names and their family relationships. This knowledge acts to "confine" in ways that the salon expresses by insisting on its boundaries.[3] Zhora says that she goes to a neighborhood salon not only for company, but because "in the neighborhood it's known that that's a good place. Miriam, the hairdresser, has always lived here. She and her husband are well liked." Neighborhood salons often purport to be the only ones that can truly protect women from being seen by the wrong other eyes. In her study of poor women in Cairo, Hoda Hoodfar writes, "Because a woman's chastity was crucial to the honor of her family and her chances of marrying respectably, in her early youth, she would be prevented from going out unaccompanied in public beyond the immediate neighborhood. Consequently, many young women were fearful of leaving their neighborhoods on their own and preferred to go with friends. Many men prized young women who knew (or, more commonly, pretended they knew) nothing of the world beyond the four walls of their homes and who were incapable of performing any task traditionally outside the female domain."[4]

Beauty salons act as spaces to enclose femininity. But the eyes of proximity can look into salons at the most unexpected moments. In Casablanca, my friend Jamila told me the story of a woman in her neighborhood:

This woman went to the salon all of the time. Her husband knew that— it wasn't a problem for him. Until, one day, he began to suspect that she was having an affair. He wondered whether she didn't just pretend to go to the salon. She must really be with him! So one day, she says she's going to the beauty salon. He waits a couple of minutes and then he goes over there. He barges in, searching frantically around to see whether she is there. But what does he see? Her purse is on one of the chairs. The salon owner is frowning at him, telling him to leave his wife alone: she was in the back room having her legs waxed. And so he left, apparently humiliated by his own hasty coming to conclusions. "But you know," Jamila ends her story, "she really was off with her lover. She had a deal worked out with the beautician. She always left her purse there just in case."

Whatever the truth of this tale, it gives us an idea of how women perceive the salon as a space not only of beauty, but of potential solidarity. This adds to the sense that it is a space set off for feminine concerns, a fact that further accentuates the reactions of those who cannot go there. In the course of talking to people about salons, men were especially keen to tell me about all of the "illicit" things that went on "in there." Although many salons sell clothing, cosmetics, and even medications that cannot be locally procured and a very few salons act as fronts for prostitution, these activities are marginal. What men's reactions lead us to notice is the extent to which the arrangement of neighborhood salons as spaces of femininity is perceived as somehow dangerously invisible, exclusive, and thus frightening for those whose presence is often evoked there, but who can enter the space in bodily form only under the most exceptional circumstances. If we notice the ways neighborhood salons work to produce and comment on the fabric of the neighborhood, the group, or the couple itself, we notice no absolute exclusions, but a gradation of gazes.

The eyes of women, young men, and children are not superfluous to the texture of judgment, even though proximity often makes them auxiliaries of men's eyes. A gradation of suspicion and of witness emerges in this universe. As we move from city to city, from neighborhood to neighborhood, the shades of this world might alter. But everywhere an uneven working of gazes contributes to reputation and decisions about how to look. We might refer to the weighting of testimony in legal battles to understand this. According to French law, a witness might be evaluated in terms of normality and sanity; the testimony of a person seen as inebriated, possessed of ulterior interest, or pathological will be doubted. There are expert witnesses and character witnesses. The Shari'a (Quranic law), on the other hand, assesses the value of legal testimony according to gender: a woman's witness counts as half that of a man.[5] But there are additional stipulations in determining the amount of trust we can place in an individual's observations or opinion. Noticing the fine nuances of evaluation in individual testimonies cannot lead us to some literal measure of the weight of eyes. But it does provide a sense of how judgments can be literally distinguished in terms of the attributes of the one who sees.

If you leave Rita's salon and take a walk down a Casablanca street, you will pass a street corner where the *drari* (young men) hang out. Their stares might be bothersome, but they bear little weight for reputation. Their words blow about like children's soap bubbles. Beware, though, of the words of the distinguished older woman, a *haja,* who leaves her home only occasionally. Her opinion might bear as much weight as that of anyone in town, for she is known as wise and modest. Her voice is carefully given space and weight for she has moved through her life in ways others have judged honorable. Her word will hold up to that of the most serious official or wealthiest of bankers. The witness of the local drunkard or the man who is known to engage in illicit traffics might, on the other hand, get short shrift when it comes to evaluating anyone's actions, character, or aesthetic choices.

The very way that information is given weight and skills assessed in salons fails to conform to the idea of knowledge as abstract and skill as measurable. The demand for universality is not primary, although, as we shall see later, it helps to distinguish what is special about neighborhood salons. Knowledge here is not warranted by diplomas or composed of lists of facts that can be verified. Nor is it evaluated in terms of an ideal dialogue between equals. This is a space dominated by certain densities, by an uneven social "surface" that the hairdresser tries to interpret in terms of style.[6] He or she shapes one's image in ways that conform to what people might say, think, do. What people should say, be, or do, however, is neither generalizable in terms of a universal subject nor according to "men" and "women," but is instead a matter of how the people present at a specific moment, in terms of a particular mesh of stories, come to judge. Iman, an unmarried data entry worker who lives in the Shoubra area of Cairo, helps us move further in this analysis when she remarks, "A wife must go to the hairdresser's because anything that she might try at home will never give the same result as at the hairdresser. Myself, I make myself beautiful to 'live my youth.' I tell myself all of the time that nothing guarantees that the man I will marry will let me do it, maybe he will be jealous, or he'll refuse me any contact with makeup." Iman's comments underline the importance of the eyes of men, of patriarchal powers. Her comments on her own actions as a youth and their relationship to the apparently inevitable moment of her marriage are interesting in thinking more generally about the idea of a "relevant other." For, as Iman shows, others might affect us long before we even meet them.[7]

Knowing up close is immediately a matter of densifying conversations and looks. This thickening does not take place within a closed set of people or places, but in terms of a set of patterns of interaction that, rather like charcoal lines on a sketch pad, deepen the shades of certain parts of the social world, a darkening that then produces points of light. The hairdresser is competent if she can assure women that coming to her will help them feel good about how they can move before others, and between, these particular points. She might be able to produce only a few types of hairstyle, but her job is not to address an empty world of fashion to invent fantastic, original works of fame. Her job is to allow women to move gracefully through the webs not of meaning but of engagements with others who are known and whose judgments count. These are the eyes and ears of significance.

At this point, you might ask whether this is not simply a description of what life is like in traditional places. Doesn't it demonstrate the difference between Muslim cities like Casablanca and Western, modern lives lived in places like Paris? The answer to these questions is both yes and no. There are indeed more neighborhood salons in Cairo and Casablanca than in Paris. In Paris, as in the world of social science, most people do not see neighborhoods as in any way binding, incarcerating, or limiting. They intimate that their worlds have all somehow completed the enlightenment process. Only in villages or small towns are close-minded neighbors watching each other all of the time. Still, even in the neighborhood where I presently live, a cosmopolitan, upper-middle-class area on the Left Bank, salons continue to play on the face-to-face. They need not be vestiges of the past nor associated with specific ethnic groups to do so. For example, a new salon recently set up shop on my street. When I went there to have my hair done about nine months after it opened, I expected to hear about how the place was working in its new neighborhood setting. I thought that the employees and owner might tell me about their move here, about the ways they were beginning to attract clients. But what I found was an already lively place full of women who already seemed to have come to know each other quite well:

> *Three beauticians in their fifties joke about the new* Elle *magazine, articles on how to keep your weight down over the winter. Most of the clients here are older women; the beauticians laugh about dieting as they tell me about how their clients bring them cakes, apples, and dried fruits. "We're going to have to have the door widened!" Geraldine jokes. The others insist that they're going to stop bringing in the croissants in the morning. But what do you do when the clients bring you such nice goodies? As I get my hair done, they gossip about the women who have just left the shop or who call to make appointments. Although I don't know most of them, I did recognize one of the clients who was leaving as I entered. I met her in the waiting room of a doctor's office down the street the week before. Because she greeted me, the beauticians all want to know if she's my neighbor. How do you know her? they want to know.*

In Cairo and Casablanca, and in Paris, the sociability of the neighborhood salon is often related to a certain incarceration not only of the feminine, but of women as representative of profession or social class, of ethnicity or generation. Today, neighborhoods are often characterized by a specific class, ethnicity, or stylistic trend, and within them, different salons themselves are diversely representative of these. The enclosed space of the salon seems to gather and intensify patterns of interaction in an effort to reinforce certain boundaries between groups. For instance, I noticed that many of the salons in Paris that provide a sense of face-to-face proximity include a disproportionate number of older women. But when I mentioned this to Sophie, she adamantly claimed that my observations were faulty, that she herself had recently been converted from a centrally located "fast-cuts" salon to a neighborhood place, where the hairdresser knows everyone. She is in her thirties, an active professional woman and mother. But she thinks that encouraging worlds where people look each other in the eye and gain knowledge about different aspects of each other's lives is important. Perhaps this is why she has chosen to live in a recently renovated part of the twentieth arrondissement that is often described as having the flavor of a village.

Moving toward Paris from Casablanca makes one more aware of such disparities within the neighborhood, as well as their distinct relationships to what we might think of as geographies of shame. The salons of the neighborhood can be seen as playing out the client-beautician relationship in light of many different eyes. People make an effort to remember one another's names and things about their life. In the context of my neighborhood in Paris, where the corruption of the mayor was an ongoing topic of debate at the time of my research, such knowledge of others, and the manipulation in favor of or against specific individuals because we "know" them, was a touchy subject.[8] Wherever we walk, we must remember that the eyes that watch might selectively turn away from certain figures.

I walk past the place where I usually get my hair cut. Their window is large, and I feel embarrassed to walk in front of it. I didn't like the cut they gave me last time, so I went to another place down the street that friends told me about. I'm happy with the cut I got, but I feel embarrassed when I pass in front of the old salon, not to mention when I see another hairdresser I've occasionally gone to at a local restaurant we both like to go to for lunch. I feel I'm being watched by the hairdressers who are fighting over the local ladies' hair. You walk through the street not feeling like you're noticed by anyone, but the people who own and work in the different shops do see where you go, even though only certain of them acknowledge you. For example, the hairdressers in the smaller salons greet me, smile. The shopowners I see regularly as well as the vendors at the open-air market do the same. Their relationship to their clients seems to rely on this mutual acknowledgment.

The people who work in the supermarket or in some of the large fast-cut salons are polite enough in the context of their work. But if you see them in the metro station or in the street, they look right past you. You exist only in terms of the role you play as client—and once they have dropped their position as employee, they no longer see you. They have made your hair fit the model, have added up your prices correctly, and have politely sent you on your way. Their work is clearly listed in a charges de travail *and they have faithfully fulfilled their contract. I sometimes wish that Francis, who cut my hair once, could be more detached, stop staring at my new haircut from some "foreign" salon as I order a salad for lunch in the restaurant next to his shop. Yes, I tell myself, he really is nicer than that young woman who did the cut, although I was happy with her work. I really must go to see him next time, even though I'll have to overcome a certain uncomfortable moment when he looks and comments on the way that "other girl" did my hair.*

Choosing to see, to stare might be the point. It is perhaps in Paris that the sense of giving a face to the members of the face-to-face world are most clearly linked to specific bodies or places, whereas Casablanca and Cairo have a tendency to be inclusive of bodies in what remains a less differentiated space of faces. This is not because Parisians are not "modern." As in Casablanca, where the question of the links between power and clientelism are broadly invoked as indicative of the need for social and political reform, the contrast of the neighborhood to the city is conceived by many people in terms of the liberty that leaving the neighborhood or less grounded zones of proximity seems to imply. But certain far-off salons in these cities can also become a neighborhood for certain people. I spoke of Lucy's salon in the preceding chapter. We might also notice how a salon space in Cairo's central Zamalek district similarly works to delimit a space of exchange, which includes gossip about movie stars, but makes me feel nearly invisible.

In a neighborhood salon in Zamalek, I go to a desk behind which sits an older woman in a hijab. The downstairs is set up for hairstyling, the upper room for aesthetic cures as well as for the styling of muhajibat. I want my legs waxed, so I take a round, narrow staircase up to the second floor. Upstairs, there are basins on the floor for pedicures and washing after hair removal. There are typical hairdressing seats downstairs, but upstairs, there are only chairs, no long couches. Several posters of women (Joico ads) adorn the walls on both floors. The door is also covered with a poster to prevent anyone from seeing in from the street. Upstairs, a large picture inscribed with the name of Allah is pasted beside these ads, mirrors, and green plants. Florescent lights illuminate the scene. A small gas stove burns to make the sugar wax (helwa).

The owner of the salon is a woman who looks to be about sixty years old. She wears her gray hair in a bun and has glasses. She and the other aesthetician are dressed in street clothes. The only "special" garment on anyone is a sort of red cape to cover women when they are getting their hair cut. One muhajibat is getting her hair cut upstairs, and a large, heavy woman with short dyed blonde hair is getting her hair done by a younger beautician who looks like she might be the daughter of the older woman. Everyone talks incessantly, calling up and down the stairs to the male hairdresser. The radio is on as everyone gossips about a woman they know who does everything to get slim: special treatments for the belly and thighs, sports. They find this terribly amusing and make fun of the upscale salons where she goes to get her special treatments.

The woman getting her hair done is finished. She covers her hairdo with her hijab and leaves. At about the same time, we hear a friend of the male hairdresser enter the downstairs room. He greets everyone and proceeds to turn on the television set; the details of a soccer game mingle with the love songs on the radio. The men's conversation floats up as the heavy blonde winks at me and laughs at my attempts to speak Egyptian as she gets her underarms waxed. Next, she moves to a new position to get her pedicure done by the younger aesthetician. Meanwhile, my waxing goes along at a leisurely pace. The boss smokes as she carefully examines the results of her work through thick glasses. At one point, she hears the call to prayer, puts out her cigarette, puts on her hijab, and pulls out a prayer rug. When she has completed her prayer, she leaves on the scarf, for the mailman has arrived. She goes downstairs to pick up the magazines he's delivered. When she reappears, she and her blonde "friend" argued about who will get to read them first. As she allows her friend/customer to look at the magazine covers, she resumes her work on my legs. She and her friend begin a passionate discussion about the marital troubles of various film stars. When, at last, my legs are finally smooth, I pay her, thank her, and get dressed to go. She thanks me, then turns again to her friend to discuss how terrible it is to hear about these sinful lives of the stars.

In this salon, we see that enclosures of several types are permeable by many kinds of voices, faces, and dicussions. Often, the relaxed, sometimes bawdy nature of discussions behind the curtains or covered windows of these women-only and "protected" spaces seems to have been rendered possible by those barriers. Here, it is perhaps not so much that all kinds of discussions have to do with the face-to-face, as that a certain geography of shame works to form how issues, bodies, and the role of the beautician are to be elaborated. My own involvement with the beautician and her clients is certainly face to face. But although I was initially an object of curiosity, I was quickly relegated to the unimportant role of a "mere" client: someone who didn't butt into their conversations, who would pay, but who clearly was of no importance. What I might say about anything really didn't matter. My words were thin.

Neighborhood salons are neither outside of fashion nor linked in a special way to the background body. Instead, they are often seen as comfortable, as safe, and as having their own personality. People in Casablanca or Cairo might go there because they are inexpensive, but in Paris their prices are as varied as those of franchises such as Jacques Déssange or Franck Provost. Back in the beauty shop in my Parisian neighborhood, the owner cuts my hair. She tells me of her recent visit to the salon in London; she said that many of the shops there have colored motifs now, like hers, and the hairstyles are wild: "We used to do things like that here in France. Twenty years ago coiffeuses weren't so classic. You should have seen all of the things we did to our hair. But then came the period of black and white—very dull—classic styles. People are afraid to be eccentric: they need to fit in to find jobs these days. But I still like some color, that's why I made the salon yellow. It's warm and attractive. The architect was surprised when I asked him for this color—he does a lot of those franchises, you know. Those places are all the same: no personality."

This, then, is a world that admits differences between individuals as involved in their personal reputation and the roles they play. These evolve according to their age, experience, and the tales told in the area. A story from other "places" in people's lives intervenes: one's reputation at work eventually becomes known; what one does on trips to other cities might also eventually be common knowledge. The boundaries of the neighborhood are thus linked to the quality of these tales and those who tell them. These limits might then be associated with specific streets, stores, or homes, but these spaces are constantly being infringed on by the movement of tales and people. People, things, and styles do not simply take on a neighborhood air by moving in. They must find a place in the world of the proximate, the exploration of which includes not only the face-to-face world of physically set-off spaces of interaction, but also legal practices, mass media, and ephemeral meetings at bus stops.

Those who hope to move out of the neighborhood tend to present the face-to-face as a substitute for the background body. They do not want to recognize that proximate salons produce bodies that are as en-lightened as their own. They remark that the shame of the face-to-face is somehow not universalizable enough to be perceived as "true" or "fair." Women who have no choice, they say, might find a welcome moment in the world of the salon. But therein they live with specific, if absent, others. Fathers, husbands, groups of friends seem to move the hands of the hairdresser in the local salon. A warm sense of being *entouré* (encircled) is produced.[9] And this is also the "problem" with these places: their constant looks at one another, the way the salon acts as a means to affirm the intelligent eyes of men—these, some beautiful butterflies might say, incarcerate beauties, self, and truth.[10]

Some people like to explain that moving out of enclosed worlds is actually the true test of the en-lightened body. Hourriya, whose name means freedom, says she "escapes" from close quarters by moving to the more "impersonal" parts of the city. There she seeks relief from the eyes of proximity. Amid the bustle of the business district or the nameless crowds in the lobbies of major hotels, she seems to think that she can find a world made not by eyes but by the anonymous movements of history, commerce, and fashion. There, it seems, she might find not just the broken-down body that any beautician works to make whole but a world of ultimate form, of modern equalities and anywhere bodies.

MADE TO ORDER

A second world of beauty appears as a double to the uneven worlds of shame. Here, it seems, only evenly lit, shameless, en-lightened bodies can survive. Photographs and video clips sit beside clients, each reflected in mirrors that often expand to form walls. Men and women appear as reflections, showing people clearly divided into those who are clients and those whose clothing, posture, and actions designate them as a part of the decor. Clients converse mainly with these specialists, who sometimes talk among each other and rarely sit down. They seem to be performing a dance to a rather intense rhythm, sometimes moving among several heads at once. This salon's reference to a rational, precisely drawn-up world of choice seems to reflect the dominant ways of cutting up spaces, bodies, and motivations in terms of isolation, labor, and choice. In a sense, this is the salon in which the "anywhere" body should be most at home. One difference or choice seems comparable to any other. Menus

Menus for style. In this advertisement in the magazine produced by the Franck Provost franchise, a "menu" for hair is proposed.

of haircuts and looks are presented to clients who order themselves "readymade."

In Paris, such fast salons have been especially successful in recent years. Indeed, the ways that France claims an *appellation d'origine* for the enlightenment epic seem to reinforce the urge to recognize not particular faces but those that demonstrate the kinds of generalizations about the polity or society that Marcel Mauss sought to develop in his work on body techniques. Catherine explains that she likes the predictability and speed of these places. Similarly, in Casablanca, Leila explains that she prefers this type of salon, for "like at the McDonald's or Pizza Hut, I feel like I'm on another planet when I go in there. I like the young male hairdressers. It's air conditioned and pretty. They don't try to sell you all kinds of additional clothes or skin products like in some salons." Catherine notes that unlike in "fancy" salons, they don't "try anything creative or weird on you. You can count on what you'll look like." Styles can be selected from a menu in a book and sometimes from in-house videos. You pick a photo, you are "done" to match it. All without an appointment, without stopping.

As I walk from my apartment on Rue Monge toward Maubert Mutualité, several chain hair salons present themselves to view. Their large plate glass window display names you can see throughout Paris, sometimes internationally. You can look in from the street and see the clients entering, then being whisked off to chairs lined up before a row of sinks in the back of the salon. You might also glimpse employees returning from their lunch break, donning their white or black smocks. You observe a series of photographs of men and women, as well as videotapes being played that show cuts of the season. These seem to be the only colors in most of these salons, where functional black-and-white and chrome tend to be preferred. Employees wear outfits coordinated with the decor. If you remember his name, request that Tom cut your hair; if Tom is popular, you might have to wait in a long line. If you are in a hurry and seek efficiency, you might as well try Pierre or Marguerite, as they too know how to do those styles you see displayed around you. When Pierre arrives, after an unnamed person has washed your hair, he provides you with a menu, which offers a larger number of styles than do the posters on the walls. You might want to combine elements or explain some slight modifications of these images, but "at least we have a basis to work with," Pierre explains. I notice that we look from the pictures to the mirror; he cuts my hair, then checks out the photo, but especially my expression. We talk about general topics, always centered on ourselves. The other beautician-client pairs are doing the same. Some of the pairs do seem to have some degree of knowledge of each other, but even after several visits here I feel no desire to speak of anything of consequence. The manager or owner of the salon is extremely friendly, but he never remembers my name. The people in the salon speak of clients in terms of their hair: "that woman with the modified shag," "the one, you know, who comes in all the time to get her roots done."

In this space clients are identified as types, and indeed, some salons seek out specific "target audiences." In Paris, for instance, Pro-Mod's low prices attract students, and Camille Aubin salons are designed to attract more mature career women. Fast salons tend to be distinguished by their mixing of men and women. In Casablanca these salons are rather expensive, but still, they are within the budget of white-collar workers who consider their looks to be a major investment. In Cairo only a few fast salons seem to work, mainly in upscale hotels, perhaps orienting their services toward visitors. But some of the relatively new sections or kinds of salons dedicated to muhajibat, to women who wear various versions of the veil, share some features with the franchises one finds in Casa or Paris. These salons identify their clients according to a (often vague) religious choice. Many of them cater to women from a variety of neighborhoods, and they offer models that, though typed as Muslim, are nonetheless often presented in the same series and publications as those in secular salons. All might not be equally apt to enter any salon, but such choices are measured by type instead of by reputation. Types of workers are also clearly distinguished within each beauty shop: aestheticians work at least part of the time in separate spaces, owners or managers oversee the work of hairdressers and assistants. These are ranked according to the work they do: in all but the smallest salons, certain people only wash hair, sweep hair from the floor, and generally assist beauticians. In Cairo especially, the hierarchy tends to be clearly visible: an assistant to the hairdresser, generally a woman, hands the beautician rollers, brushes, or curling irons rather as a nurse prepares instruments for a doctor engaged in a delicate operation. As in proximate salons, people who work in these salons are usually called by their first name. But here they often wear name tags because unlike in the neighborhood places, you might see them only this once. Speed, efficiency, and clear choices predominate in these spaces. The charm of the anonymous number is sometimes apparent:

> As I have my hair shampooed, Nadine, the colorist, reminds Ghislaine, who is giving my neighbor a shampoo, that she must give her a "346." This code refers to a series of products that correspond to the computerized payment system. Indeed, once she has given her client a "turban," Ghislaine takes the client's form from the pocket of her white robe. She carefully inscribes "346" and then takes her to Pierre, who will cut the newly colored hair. I notice that Nadine keeps careful notes of these different codes, plus her own comments, on an index card. I wonder what the account's version of all of our hair might look like.

Our faces and colors dissolve into numbers that can in turn generate statistics for salon owners and cosmetic companies. Similarly, when Pierre talks with the client about how she wants her hair done, he proposes a set of photographs of "types" of women reproduced in the publication of the franchise. He seems intent on reproducing one of the haircuts with names like "Alexandra," "Chantal," and "Jessica."

Indeed, this same abstract mode of evaluation is applied to the competence of the beauticians. Some franchises, following an approach first developed for fast food by McDonald's, have developed their own training centers.[11] They retrain beauticians to use their methods, tools, products, and procedures. In the fast salon, knowledge gained through reading, attending seminars, and gaining diplomas is highly valued. This means that one needs to have attended school for a fairly long time. You have to follow the latest innovations by reading the specialized press, not simply by listening to the radio programs that just anyone can follow. This seems to be particularly the case concerning the specializations like aesthetics and hair coloring that require constant attention to new products and techniques. As one aesthetician explained in Casablanca: "To be a good aesthetician you need to be able to read the manuals in French. It takes at least a year of training—I myself went to Paris to do it. Hairdressers can just learn here in Morocco—they don't even really have to know how to read. Girls who don't know how to read French can't get far. To keep up with the literature, especially for aestheticians, you have to read the latest magazines. As I know French I was able to actually go on and get my diploma in France. That counts a lot in finding the best jobs."

There are many implicit references to medical practices and equipment in the chrome-clean look of the salons, the clothes of the workers, and the shape of the aesthetician's chair. In Paris, Sandrine explains to me:

> There are a lot of similarities between the work of a physical therapist and that of an aesthetician. But they [the therapists] don't really treat the entire body. You go to them with a problem in your leg, for example, and they massage you right there, at the point where you have a problem. We would deal with that, but also give you a whole-body massage to relax you more. The person has to be treated as a whole—this is what the ying and yang approach of the Chinese has taught me. After I had my daughter I went to a *kiné* [physical therapist]. I couldn't believe it. Ten minutes of massage on my stomach and up—I was done. He kept bright lights staring at me the whole time. It produced more, not less, anxiety—like getting an operation.

In addition, you know that certain gestures are forbidden to aestheticians. For example, the kiné can make your circulation move toward your heart; we must move it toward the ganglions. By restricting our movements the profession of kinés tries to preserve their clientele. Of course, they are also reimbursed by social security insurance, whereas our clients have to pay for our services.

Sandrine complains that her boss "calculates everything by the hour." "I'd like to spend, say, an hour and a quarter with the client for a massage, but she [the boss] won't let me. Sometimes this is disruptive of my work."

The legitimacy of aesthetic knowledge is thus set up against what appear to be artificial barriers by the medical professions. Indeed, to Sandrine, her work is more valuable than that of the physical therapist because she works with the body to make it not only better but whole. At the same time, fast salons especially play on the use of uniforms and shoes, shiny appliances, and mystical devices in ways that imply that they, like modern doctors, operate on given body parts with expert knowledge as a means to create a healthy, beautiful, total look.

Hierarchies among professions are not only located outside of the beauty industry, they almost always enter into the composition of salons themselves. Aestheticians are the most independent workers and their work less subject to the scrutiny of others than that of hairdressers or colorists. Manicures and pedicures are often performed in the open, central section of the salon, whether they are associated with hairdressing or not; other treatments, such as waxing, massage, and facials, are performed in separate rooms. In these spaces, where lights are often dimmed and soft music is played, aestheticians are often alone with their clients. When there are several clients in the same room, they may be separated by curtains. Aesthetic treatments are not visually measured in terms of how they can "copy" pictures. Instead, many of the procedures involve tactile sensations that may or may not have such "visible" results. This leads us to pay attention to some aspects of fast salons generally to which their intense appeals to sight might initially blind us.

The correct reproduction of pictured styles is the most salient feature of fast salons. Indeed, many clients of these salons said they went to them because they were sure to leave with the look they wanted. They often said that the neighborhood places didn't always know how to do this, and more elite establishments presented hairdressers as "artists" who didn't care about what their clients wanted and produced all kinds of unpredictable, eccentric hairstyles. But in the course of observing fast salons I became aware that it was a special relationship to the hairdresser or the aesthetician that I observed in their reflections. In the fast salon, a glance at the mirror shows the extent to which the gazes that meet are those of beautician and client. Like the backroom touch of the aesthetician on your face, these exchanges are the point of coming here. Clients might observe other clients in the glass, but the only groups of people one observes here are composed of employees, and even then, they often meet to discuss how the coloring of a client will be coordinated with her cut or permanent.

In fast salons, not only are the technical jargon and shiny symbols of efficiency and medicine employed to signify modernity and cleanliness, their association with a specific kind of dialogic relationship is similarly reproduced. The beautician and client work together to produce the "true" face of the client. They do this by repeated looks into the mirror to evaluate the movements of the hairdresser's hands that the client controls through his or her verbal and sometimes facial expressions. This specific competence that men and women ask of their hairdresser is thus not simply an issue of the professional mastering of the reproduction of models. Rather, like a therapist, the beautician is expected to know how to "listen" to the client and to work with him or her to effect this reproduction.

This form of salon does not involve people in the kinds of collective verdicts that inevitably enter into the development of style in neighborhood salons. There, even the most intimate and intense exchanges between client and hairdresser are woven into a fabric of looks, ideas, and judgments that involve many people. In fast salons, however, efforts to replicate photographs or interpret the ideas expressed by the client are related to collective modes of producing beauties in a very different way. Their more "individualized" approach to and discussion of style involves images in magazines, television, or film in terms of how they can be decomposed and reworked on the body at hand. In selecting who one will be from the panoply of pictures, impediments to these choices and motions appear. Others absent from the salon suddenly enter it. Husbands, colleagues, and visions of other women in offices, on the street, or on television intervene in determining the limits of the possible for a specific woman. Choices are made, freely, but freedom is built from a mimetic process involving the history of the individual within a social milieu. For the hairdresser, this milieu is formed of types, not of known people.

Latifa, who owns a salon in Casablanca, remarks that one must maintain a friendly relationship with the client without becoming her friend. This, as one hairdresser whom the journalist Bouchra Lahbabi interviewed said, "allows you to give good advice without a personal stake in it. Sometimes a hairdresser discovers a latent depression in her client and so she tries to guide her. Listening is very important: when you don't know how to listen you cannot know how to style hair."[12] So, though one does not become a friend, one must address how to make one's client similar to the model she chooses to become. Conversation and listening are helpful in softening the edges of the image, in making it into something a bit more human, a bit more whole than the disconnected specializations of the salon itself might be able to do without this kind of talk. And in some instances, the beautician too gets tips from clients, or has a chance to express her own thoughts or hopes to them.

The last time I saw Sandrine she was upset and angry because her boss had told her she had to leave at the end of the month. She told me it was a "personality problem," but she felt that the owner just didn't give her credit for her competence as an aesthetician. Today, she lights up when I see her; excitedly she tells me she's found another job already, across town, in a small place:

> But I'm going to work with the best brands: Guerlain, Chanel. . . . and the place is wonderful. Each *cabine* [vestibule] is independent, not like here where, when you're doing a waxing, you can hear the conversations at the front desk! There they really treat the clients right, they give them all of the comforts. Each cabine is spacious and has nice armchairs or couches. There are no strict time limits—the owner leaves plenty of time between appointments so that you don't have to rush clients to keep on schedule. I won't have to do just the standard treatments; instead, I'll be able to adapt what I do to the client's individual needs. For example, I'll be able to use all of my different massage techniques instead of just two, like I do here. And I'll be working with important brands. You should see—they gave me a waxing with their special wax: you can't even feel it! It leaves your skin smooth and satiny!

Sandrine's comments express a certain frustration with the rigidity that sometimes comes to characterize these efficient but often too fast salons as well as divisions of knowledge that she does not see as valid. In one way, treating the body as a whole, massaging it back together, seems to work against the basic model of the beauty salon. Yet as in the mirrors of the hairdressers who work in fast salons, she sees her relationship to her clients as central. This is not unlike the special relationship that is often formed by hairdressers in front of the mirror. They, like Sandrine, get to know their clients. They exchange information and sometimes develop quite a collection of stories about funny, sad, or interesting tales that they exchange with fellow professionals. But these stories remain just that: tales without direct consequences. Like the names given for the hairstyles—"classic" or "sporty" or "Christy," "Natacha," or "Bianca"—the stories are anecdotes of types, possible lives, and possible looks. They say "This can be done" or "This can happen to anyone." These are not the stories of gossip, of potentially reputation-molding information, which are exchanged in the first kind of salons. The consequences of choosing a style and of telling about one's life seem attenuated here.

Deconstructing and putting the body together again takes place in an enclosure that offers more, not less, protection for the "secret" world of the individual. Like the office of a doctor, a psychotherapist, or a university professor, the judgments made here tend to be disconnected from a context of specific faces, while intensifying the relationship with the knowledgeable face of the specialist. Speaking and touching with knowledge, the specialist's hand forms a point of contact with norms of practice and of thought that are perceived as invisible, universal, and readily reproduced. We remember other worlds and this memory allows us to work with the specialist to form ourselves. These worlds are those we forget, those of the background or of the proximate salon that "fast" people often assimilate to heaviness. They are those we flee and think of as heavy with fathers' eyes, gossip, and pettiness. But in spite of their apparent comprehension of all spaces, of any looks, the specialists of the fast salon cannot promise entry into all social worlds.

Let us turn now to yet another kind of salon that might also emerge in the flight from gravity but that, rather than confining the face-to-face to an intense, dual relationship, renders very special faces for all to see.

It might seem that a contrast between abstraction and proximity would be sufficient to explain how salons give form to different bodies with their distinct modes of socializing. These might be linked to two different concepts of space produced by the emergence of the "world as picture."[13] Such a two-step account would easily echo the work of en-lightenment, perhaps developing a more thorough understanding of the relationship of light to heavy bodies under changing global conditions. However, to leave our analysis of the power of reproducible and easily transmittable images of beauty at this would be to forget the apparently magical way in which the even spaces of modern sights in the age of mechanical and electronic reproduction can be focused on the personal name as a claim to fame. In certain salons we cannot trust the centrality of the face-to-face looks of friends and neighbors. What we observe there makes sense only in terms of networks that spread out from radiant centers of renown.

Working with Guerlain is what Sandrine emphasizes when she talks about moving to a new kind of salon. She expresses an idea of being moved to "another level," as she says. Guerlain, it seems, will lift her out of the world of the ordinary and to a new experience in her career. She does not mention the name of the owner of the salon, or the name of the salon. But the association she makes between the brand and the luxurious space in which the client will be pampered, given space, made comfortable brings us to the third type of salon. It centers around famous products, hairdressers, and clients.

Véronique, who goes regularly to a Guerlain institute, explains that she feels comfortable there because she is treated warmly and no one tries to get her to buy particular products. While talking to Małgorzata about her experience there, she spontaneously compares the warm atmosphere of the institute to those of the fast hair salon where she sometimes gets her hair done: "They just don't take the time—they need to be more soft." Emilie echoes her preoccupations, saying, "People are too quick and too cold" at the Mod's hair salon she used to go to. She wants to find a place where she can "appreciate the time at the salon."

Indeed, the insistence is not simply on brand names, but on the luxury of spending time in a calm, uncluttered place. If the timed and numbered work of the fast salon corresponds to tightly scheduled lives, special salons that associate people with famous names act to suggest that such precision is bad, vulgar, and simply not to be allowed on their premises. There is a Moroccan saying: Haste comes from the devil. For many, these luxurious salons promise respite from the clock that is redolent with sweet scents and heavenly timelessness. Many women in the cities I moved through said that they prefer deluxe salons because they promise a pause from the press of the clock and demands for measured efficiency. One parisienne working mother's remarks recall the demand that Moroccan women be paid more so that they are able to purchase women's magazines to follow fashion. Hélène complains that the nicer institutes in Paris discriminate against working women because they often close at 7 P.M. She wishes that they would stay open longer so that she could have some time for herself. Spending time, then, seems to be related to a sense of moving away from the world of work and into a realm of reputable brands. In this world, hairdressers and aestheticians are known by their association with such brands or according to their own reputable names. And no matter how famous they are, they not only ask your name as soon as you walk in, they eagerly work to learn about your profession or that of your spouse. They quickly find out where your children go to school and where you go on vacation. This is a part of the process of situating who you are, of preparing to work to produce that special look that is uniquely you.

Salons like this are generally expensive and located in central or upscale shopping districts. People come from all over the city. Information is not obtained from neighbors but from the milieu who make the news. Here, inside information on fashion, politics, and deals between companies are available not only through the mass media, but by word of mouth. Like the neighborhood world of face-to-face contact, these salons also claim personalized knowledge. But the configuration of the person's relationship to others' eyes and his or her own face is not the same as in the close-eyed world of the proximate. This salon's meaning does not depend so emphatically on the creation of a sense of place or of a therapeutic relationship to the hairdresser as do other kinds of salons. Here, it is not so much your problems or ideas as your irreducibility to category that is emphasized. Instead of focusing on pictures or types, special salons work with relations. Lamia lectures me: I really should go only to certain kinds of establishments in Casablanca if I want to get my hair done right. Lamia hates salons "where everyone gossips." She says, "Sure, for your research it must be interesting to go to those funny neighborhood dives. But for yourself, there are only three salons in the city where you can expect them to know how to cut your hair like they do in Paris. If you go to Kenza's you can be sure to get the kind of attention you'll need. They take their time, not like those places where they produce haircuts like on the assembly line. Everyone comes out with the same haircut!" Samy, Jacques, or Max might be more expensive than neighborhood salons or fast shops, but this is not the key to their exclusivity. This they achieve by developing their reputation. They do this rather like their clients do: not by working on people sitting together or on the development of abstract excellences theoretically available to all, but by working on their image, its diffusion, and its difference from all others. In these salons clients might not know one another but they *know of* each other.

The special salon extends one's relationship with the hairdresser beyond its walls, rendering any Goffmanesque approach to interaction impossible. It might appear like a knot in a net that is loosely yet strongly woven. It involves you in a logic of names and faces that cannot be reflected from any given mirror. It is the stylist who pulls it all together for you: he or she acts to master the movements of fashion not as a general but as a particular art. The point is not to copy or to follow but to implicate the client in the styles of the day in ways that work "for her." Movement is essential to the body of this client. But actual displacement of the body is not. For her name can travel over the Internet. It can multiply like the stocks she purchases on the other side of the world. It can flutter about cocktail party conversations or diplomatic dinners, board rooms, golf games, or afternoon teas. And so can the names of those who style her. Jacques and Max and Samy are themselves a part of this commerce between people who see themselves as those who count. Rock stars, heads of state, mistresses and wives of princes—these give definition to the circles of fame and lineages of notability that set off this net and give it definition. But many lesser-known names and faces partake of this logic that creates and gravitates around multiple centers woven of repetitive attractions.

This world is at once constituted by the moves of the mechanically and electronically reproducible and the spectacle of its ritual use to render bodies differently. This depiction depends on the touch of the artistic stylist. The hairdresser acts to produce public art. His artistry involves working with you not as a therapist working on interiority, but rather, as one who must know you in terms of how he can produce you as style for stages of photo opportunities, even if only as a bit player in a wedding video. This work can gain momentum if it is reported in the local or national news. Clients, like hairdressers, work with repetition and types to reinscribe the idea of the original. In this, the stylist is more like the designer than the brand. Having one's hair done by the "real" Jacques Déssange is different from going to one of his many fast shops. His "touch" might be made ever more famous by the success of these franchises, but it is also what validates the quality of the fast salons. And it is what sets him off in another world from his own name used as brand.

To bring people to his salon from all over the city, and perhaps the world, Max must work on his name and image in ways that mirror how clients conceive of their own value. The echo of one's voice, the radiance of one's face—these move like investments in faraway places to deny the gravity of place in ways that seem to work closely with en-lightening processes. The body is cut up and reworked in ways similar to other salons. But here there is a sense in which the putting together works not with types or forms but with the networks of disembodied (and thus doubly powerful) information. Value accrues not from matching but from the movement along these lines. Bodies and their shadows expand according to where they have gone. But it is not quite a life story they tell. Looks are inscribed by travel and the hands they have touched. These must be shown and worked with in ways that cannot always be stated. The stylist works to make these apparent as points of origin or passage. He must do so in ways that work these touches and passages into who you are. You become a bundle of information of a very special kind. The work of the stylist stretches the walls of the salon to reach for the breadth of your extended body and the particularities of the circuits by which you have taken form. It works with you to include the hairdresser in your moves. So it listens in at receptions where you thank people for their compliments on your style by saying "Oh, it's Max who did it" or comparing the work of Max to that done by Alexander.

The reproductive capacities of photography, video, and film might forget the aura of the original, but this also allows them to be set on edge, to establish their own magnetic force. These special points promise connections. Closeness to one special name gives one access to other names in its knot. We might relate it to an older version of sight, for example, the way the ninth-century scholar al-Kindi spoke of sight: " 'It is manifest,' al-Kindi asserts, 'that everything in this world, whether it be substance or accident, produces rays in its own manner like a star. . . . Everything that has actual existence in the world of the elements emits rays in every direction, which fill the whole world.' This radiation binds the world into vast networks in which everything acts upon everything else to produce natural effects. Stars act upon the territorial world; magnets, fire, sound, and colors act on objects in their vicinity. Even words conceived by the mind can radiate power and thus produce effects outside the mind."[14]

Such accounts are no longer pertinent to optics, but special salons' pretentions might be understood with reference to radiant objects that burn, trace orbits around greater stars, and sometimes implode. The body of this space is never in place. If it is to maintain its centrality in a world of easily producible faces, values, and fame, it must constantly glitter and glow in ways that transform its qualities to maintain the impression of solidity. Repetition and placement are essential to the altering of the import of the image or the sound that fame entails. Sometimes, for example, in the use of the images of political leaders, such repetition is enforced by arms, coercion, or censure. It generally involves some accumulation of economic power. Such political and economic aspects are a part of the tying of the knots of fame rather than fame's being their representative. As I noticed concerning the image of the Moroccan king, one of the ways that pictures impose their gravity is by pretending that there is no outside. By crowding our vision with seemingly infinite versions of a single face, we begin to forget what is outside the picture frame. By associating certain images with one another, attempts at recreating the centers of meaning and power can move beyond such limits.

How we use and react to the juxtaposition of pictures often reveals how reproducible images retain a sense of "touch" and influence the people they represent. Virginia Danielson writes of how Huda Sha'rawi was hesitant to allow her photograph to be published beside those of actresses in the theater magazine *Rus al-Yusuf*. She was afraid that their "light" reputations would tarnish hers by simple association (she later overcame her fear and let her picture be printed there).[15] A more recent example of how images' juxtaposition can be used is a series of drawings for an ad for the

Faithful fame. In an advertisement for the *Quotidien du Maroc* we get a glimpse of how the menu format can be used to express complex ideas about fame, power, and truth. Here, individual portraits are hand-drawn rather than photographed. Each is set against a white background in identical frames. The equal treatment of each image suggests equivalence between the internationally and nationally known faces. The moving of the famous onto a single plane suggests a single world, but one that might include other, additional faces. This contrasts markedly with the way photographs of fame usually emphasize the distinctive and central nature of particular people, a good example of which can be seen in portraits of the Moroccan kings (see my *Picturing Casablanca* for more on this). It is interesting that words in this ad dwell on the newspaper's "faithfulness": in its portrayal of these faces, in its reporting, and to its readers.

Moroccan newspaper *Le Quotidien*.[16] Here, instead of presenting photographs, each face has been drawn by hand. This is no mere set of mug shots, but each image is drawn in the same style; no distinction in size or technique differentiates them. Most of the faces are recognizable. These are people we see on the television news. Looking at the images, most will recognize Yasser Arafat and Tony Blair. You might not, however, be able to give a name to several of the pictures of people from Casablanca and Rabat: a journalist, a politician, a playwright. People involved in political or artistic networks in and around Casablanca will recognize these faces.

What emerges is not a menu of types, like the fast salon menu, but a proposition. The image acts as an argument for networks of fame surrounding these figures, which seem to absorb some of the heat and light of the bigger stars. The point here is to be there. What one does, says, or thinks to get to this space is less important than the simple fact of being drawn into it.

Hairdressing itself might become radiant: an article in another paper writes of "Moroccan hairdressing at the top." The article talks of M. Skander, "thanks to whom [Moroccan] coiffure has been able to win several medals in international festivals (Egypt, Japan, France, Italy). His celebrity goes beyond our borders. We could easily consider him the Déssange of Morocco, because he brings a prestigious *griffe* [signature, mark] to each style he signs. His professionalism, dynamism and his open spirit give him a great adaptability. . . . 'My only goal,' he admits, 'is to show that Moroccan hairdressers are talented, and that there are geniuses among them.' "[17] We see how Déssange acts as a model of radiance and genius, and we might imagine him and M. Skandar on a picture similar to the one printed in the newspaper portraits. Already, being written about is itself a way of increasing fame. And the comparison to Déssange sets up a relationship between the two hairdressers, who probably have never met. Placing the names side by side, like presenting one's national name amid those of international repute, proposes the possibility of the apprentice overtaking the master, the copy becoming brighter than the original.[18]

The space of radiant bodies is reworked in beauty salons not only because they cater to people who are pictured in this space, but also because they work according to a shared logic. In these select salons the point is not so much to "succeed" in reproducing models of namable styles, as to be worked over by the same hands that have coiffed a princess. The issue is not that people appearing in the press or on television might not care who does their hair; rather, it has to do too with the establishment of the stylist as artist, as himself a point of gravity. His hands assure that you will be extracted from the reproducible, your originality expressed as neither representative of a neighborhood nor of a type.

Special salons might propose expensive creams or shampoos to their clients, but they also take part in the purchases clients make when they go to New York or Milan for a weekend shopping spree. Beauticians suggest new products and know where you can go to get them. Some people do cross continents in pursuit of the latest face creams or cut of trousers. But although following such fashion victims alerts us to the third kind of beauty space, it would be erroneous to make too direct an equation between special salons and the bank balances of clients. If the "symbolic center" of beauty is radiated by a salon they can drive or take a bus to, women without passports or extensive investment portfolios do participate in the elaboration of this kind of salon.[19] Some well-off women prefer the neighborhood feel of the local salon, and many career women feel reassured by the quickness and predictability of the fast salon. Similarly, some young secretaries or clerks who in urban Morocco often spend more than half of their earnings on beauty products, salons, and clothing might frequent such establishments. Many women alternate their visits to special salons with those they make on a regular basis to fast or neighborhood salons. Amina says: "You know, I really like Fatima's salon down the street. I like the feeling there. But I really don't think she's a good hair cutter. Like many of my friends there, I go to Jacques to get the cut done. Every couple of months I go downtown and see him—it's expensive but it's worth it. I get my hair cut there and then I go to Fatima's for the regular washing and styling. I can't do my own hair, so it's nice to have someone close to home who can do it for me inexpensively." Obviously, one needs to be able to find the money to go to see Jacques, even if the visits are only occasional. But in considering who can pay for what services we must remember that age or occupation can play very important roles in determining the hierarchies of spending. Even someone on a modest salary, if given the opportunity to attend a special event, to be interviewed for just the right job, or invited on a special date, will often make an effort to do the things "necessary" to look "right" for the occasion.[20]

Here, the art of the stylist is not to work on interiority, but rather, to produce you with his special touch. He marks you with his name at the same time that he situates you in a net of other names. The point is not to enclose you, to avoid contact or mixing, but instead, to radiate your apparently irreducible difference and put you into contact with the brightest stars. Measures of radiant intensity, no longer of dimensions, are at issue in this extensive space. In linking oneself to a logic of celestial spheres, the body itself seems to lose some of its materiality and mortality. Even the dead can offer direction and provide light here. This reminds me of how Margot Badran describes Eugénie Le Brun, the Frenchwoman who held Egypt's first literary salon, continuing to live in the mind of Huda Sha'rawi even after her death. Sha'rawi wrote, "I had come to rely heavily on her good counsel but even after her death I felt her spirit light the way before me. When I was about to embark on something I often paused to ask myself what she would think, and if I sensed her approval I would proceed."[21] This relationship of the living with the dead must be related to a renewed sense of what beauty can be. It moves us out of salons to think about the distinct landscapes, times, and relationships that their bodily techniques help to form.

TYPES AND LANDSCAPES

We could chart the three types of salons in Casablanca, Cairo, and Paris. We would then notice that their distribution varies in each. It is possible to develop a map that would graphically express the ways in which certain types of salons take root and flourish in specific cities or neighborhoods. We might also establish these according to the changing configurations of salon types over time. We would notice that, for example, fast salons are rare in Cairo, have become quite numerous in Paris, and have begun to flourish in Casablanca. We might then come up with the idea of charting bodies as types, according to their frequency of attending specific kinds of salons. These maps could in turn lead us to relate classes or civilizations to ways of organizing the density of talk, the quality of relation, the character of individuals' relationships in specific cultures. We could envisage the possibility of developing geographies of taste, which provide a clear vision of the links among the habitus of these different groups that might in turn lead us to comment on the way classes are constituted. We might, based on the relationships observed in salons, even hazard to discuss how they are more or less typical of a specific place at a given point in history. Alterations in maps would then be used to chart civilizational changes. Our tracking and arranging might thus lead to painting impressionistic understandings of some important relationships and developments. However, by adopting a common representational matrix and forgetting how people move between salons, such maps focus too much on placement and access. As Michel de Certeau points out:

It is true that the operations of walking on can be traced on city maps in such a way as to transcribe their paths (here well-trodden, there very faint) and their trajectories (going this way and not that). But these thick or thin curves only refer, like words, to the absence of what has passed by. Surveys of routes miss what was: the act itself of passing by. The operation of walking, wandering, or "window shopping," that is, the activity of passers-by, is transformed into points that draw a total-izing and reversible line on the map. They allow us to grasp only a relic set in the nowhere of a surface of projection. Itself visible, it has the effect of making invisible the operation that made it possible. These fixations constitute procedures for forgetting. They trace the (vora-cious) property that the geographical system has of being able to trans-form action into legibility, but in doing so it causes a way of being in the world to be forgotten.[22]

Linking comparisons is a process not of charting, but of following. It is itself mimetic. Access to forms, things, and ideas is essential to take into consideration, but only from the distant position of the mapmaker can the ethnographer herself observe these all at once. Ethnographic knowl-edge is made by moving through, not over. Following pictures, people, and things out of Casablanca, out toward Cairo and Paris, one quickly realizes that shaping beauties relies on a dynamic movement in which all salons take part. Although some women are closely identified with par-ticular kinds of salons, many of us move among types. In this we are like the styles, recipes, and products beauticians use and we engage in our quest to develop ourselves.

Each salon sets store on different sets of intelligent eyes. Each bears a distinct relationship to physical and social space. The worlds in which these different salons work might effectively limit the kinds of style or models people who wish to enter them adopt. But many models are found in all worlds. Still, the similar is not judged or selected in the same way or for the same reasons within each world's distinctive moral landscape. Nelson Goodman writes, "Some relevant kinds of the one world, rather than being absent from the other, are present as irrelevant kinds: some differences among worlds are not so much in entities comprised as in emphasis or accent, and these differences are no less consequential. Just as to stress all syllables is to stress none, so to take all classes as relevant kinds is to take none as such."[23] These remarks help in understanding how the single body of the salon takes on meaning in different worlds of beauty. They lead us to think about how the three salons attribute significance. But they do not explicate how these different salons and the "worlds" they are a part of themselves interact to produce the beauties they worship or revile. To hear the stress of the syllable or a remark on the shade of lipstick is only a taking-off point. The more important step comes when we try to understand how the shared, en-lightened body is produced in all of the worlds at the same time, but differently. By thinking about these differences in terms of "worlds" we can think about how in a single city, different modes of judgment coexist. To think about judgment, of beauties or of people, we need to be attentive to the weighting of voices and how it is expressed in bodily attractions. Much recent research on beauties, and polities draws attention to the need for such sensitive interpretation.[24] But thinking about such distinctions in terms of worlds can, I think, help us to better grasp what "sensitivity" entails. It can explain how not all elements of a social body can be held together for long—and why they cannot all be laid side by side on a single plane. It helps us notice how ideas or forms move among "spheres" of law or art or politics with ease.[25] It draws attention to how social groups or statuses rely on mastering moves among worlds that are irreducible to cultures, cities, or nations.[26]

Three kinds of salons and the worlds they help to form produce and contest a single body. They involve similar images, things, and people. These pass from one salon to the next. The salon can itself facilitate these passages. Much like the universalizing philosophies that Benhabib says render femininity as the shadow of the public realm, each salon's world seems to hope to appear as the true, original, or best form of this pervasive institution. Other salons and the bodies they work with then assimilate with various aspects of the common background. Those bodies, stuck in place and stranded, are thus associated with worlds of which they know nothing. Proximities might associate them with the way that fame often dwells on genealogical claim. Fast salon owners might phrase the neighborhood salons as tradition, unwilling to notice their similarities to bodies they seek to portray in the form of a chrysalis not yet out of its cocoon. Circles of fame often fear the implications of touching and of smell in face-to-face encounters and berate the uniformity and naïveté of worlds that see excellence in typified forms and dyadic interactions. The en-lightened body uses a common background body to develop a universalist rhetoric in the service of its own expansion. But its embodiments rely on distinctions that are only partially explicable in terms of the separation from background recounted in epics of opening. Using the three kinds of salons and their worlds as a basis for further investigation, I can now notice how forms, people, and things move through salons to enter different kinds of worlds.

Aïcha and I walk around the Boulaq neighborhood of Cairo for a while. We stop by one salon but they do only manicures. We ask where there is a hairdresser, and they point across the street. We go toward the salon, and a man in his early thirties in jeans and a colorful shirt greets us at the entrance. He smiles and asks whether we both want our hair done. Aïcha refuses, saying she's from a nearby neighborhood and I'm the one who needs a haircut. She seems a little annoyed by the hairdresser's attitude. She says that I'm her friend, on a visit to Egypt, and that I'm studying ideas of beauty here. I tell him I'd like to get my hair trimmed. He says fine, still smiling, but obviously curious about these foreign ladies.

Aïcha sits down in one of the two waiting chairs, as I set down my jacket and purse and sit in the barber's chair in front of the mirror. He drapes a large white smock around me and wraps a towel around my neck, and I meet Aïcha's gaze as she glances into the corner from which he grabbed the towel. I see that she is upset because the laundry is clearly not done with the same regularity here as in many of the other salons I've visited. Aïcha is being careful. Her eyes lead me to inspect the bare wood floor of the room. My own gaze follows the painted walls to the single poster in the place: a painting of a woman with luxurious multicolored hair. I also notice a framed verse of the Koran. These are the only decorations, although a random pile of old magazines is stacked next to Aïcha. The hairdresser, Jamal, calls a younger man from the street—his assistant? a friend? He tells the youth to get water, and he himself moves toward a shelf where there is a bottle of shampoo. Aïcha, oblivious to my right to choose, interjects, "No, her hair is clean—it does not need to be washed!" In French, she exclaims to me that I will catch something if he uses these towels on my hair. "Did you see those towels?" she asks. "Who knows where he's getting the water?"

Jamal can't understand what she's saying, but he can sense her critical eyes watching his every move. Aïcha has assumed the role of my guardian angel, and this frees me to smile and converse with Jamal. He is curious about me: Where am I staying? What have I visited in Cairo? When the water arrives he dabs my hair with it. He starts to cut my hair, chatting all the while, and explains that he's not used to having clients with such "fine" hair. This concerns him, as he is used to using the curling iron to straighten and shape his clients' hair. In my case, he has to find his blow-dryer, which he had stashed away in a back closet. He takes it out, plugs it in, and tries to style my hair. The plug keeps coming undone, the current stops, and he has to readjust the blow-dryer and the position of his hand on the comb. I feel very uncomfortable thinking about the problems with the electricity, the water.

While Aïcha surveys the shape of my hair, another client enters and says she wants him to do her roots (her hair is colored reddish brown). I can watch them in the mirror: he jokes with her and asks her how she is, then tells her to come back in a few minutes. She takes a good look at me and asks where I'm from. Jamal explains I'm with Aïcha, who, although she is not Egyptian, lives nearby.

When he completes his work, I ask how much I owe him. He says that for the haircut and hair spray, without washing, it is 20 pounds. This is about what I would pay in a downtown salon with running water and functional blow-dryers. Clearly, he knows the prices, and decides that this is the price someone like me is used to paying. I am tired after a rather difficult haircut and the effort I must exert to converse in Egyptian dialect. Aïcha is a bit disgusted with the high price, but Jamal is nonchalant. As I pay and leave, he asks me if I'm satisfied with the style. He smiles and tells me that if I'm in Cairo again I should stop by and see him.

Moving through beauties as they are formed in salons blurs the contours of this study. As we move out of Casablanca in their midst, we might meet no resistance, no boundary that signals our arrival in the "new worlds" of Paris or Cairo. Alternatively, we might never achieve a sense of smooth motion through space at all, once embraced by the warm eyes of careful vicinity. We move among salons with varying impressions of being out of place. Sometimes, a change of place permits us to relax our defenses

against the strangeness of worlds we don't know. A foreign-sounding name or an unfamiliar dialect enables us to avoid thinking about our inability to rely on ways of being that are familiar. But this is a relatively unusual occurrence. Most often, we move amid familiar routines and objects. This is a far more delicate affair than engaging with alternative ways of life that, national discourses and tour brochures assure us, are merely temporary excursions. What does it take to delineate social and cultural fault lines? Can we identify certain kinds of people who might be associated with their distinctive landscapes, evaluations, and intelligences? Or is the fact that practices, styles, and people might pass so easily among these different spaces problematic? Who keeps people in place, and to what aim? Why these three kinds of salons and no others?

The beauty salon can pull together neighborhoods, people, and nations. If you know how to enact its routines you can pass into worlds that might initially seem quite strange to you. You might not feel comfortable with a salon's decor, its language, or how people gaze at one another, but you do know the steps, and they guide you through the process of getting your hair done. The salon is itself a means of passing between worlds.[1] My visit to Boulaq in 1996 showed that even when the resources for following through with the basic choreography of greeting, putting on smocks, washing hair, and styling are extremely limited, forms tend to be preserved, repeated, pointed to as a shared "third."

With no water, with faulty electricity, and in the midst of the crisis of having a foreign woman come to get her hair cut, accompanied by a skeptical local resident who was clearly critical, Jamal faultlessly performed the dance of greeting, discussing potential styles, washing (or wetting), cutting and drying my hair, then politely asking me to come back again. The resulting haircut was not *copie conforme*. Indeed, the ends were uneven, and I had them straightened out the next day at another salon I visited. But the routine was faithfully reproduced. This made it possible for us to get through the encounter, which was carefully observed not only by the skeptical Aïcha, but by Jamal's regular client and several people in the neighborhood who peeked into the salon to get a look at his unusual visitors. Clearly, certain bodies are expected to go to certain types of salons. What kind of salon was Jamal's? What kind of desire animates the desire to visibly transform bodies even in such difficult landscapes? Remembering the second-hand barber's chair in the bone-dry salon, I cannot help but think that if the salon could take root in such difficult climates, it must serve some quite profoundly felt need. But this need is perhaps not, as many sociologists have surmised, reducible to a matter of evaluating cost. Nor does it have to be felt by a whole "population" to be worthy of study. Here, we follow the routine; we notice how very important its progress is in establishing communication between Jamal, myself, and Aïcha. At many points, the expectations we bring with us begin to make exchanges difficult. Aïcha's eyes on the towels. How I feel when the electricity falters. The way the client sizes me up—ironically—knowing perhaps that Jamal will be duly paid for his reception of these odd women who have strayed into the neighborhood. The entire scene is done in passing. But this does not make it meaningless.[2]

The process of research might be seen as one in which little-known worlds are entered or the links between the same shown in new ways. Most of the time, however, people establish patterns of interaction with and between worlds. These integrate various kinds of constraint and enclosure and rely on forms to make these passages, as in the case of Jamal's salon. Indeed, one of the interesting things about his salon is precisely his insistence on maintaining the form in spite of his limited infrastructure. One might have imagined that he really couldn't have a salon—without water, without being able to keep it clean. But the form provided what he needed to pull it off. The routine pulled us all through the place. Still, though the routine smoothed our exchanges, attention to it alone does not explain why it has been adopted throughout the world. It does not explain the ways people come to learn to use such scripts to "pass" between worlds and, indeed, why they should want to do this.

STAYING PUT

Attiate, a Cairene factory worker, says, "We are a tight group. We keep together and on most subjects we think alike. We defend each other's right. If we see a fellow worker poorly dressed whose husband is taking her salary, we show her the unfairness of it and encourage her to ask for her rights. All of us work hard, we have earned these rights. You see us all with strong personalities. Aren't our eyes opened wider than housewives'?"[3]

In Casablanca, Latifa and her sister Souraya hardly leave the neighborhood where they have lived since they were born. Now in their twenties, they lost their father in their teens. They were always a little shy, they both admitted. Living "alone" with their mother, without any brothers, they feel that they must be especially careful to maintain their good reputation in the neighborhood. Without a father's eyes to show the neighbors that they are looked after, kept in line, they must vividly display their virtue.[4] Latifa goes out only to visit another sister who is married or to buy things at the market. Souraya does go to the local beauty salon to get her hair styled. Both enjoy a weekly visit to the hammam. Although both women have received a few years of schooling and can make their way around town, they just don't go about much. They are afraid; a local pimp has tried to come into the house to convince Latifa to join his group on several occasions. The fate of ending up "like those girls" acts to keep them and other women in Casablanca in place.

Some women from Latifa and Souraya's neighborhood move about town to go to work every day. Some men require their wife to stay put, but increasingly, women in Morocco's cities work outside of the home. Some find work as maids, others teach. Educated women who go downtown to work and have their hair done over their lunch break are not seen in the same way as the young women leaving the neighborhood to meet their friends. But once on the bus, it is difficult to identify who comes from where. Anyone might go to fast salons in the city center, the same kind of place that my rather well-to-do friend Isabelle goes to in Paris.

Isabelle doesn't have a favorite salon, she says. But when I asked her to visit a salon in the Saint Germaine des près area recommended by one of my colleagues, she said that she "couldn't" go to such a place. At first, I didn't understand. Véronique goes there regularly, and I know that her financial situation is much less stable than is Isabelle's. I insisted: "But you know, it's not all that expensive." "No," she said, "it's that I feel out of place. I wouldn't know how to act." She explained to me that she likes to go to salons "where it's not so snobby." Isabelle prefers fast salons where she feels more at home. She does not revel in the kind of attention she imagines she will receive in "that kind" of upscale salon, but instead, is threatened by it. The routines in the St. Germaine salons are similar to those where she ususally goes, and indeed, are quite similar to those I acted out when I visited Jamal's. But Isabelle says, "I wouldn't know how to act, what to do. All of those rich ladies and *Vogue* magazines. Fashion isn't my thing."

In spite of her wealth and her extremely abundant "cultural capital," Isabelle is unable or unwilling to step into a world of special selves. She will not conceive of herself as authentic artwork that can be touched and remodeled by the hands of the beautician as artist. The standard hands of clocks and mechanical reproduction and standards of equality keep her safe, make her a part of the serial social body. They establish her connection to the hairdresser without any echoes of what she thinks of as "complicated" and often pretentious approaches to looks. To enter the space where one's own "special" face mixes with those of the rich, famous, or merely successful might be to find oneself wanting in ways one would not otherwise suspect. It could also be perceived as a way of promoting the forms of judgment and sight that orient that special world. Isabelle seems prepared to engage in neither of these possibilities.

The same moves take on a different rhythm once they cross the borders between different salons. I think of how Jamal proudly prances through his salon and calls to people in the street to assist him in obtaining what he needs to do hair. I compare his gait to Isabelle's discrete way of winding through the crowds. His brightly colored, soiled shirt; her carefully cleaned clothes in subdued tones. Her talk about capitalism and how we are all taken in as consumers and the way she knows about every discount shop where you can get more for your money. Michael Oakeschott also thinks in terms of markets and their way of attributing value in the context of his complex understanding of ethics, philosophy, and the distinct worlds of science, history, and practice. Although he does note that all worlds tend to present their modes of experience as complete, in fact, "What is true for one of these worlds can be neither true nor false for any other; it is merely irrelevant. To carry a practical attitude into the world of science or history, or to carry a scientific or an historical attitude into the world of practice, in every case, turns what is significant into nonsense, turns what is valuable into something worthless by dragging it into the wrong market."[5] Must we admit that noticing three kinds of salons, three worlds, is a matter of thinking about who can see what when? Bargaining may very well be a part of these movements. But there is also some kind of effort to create a unity, oneself, which can traverse while remaining recognizable as itself in all worlds. Moving from one world to another might turn the "significant" into "nonsense," but it could also introduce changes in both. Worlds are constantly in the process of sharing, copying, critiquing, and altering each other's values and meanings.

Still, Oakeschott's claims about "dragging things onto the wrong market" at the price of translating them into nonsense points out an important aspect of how worlds are consolidated, their excellences developed, their edges kept clean. Meaning, then, might be perceived as a matter of producing styles within a well-defined world. This world is not one of class or culture, but a development of distinct aspects of reality, a set of propositions about beauty, self, and propriety. Developing looks according to these protects a way of being. The beauty salon might itself appear as an icon of such protection. Diverse salons guard not simply against the entrance of specific kinds of looks or evaluations. They also avoid contradictions arising from different versions of a given style. Separation and segregation can help to keep things clear. Nelson Goodman expresses this when he writes, "Versions not applying in the same world no longer conflict; contradiction is avoided by segregation. A true version is true in some worlds, a false version in none. Thus the multiple worlds of conflicting true versions are actual worlds not the merely possible worlds or non-worlds of false versions."[6] Contradictions and conflicts cannot arise unless there are passages among these diverse spaces. But to speak of versions implies the possibility that although certain things might not be recognized in all worlds, at least certain others move between worlds and receive identifications that allow us to perceive them as distinct versions of some kind of sameness.

Goodman's ideas on versions point out how contradiction can result in meetings of worlds. Still, he allows us to imagine how a single style takes on meaning in several ways. By suggesting that worlds involve a sense of segregation, but that crossing them is a matter of contradiction rather than nonsense and wasted energy, he gives us clues to understanding how salons and en-lightened bodies act to pass people, styles, and ideas from one world to the next. Noticing versions allows us to think about how passages are made. Salons themselves show various kinds of segregation: from their immediate physical environment, in the aspects of style they perform, and, indeed, from one another. And yet, as my meeting with Jamal shows, they can also be an incredibly powerful medium for moving between worlds. Like pictures, salons develop distinct styles congruent with aspects of experience and modes of judgment. Like pictures, they allow for additive logics within their varied frames in ways that allow for what Goodman calls contradiction. They translate or adapt, incorporate or revel in the arrival of ideas, styles, or people that come from other worlds.

Movements of people, things, or ideas between worlds are not fortuitous. Although each world provides a specific version of a given style, passages alter how they draw up their singular beauties out of what might appear to be a single image. Worlds of beauty draw constantly on one another. In so doing they contrast various ways of being distinguished, beautiful, or honorable. They set mimetic chains in motion with respect to each other, but without giving these terms a single valence in all worlds. These moves are not just about style or literary texts. Talk about women's looks and their ways of playing with worlds through them show us how powerful understandings of the coherence of coexisting, competing, and mutually influential worlds are a part of all aspects of life. Take, for example, the way Halima, Fedwa, and Nejiba discuss the use of makeup in terms of the world of proximities that gives special weight to the eyes of husbands, actual or potential:

HALIMA: My daughters don't use makeup except on certain occasions. Young women need to make up to show themselves off.

FEDWA: Why does a woman have to use makeup?

HALIMA: To be beautiful. There is a difference between a woman with makeup and a woman without it. The one who is made up, you see the light of her face. Women mainly use makeup for their husbands. And the woman without a husband uses makeup to find one.

FEDWA: When does a woman start to take care of herself in this way?

HALIMA: Beginning at eighteen years old, to try to find a husband. The rural [beldiyya] woman, she uses makeup from her youth, khol never leaves her eyes, and she always has henna on her feet and hands. The young urban girl makes up too, with beauty products that she finds in the market. Personally, I see nothing wrong with it. On the contrary, the girl who knows what she's about (dégourdie) is the one who knows how to use makeup well.

NEJIBA: As for me, on Saturday I go to the baths and then I put on makeup. I use khol, mascara (Pinaud brand), and blush. My husband doesn't like to see me make up to go out, it seems to make him have doubts about me. . . .

HALIMA: We already told you. Before, a woman got up too early to prepare breakfast for her husband. Today, women get up at the same time as their husbands and they go together to do their shopping. Before, women had to figure a lot out to get things—now she just goes to the store where she can find everything. For example, it was shameful for a woman to buy bread, she was supposed to make it herself. And anyway, before, you couldn't even get bread at the corner store. . . .

Whether these women move into other worlds of evaluation at other moments, in the context of this interview they share a sense of the boundaries of proximity, clearly stating how the use of makeup relates to shame at distinct stages of a woman's life. They show that within this world where a husband's eyes change everything, the epic of opening has altered the very sense of proximity. While protecting the sense of a world in which the actual gaze of a known man remains the guiding principle for how everyone sees, the eyes of this version of shame have nonetheless evolved over time. The space of women's walking has expanded, as perhaps have the ways that the eyes of husbands and fathers are carried along to the places where women go. Within the world of known persons and the eyes of fathers and husbands, what might at one point have resembled a contradiction has been incorporated into a world that permits change. This is not simply a change within a given world, but a transformation of versions because worlds coexist and people use worlds against one another to achieve a variety of effects. Think of how Jamila, a middle-aged housewife in Casablanca, works with herself and the eyes of her husband:

As for me, I have always gone to the beach. And I always wear a bathing suit; even after my wedding. One time we all went in a group to the beach and my husband was supposed to arrive later. I wore my bathing suit and I started to swim, when I saw my husband arriving in the distance. I ran to get dressed. He doesn't like to see me nude.
Before, there was respect and shame, and a woman couldn't do anything in front of her father. We were shameful and respectful even in front of outsiders or foreigners [berrani]. Before, when we were young girls, we couldn't drink tea with a male guest. Today, the kids, if you don't serve them immediately it's a scandal!

To cross worlds is to make claims about their hierarchy. Jamila's comments summarize many events, interviews, and situations I have worked in and with throughout this project. Her words dwell on shame and the eyes of her man [*rajal*]. She clearly associates this view with the past, with fathers. Even after her wedding, she says, she continues to wear her bathing suit. She adopts the idea of her body as open to the even world of the fast salon, knowing full well that her status as a married woman and the eyes of her husband will judge such behavior as shameless.[7] The negotiation of this reality, this context, or the "true versions," does not take place on an even plane. Thus, we cannot simply speak of various settings and analyze Jamila's distinct roles or routines. She encompasses her account in a story that tells of change, joining the narrative of en-lightening, of the opening of alternative spaces she associates with kids and today. She recognizes different versions as correct.[8] She does not engage with this narrative primarily in terms of the pursuit of a collective truth set on developing criteria that would include all worlds. She experiences her body in terms that set her into the even light of the fast world of equalities, and yet she gives priority to her husband's gaze.

Styles might be perceptible as palettes for mixing what seem to be different ways of conceiving of worlds. But they can likewise appear as sparks that fly when coexisting worlds are pushed into coming to terms with each other. The undressed, adorned, clipped, and colored body can be seen as arguing for certain forms of sociability. There is a sort of "conversation" of style, but it is rarely expressed verbally. It is not immediately enmeshed in a quest to find an overall truth. Nor is its way of working with reality simply a matter of playing with frames. Indeed, to think of context as determined by the frame is itself to favor a certain world, a certain approach to truth, style, and meaning.[9] For Jamila, it is the eye of the very real husband that makes her say that there is a shift in her practice. We have no idea whether her husband is really opposed to her wearing a bathing suit. His opinion is not a part of the definition. Instead, it is his eye as a beacon of a certain order, a certain texture of sight and judgment that signals the move between worlds. Goodman writes that these are " . . . made not from nothing after all, but from other worlds. Worldmaking as we know it always starts from worlds already on hand: the making is a remaking."[10] If so, then it is in the moves between worlds, in their examination and strategic uses of each other's versions that some kind of reality might be pointed to.

Working within a primary world of reference does not necessarily, or even generally, imply the utter rejection of the appeal that certain versions of a style, of beauty, or of oneself might produce in another world. Remember that Isabelle refuses to enter a world of purported fame and luxury. She is not opposed to a neighborhood world of known faces, but her ways of envisaging claims to truth and beauty are clearly set in criteria based on notions of equality, autonomy, of an evenly lighted social plane in which each individual can trace his or her life story.[11] We might interpret her unwillingness to enter the world of uneven prestige and spheres of fame as a refusal to become similar to and different from others in terms of modes of valuation that she does not feel comfortable with or condone. Her reticence could be read as a kind of logocentrism. It might be understood as a kind of militancy, as an effort to expand the boundaries of the fast salon in ways that are multiple but that make sense even of their oppositions with reference to the coherence of certain ways of thinking, watching, and walking. To work within a single world makes it possible to think about truths and beauties in terms of contradiction. On this single spread of fast beauties, we can come up with ethical or political differences, but these can be viewed as holding specific positions on that flat page. Indeed, it is within and not between worlds that contradiction becomes pertinent. Isabelle has a strong sense of the values of the world to which she wants to belong. She interprets participation in several worlds as problematic, given that her measures are so strongly set in the world of single measures and equalizing lights. She sees a move toward the claims of exclusivity of the elite salons as unjust, and her own involvement there as irreconcilable with her own ideals. Her refusal might be related, as I have already suggested, to the fear of entering new mimetic worlds with their unfamiliar modes of competition. But it must also be related to the fact that for Isabelle, to live in several worlds is to appear as something she is not.

The borders of worlds can be carefully guarded by insistence on coherency, by accusations of two- (or three-?) faced behaviors. And yet, consistency does not seem best served by copying a given model or following a rule. Those who criticize the efforts of provincial or poor girls to "walk like the movies," who damn them for their impertinence in copying the ways of worlds in which they should not matter, play on a specific understanding of mimesis. So do people who criticize fashion designers for gathering ideas from around the world. Yet, there are other ways of comprehending the implications of that term. As Samuel Ijsseling writes, "It is very tempting to interpret the form of mimesis invoked here—that is, mimicking, following or imitating others—according to the traditional scheme of an original example and an unoriginal imitation, or in light of the opposition between real and unreal. It is correct to say that mimesis is characterized by a fundamental ambivalence. It is possible that someone who imitates someone else according to a prescribed protocol, neither daring nor being able to say or do anything not already said or done by others becomes estranged from himself, loses himself and founders in a world of appearance—or even worse, never becomes himself and never rises above the world of this appearance."[12]

Mimesis has many meanings. It is not a simple imprint of a model, except in a version of the concept that is congruent with the menus of fast salons (and even there the problem of realizing such an idea is problematic). Ijsseling alerts us to the idea that "mimesis is displacement, transposition, to another level of reality—without the new level necessarily being either higher or lower than the first."[13] But although the ideas of motion, of following, of transposition are clear in what we see in beauty salons and beyond, we might question how the desire to engage in the moves of mimesis is produced if at least some temporary prestige of one another world is not involved.[14] Is mere novelty enough to make versions pass from place to place? Are all moves of any kind between every world equally important? How is it that certain worlds, certain truths, and certain eyes come to hold power over others?

POWERFUL MOVES

Contrary to the philosopher's insistence that a hierarchy of worlds is not to be found, the sharing of styles, and indeed, the sharing of a single enlightened body has profound implications for power relations between worlds. We cannot always easily glide from world to world. This is not only because it might be difficult for us to learn to walk in new ways, but because others try to brand us as mere imitators. Not only individuals or groups of friends determine which worlds are given precedence. They are helped in this by powers and institutions that play worlds against each other. Laws, urban design, and the way some worlds seem to work more easily with materials intended for others and master world walking are intimately related. This does not imply that all power is gained by developing an objective distance from all worlds. Rather, individual power can result from a firm association of oneself with a specific dominant world.[15] It might also involve a particularly astute approach to the ways of negotiating passages across worlds. In this case, the creativity of world building is linked to a more dynamic power. The guardians of style are many. And recognizing their ways can help us to understand why distinctions among worlds bear a relationship to processes of social distinction in ways that use words like "economy," "culture," or "nation" as a part of their world-expanding strategies.

The experience of Leila offers a glimpse at how laws of state can intervene to define the order of worlds in people's lives, how laws themselves are negotiated too in terms of the work between standards of judgment and of power. A friend of a friend, Leila heard about my work on immigration in Morocco and asked me to interview her: "You must wonder why I wanted to talk with you about my experience. You know, many people talk about the question of immigration and wanting to leave Morocco. But they don't always hear about girls like me." Leila talks openly as her sister and other relatives serve tea. She is dressed in a very short skirt and platform shoes. I know that her family is wealthy. She explains that she attended an elite private high school and then deciced to pursue her studies in France. This was not unusual in her family, which counts many foreign-trained professionals among its members. Less a scholar than many of her relatives, Leila admits that she wasn't a model student in Paris. She preferred socializing. She loves to dance and party, she says, and she also likes to experiment with all kinds of clothes and hairstyles. "I was over there in Paris, and I had lots of friends. I wanted to invite them to see my country, where I came from. So we all came down here one summer. But after my friends left, I had to stay on longer to take care of some business. As I was packing to leave, my father appeared and told me I was not going anywhere. Like that. Out of the blue. He just said I couldn't go. No explanations. He took my passport." "So what did you do?" I asked. "I was outraged. I locked myself in my room. I refused to eat. I went on a hunger strike. I couldn't understand it. I had done nothing wrong. If only I could get back to Paris—I could work, I didn't need his money. But he wouldn't let me go. I stayed in my room. I didn't want to see anyone. My cousins tried to intervene, but he wouldn't listen." Her sister comments, "It's true—it was terrible. She wouldn't come out for at least a year. We tried to convince her that she had to live. That it wouldn't be so bad, but she wouldn't listen." Then Leila continues: "I lost all of my papers, my diplomas, my personal letters, clothes: all of the things that I had in my apartment in Paris have been lost. For a while friends there kept my things, but eventually we lost touch. In the meantime, I found out that my father had changed our name. During the protectorate my grandfather had collaborated with the French. Thus, with Independence we had our name changed. Of course, I was born long after that so I always had the new name. But, suddenly, my father decided to take back the older name. I guess that the protectorate has been forgotten and the old name was okay again."

So just at the point at which Leila brings her friends to visit her native country, her father is himself involved in reworking his own position in the world of names. Leila says she wondered who she was. She felt as if she had lost her identity: "My papers were lost, but they were no good anymore anyway," she says, "since I wasn't that person anymore." Indeed, it seems that her father considers the eyes of others seeing Leila in his determination to keep her in place, to keep her under his gaze, but he is not as concerned about her "morality" and modesty as he is about his own reputation. It is when he decides to redefine himself in terms of a famous lineage that he begins to "see" and take offense at Leila's short skirts, foreign friends, and love of dancing.

The map of Morocco provides a sense of control here, but one that uses borders to play a complex game with how we think about locality, meaning, and power. Moroccan law enables the father to define a space of sight and control that is congruent with national borders. From the point of view of the proximate eyes of patriarchy, the nation might appear as an extension of his own sight, or it could be conceived as a pattern of circles within the frame of a national territory. In any case, what is important is precisely the fact that people in these circles might witness unbecoming looks. But the father's sudden decision to inhibit his daughter's movements does not so much seek to be efficacious at the level of who sees her in Morocco as it uses the nation as a means to contain movements that, as they include the globe as space, might reveal her clothes and comportment to the eyes that count. Leila still wears miniskirts in her neighbor-hood for all to see. Her sister says that both of them "just wear anything here. We don't care who sees us. It doesn't matter at all. I either wear miniskirts or just sweat pants. I don't worry about making up—I don't care at all what I look like when I'm in Morocco." It seems that her father does not care that the eyes of proximity judge her wanting. But we can guess that in Paris or London, he does care that his daughter dances in discotheques where people who are important to the networks he seeks to cultivate go to be seen. His actions and his daughter's make sense only as an attempt to safeguard his name in the world of fame. However, he uses the law as a means of controlling his daughter in a way that is not con-gruent with any claim to charismatic authority. He neither locates his daughters in a neighborhood setting where the eyes of the face-to-face might reinforce his right to dictate to his daughters, nor does he manage to make them respect his name and the ways that money might make it shine anew. His daughter reacts to his clumsiness by first retreating then rebelling and seeking to denounce his despotism by telling me of her tale and publicizing her indifference by provoking looks at every streetcorner. Might not her provocations in the proximate achieve such a momentum as escape those eyes that her father seems not to see and cross into the worlds in which he seeks recognition? People and talk circulate, moving beyond the borders her father uses as a rampart of reputation. Might not the potential for authority involve marks of mastery in all worlds? Might it not involve a sensitivity to how movements of people, ideas, or pictures can be carefully worked in ways that tie together several worlds?

We can use what we have learned in salons to make sense of political and institutional plays beyond this instance of law within a single state. From Casablanca, where I was living in 1989, I read of the first of many "veil scandals" in France. The crisis began when three junior high school girls were expelled from school for wearing the hijab. Why, I wondered, had young women wearing scarves to school catalyzed such intense pas-sions? Signs of belief and belonging among Islamists are also expressed in postures, prayer marks, beards, and hairstyles. Islamic "brothers" often wear a distinctive *kamise*, leaving their beards ungroomed.[16] Yet in France, as in many parts of the Muslim world, it is the image of a veiled girl that is problematic. Indeed, since the late 1980s, a series of what have been called veil crises have set off an ongoing debate about whether this head covering is a challenge to the nation. The event that periodically sets off talk about the hijab occurs when one or more adolescent girls wears the hijab to school.

For some, the veil is sometimes presented in terms of equality and the common right to dress as one likes. But as the repeated veil crises show, for many, the hijab is perceived as rejecting the principles of the modern polity. Some voices point out the girls' rights to choose. Then, debates ensue concerning whether it is the girls who choose this attire or their fathers who force it upon them.[17] But such ideas of choice, the hijab version of fast style, cannot be heard by those who view the veil as an exclusionary tactic. For there is a way in which the hijab expresses not only religious choice, but also the exclusivity of the body of the girl who wears it. In these debates, the hijab is perceived as introducing the background body into a space that has long been "open."

However, if we consider the direction the discussion concerning the veil took and continues to take in Paris, we are forced to acknowledge that that opening is a limited one. In reaction to the first veil crisis, it is telling that the socialist Michel Rocard, then prime minister, made a point of saying that girls should not be excluded from schools, because as future mothers they pass on "cultural models."[18] At the height of that first crisis, Morocco's King Hassan II was also invited to speak on the issue on one of the French public television channels. He and Rocard displayed a similar concern for the way young ladies should be perceived. The monarch drew our attention to the fact that the prophet Mohammed placed men and women at the same level. And he used his own daughters as examples. The princesses, he said, were very modern young ladies: "My daughters swam. They've played basketball in shorts, and have played tennis in tennis skirts . . . on the condition that there is of course no provocation." He went on to explain that he has introduced "the mother of his children" publicly because she is "well brought up and presentable."[19] Clearly he, not she, determined which outfits were "provocative" for their daughters. In reading these comments, it becomes clear that each of these political actors pays homage to the idea of "integration" into a world of open horizons and anywhere bodies. And both also work together to bring out the proximate or the radiant qualities of patriarchal eyes.

Hijab or not, the idea of protection is present throughout these debates. The crisis serves to work through its various versions and consolidate a centrality of the Moroccan monarch, who demonstrates his understanding of the fast and open world of modernity while appealing to the fatherly eyes of proximate men. Rocard and other leaders in France, meanwhile, focus on the world of open and equal bodies, yet work to tie these to the nation's centrality, a community those girls should serve in a special way. It introduces a sense of the proximate eyes of the neighbors watching, wondering when the new bride will get pregnant and give birth. The fatherly eyes of the neighborhood and the burning eyes of the radiant leader are used to identify certain styles as more en-lightened than others. They work together to confine the world of equality as someone like Isabelle imagines it.

PUTTING ON NEWNESS

Hourriya, whose name means freedom, plays with worlds to provoke us to think always about backgrounds. She reminds me of what Georg Simmel wrote in his 1904 essay on fashion: "The imitator is the passive individual who believes in social similarity or adapts himself to existing elements; the teleological individual, on the other hand, is ever experimenting, always restlessly striving, and he relies on his own personal conviction."[20] Although I don't agree with his account of similarity, I must admit that certain people do seem more inclined to strive, to experiment. Hourriya is one of these. Educated and moderately well off, she sometimes travels to Paris for work. She takes advantage of her time there to get her hair cut and buy new clothes. But she also goes to Samy in downtown Casa, and sometimes does not cut her hair at all for a while; she lets it grow and her curls spring wildly out around her face. She doesn't need designer labels, she says. She laughs at the "wives of government ministers who think that they can't go out without a dress from Yves Saint Laurent. It's like they all have a uniform." Indeed, when she appears in a simple suit at their party, she looks the "lightest" and seems "most special."

Hourriya is not outlandish. She does not, like Leila, knowingly provoke the eyes of the proximate in a last-ditch effort to free herself. Nor does she decide to take on the role of the painted lady, or bohemian, as some women do in every world, as a way of countering prevalent versions of the belle dame or BCBG matron." And yet, she does seem to incite people to question their most familiar ways of viewing what she perceives as too easy acceptance of the worlds that be. Sometimes she inhabits a Chanel suit, at others a beautiful caftan, but she does it in a way that is so conforming to the ideals of each world she enters that she points out features of the eyes looking at her that are unsettling. She comes off as somehow strange, deranging by her mastery of the ways one "ought" to look because of how she uses her style to bring several worlds into contact.

Like Jamal in his basic beauty shop, Hourriya seems so very sure of herself. She masters the moves she effects, whether these are versions of a haircut or of herself between diverse social networks or enclosures. Unlike Jamal, she does not depend on a specific routine, a given space. Her ease also comes from knowing the steps of many different dances. This is no fixed performance but a supple set of moves by which she introduces something new into any situation. Hourriya is provocative and beautiful, sometimes shameful, and generally effective because of the way she orchestrates crossings between distinct modes of evaluation. This ability is what gives her a very personal style. It does seem linked to a special conviction, but one she cannot articulate in words. Of course, her voice is as supple as her feet over tile or wood or carpeted floors. But for all of her talent with several languages she cannot verbalize the reasons for the looks she receives, knowing that the judgments of each world will find her odd and fascinating. Her ways of walking draw her, like us, toward her but then beyond. They lead to the idea that there must be yet other worlds, as yet unknown spaces where other eyes might reign. Hourriya's style pushes us to notice similarities and differences of many kinds. She gets us to ask Difference from what? instead of simply designating alternatives as oppositions within a single and set symbolic or social system.

But might not this distract us from remarking what Marcel Mauss wanted to generalize and what the well brought up ladies we visited earlier claimed: that certain kinds of people have a seemingly natural knowledge of how to walk in certain worlds? This naturalness, they agree, that comes from training and tradition. It is the result of a special relationship to cities and to early en-lightenment. To focus too intently on Hourriya is to look to the edges of our social life, they might say. Instead, we must also consider how "vast groups of people move together through time," as Jean Marques so clearly stated. History might alter the ways in which orders confront one another, and thus, how these changes are expressed. The "personal style" might then simply indicate a change in status, a new class position gained through the accruing of economic or cultural capital. Pierre Bourdieu accounts for distinctions of taste and habit in France in terms of such positionings and trajectories: "Each individual system of disposition is a structural variant of the others, expressing the singularity of its position within the class and its trajectory. 'Personal style,' the particular stamp [*marque*] marking all the products of the same *habitus*, whether practices or works, is never more than a deviation [*écart*] in relation to a period or class, so that it relates back to the common style not only by its conformity—like Phidias, who, for Hegel, had no 'manner'— but also by the difference that makes 'the manner.' "[21]

This definition is significant, for it presents the characteristic rhythm of Bourdieu's way of taking Mauss in stride while accounting for the disgust the urban ladies feel at the look of young *'aroubi* girls. Style is a *marque*, a word that in French plays on the idea of the brand. This brand "marks" those of a single habitus. To see this we must form an idea of the special style of the times, the class, or, presumably, the cultural group.[22] Personal style can then emerge in relation to this common ground. This selection from Bourdieu goes beyond the explanation of this ground to suggest why style might be interesting at all. Style, he writes, is an *écart*. By putting this word back into French, and keeping in mind that it is related to the scar of the branding iron, we might better understand both what is said and what is set aside in this definition of style. We might also use the term to move beyond Bourdieu's intentions to take our own deviation toward a rather different dance of variety and versions across worlds that help to give form to what *we* might call societies.

An écart can simply mean a relation between two things, in this case, the personal style and the style of the period or class. To see an écart in this way is to set it between a generality and a particularity. But this word joins the background to the body of style in a special way. For it unites the idea of distance to notions of delinquency or flights of fancy. To signal style as a breach captures the potential danger of creating style, but also assumes that the background is already understood. Style is merely an écart. It takes on meaning only by its way of working with how it has been branded and the small moves it can make over the background. Style here is a symptom rather than an experience. It produces meanings about things beyond the body of the stylish, exceeding the understanding of the beautiful.

For Bourdieu, the result is an account of style as indicative of movements within an enclosure, a taken-for-granted society.[23] Alterity might be involved, but its workings are vague and mysterious, something on the order of a belief in a heaven the scholar holds onto, rather like the enlightened body retains a special tie to the heavy background by spinning sentimental and nostalgic narrative. As James Faubion writes, "For the Bourdieusian, the other is in the modern as the Orthodox saint is in each of his iconic refractions, a naked presence cloaked beneath a pageantry of costumes, some plain and humble, some at the height of fashion."[24] This naked presence helps the scholar get through the motions of the society at hand. But its lack of definition adds to his own reluctance to see not merely his scholarly position, but how he, or the "other," might actually make a difference.

To think about the moves of style that makes us into something, we must pursue the word écart in its verbal form. *Ecarter* means to push aside, as, for example, to push aside a rival in a race. It can be used to indicate the setting aside of a possible course of action. Style in the verbal mode might force decision, force articulation, and favor the development of worlds in which the personal style makes sense, as it does for Hourriya. It might convince some people that they are not possessed of what it takes to make the leap across the cracks that are opened up by the process. To do this might imply delinquency or flights of fancy. It might mean risking the *grand écart*, that is, doing splits, one foot on the ground that calls your looks delinquent, the other perhaps set in a world where your looks appear innocuous. At once delinquent and unremarkable, such a split is not uncommon even among people we might place in a single set based on their income, the dialect they speak, their kin, or their relationship to central points of symbolic power. But all delinquencies, all flights of fancy, all means of setting aside certain agendas for beauty and for possible worlds make us notice them as style, or as meaningful. All styles cannot work with the same efficaciousness. The only way to account for this is to notice how periods and societies form "general" styles, not as grounds, but in a process of joining a variety of worlds of judgment. Once we begin to notice that there are several coherent worlds at work producing our beauties and how we judge them we can begin to think about marginality and edges not only in terms of unified criteria and rankings, but as produced in the meetings between these worlds.

Producing different versions of oneself and one's projects is a means of power for Hourriya, for a prime minister, for a king. Passages of institutions, of people, and of ideas from one world to another encourage noticing differently ordered others and their eyes. They might introduce not only new things into distinct worlds but affect the relationships of individuals or groups to these different ways of judging, thinking, and becoming. Passages often intensify our gaze and densify our talk. They alert us to help validate or alter criteria reigning in each world they cross. They fight within worlds to gain attention, wealth, or perfection. They seek to move institutions or ideas among worlds. But certain aims can be reached only if a world becomes a world of reference for many people. This involves the consolidation of criteria from a world, a process that involves work not only within but often among worlds. Strategies of confinement and movements toward coherency are a part of what makes each world possible. Yet, these only become clear as we move from one world to the next. Moves allow us to experiment with nonsense, or transport rules or beauties to renew their possible versions. Crossing between worlds can incite forceful reactions or the stirring of new desires. Dancing from one world to another does not take place in some ethereal concert hall, nor in some in-between space, but on grounds that we bring together from already relevant worlds.

The play on worlds we live with now often assumes that backgrounds are set in time and kept in place. But what I have learned about beauty leads me to think that, in fact, we draw our backgrounds from the worlds that we move through and not from a grounded, heavy body. Adopting styles or ways of walking implicate us all in making worlds out of other worlds. And the way we do this involves promoting, styling, and perfecting certain worlds and particular passages as regular, good, or gracious. The other worlds serve to highlight this when we spin them around and use them as backgrounds. We seek to make existing worlds expand or shrink to gain power or acquire things, but also to develop a sense of how the world in general ought to be.

If, to us, studying a racing form seems a practical activity and chasing butterflies does not, that is not because the one is useful and the other is not; it is because the one is considered an effort, however feckless, to know what's what and the other, however charming, is not.—Clifford Geertz, "Common Sense as a Cultural System"[1]

Images of beauty can be as elusive as the butterfly. And have just as short a life span. Like a butterfly hunter, using Casablanca, Paris, and Cairo as my territory, I have stitched nets to capture such ephemeral pictures and to record stories people tell about their life cycle. In imitation of those capricious creatures, I have taken flight, then hovered over where these beauties meet. What I am left with is not a collection but a record of a peregrination, a diary of patterns of flight. Engaging in what might seem such an impractical activity as chasing these winged and restless visions, listening to tales of one man's mindless rush into the winds of fashion or another woman's urge to don cloaks of timeless tradition, I have listened to such diverse accounts of the makeup of beauty, as a concept and an industry, the object of competition, and a locus of the most intimate emotion. Beauty appears as a movement, and as a means of attraction. It is a lure we hope to become in the process of pursuing it.

Today, the places we inhabit might play on mirrors that reflect the anywhere ways we often make up our faces. They seem to gain in unity in a process that is like the light of the sun gathered in a lamp that shines from everywhere. A celestial slide show of infinite looks denies the power of earthly gravity. Apparently beyond nature and bodily need, we yet mourn how lightness seems to sweep our feet off the ground. We need the contrast of the heavy body to find some definition. We might find it in our own moments of heaviness or see it in others whose timelessness keeps them in close touch with given lands. In between the light and the heavy, performing an endless pas de bourrée between lithe dances of disinterest and the heavy pull of need, between airy flight and connections to terrains, we tell epics of opening to explain our forward motion. These tales animate how we walk down streets or envisage future worlds. In the tow of those stories I have moved from Casablanca to Paris to Cairo as though through an ever widening clearing, a space of sharing and possible complicity, but one that seems to have no middle ground. Following beauties in others' eyes and mirrored hands' reflections, I found the two-step did encourage kinds of talk and common ideas about bodily alterations. But its freedoms and enclosures were not adapted to noticing where that in-betweenness might be found. Watching the movies and the ways girls walk, I found worlds where waltzes animated and confounded the enlightened interval. I began to recognize the play of light here, of several ways of playing on reflections. In the tangles of opening stories strewn among beauty's butterflylike movements, I was taught how to step beyond the in-between to find inspiration in the gifts our ancestors did not quite bequeathe to us.

To generalize and to understand how species or cultures move together, I moved back in time to search out Marcel Mauss in an American hospital. Deadly bored, he explained that at first no particular movements there attracted his attention. To tell time he listened for the regular tread of rubber nurse shoes on the tile floor. But then, those padded timepieces led him up the ladies' legs, returned, then followed him back to central Paris. There, those kitty-soft steps set the lines of his thought, set him noticing scenes in the street and girls in the movies he might never have noticed—got him thinking of how to move over the world without ever going away. He wrote the famous essay on body techniques we still read today. In it, we read of his watching, swimming, and marching, but unfortunately, too, his manner of moving out of these toward "generalizations." It is, above all, a manual of how to get away, to distance oneself from the sources, the 'in, or eyes, of his inspiration, in favor of read accounts where there is less chance of conceptual disarray. So easily laid aside, those profound and promising moments are not where his eye lingers. So fitting of the scientist that his collections are always clearly labeled, his landscapes, except the movies, all of a piece. Culture to culture he provides information, pulls his armchair closer to his desk to examine each new account of peculiar muscular motion. His writings gather then order specimens from around the world, but his own moves involve no exuberant expense of energy, no romantic references to exotic locations. Mauss's gift is one of good measure, careful balance, and eyes without bodies. Like a latter-day Léa he becomes so light and so general that he loses any claims to style at all. His face is the one Herzog recognizes in eighteenth-century London's barbershops. His eyes display the kind of intelligence that Habermas dreams of meeting in some café. His face becomes that of *l'honnête homme.*

This is a vanishing act that might inspire us to see our position as one that can never reach or perhaps willfully rejects such a perfect conception of extensive, general, and faceless knowledge. Or it might, as it has in much recent scholarship, incite us to focus on our own experience (glancing back at our predecessors). Today, in a period when uprooting and exile seem the lot of en-lightened existence, and when we think it so important to hear the voices of all subjects, whose version of their walks might be quite other than those that doctors of medicine or philosophy describe, we tend to equate disappearance with concealment. Instead of engaging in dreams of exploration and generalization, we develop dissertations on the particular figures who show the workings of the powers behind the ways we can learn and come to know. The marginal or the exile comes to stand for a different kind of entanglement with heavy background bodies. His or her path is peculiar; it indicates a special kind of link to lost wholeness. It is a movement away from that heavy place, a place become forbidden, dangerous, unlike itself, so that one's marginality and novelty in the new landscapes one inhabits is full of import. That new place is never quite one's own, and yet one offers it strange kinds of beauty it did not possess until one's coming. Homi Bhabha expresses this when he writes about what interests him: "I am less interested in the metonymic fragmentation of the 'original.' I am more engaged with the 'foreign' element that reveals the interstitial; insists in the textile superfluity of folds and wrinkles; and becomes in the 'unstable element of linkage,' the indeterminate temporality of the in-between, that has to be engaged in creating the conditions through which 'newness comes into the world.' The foreign element 'destroys the original's structures of references and sense communication as well' not simply by negating it but by negotiating the disjunction in which successive cultural temporalities are preserved in the work of history and *at the same time* cancelled."[2]

The kind of unhinging process on which Bhabha hangs this passage reminds me of the extra meaning that new colors of hair produce. Canceling and reiterating attract attention to complex moves between the heavy and the light. They add an interesting twist, for it is no longer the land as background, but the body taking on the landscape that we observe, its velocity meteoric as it crashes the system it meets in its path. To speak of the "interstitial" not only refers to a foreignness designated by what it is not but also conceives of the new as originating in an abyss. Creativity emerges from the crater that the foreign creates. But are such fissures the most likely places from which newness can be born? If the alien and the strange alters structures, its lack of lightness seems to set it apart from other airy bodies. Its stubbornness might produce new things, but such a body must also live entrenched, so heavy as to find the expression of nostalgia problematic. This is an "element" or body that seeks to regain weight and gravity through motion. It draws memories of a land into its body and scoffs at the carefree mysteries of making one's own face. But it thus eliminates the possibilities of maintaining any background beyond the "systems" it encounters. This exile, this strange wanderer can never go home, for its body is its origin and its value.

We might find alternative modes of travel to this heavy moving figure in those who seek no grounds, those who not only say their faces are from anywhere, but who often move from place to place to prove it. Unlike the party-crashing foreign element, this beauty observes the dance floor from several sidelines. Reinventing the wallflower, she thrives on watching others dance. Her own momentum seems to come not from multiple engagements but from this contemplation. She neither breaks the case of the glass that protects the specimens she cherishes, nor does she carefully open it to rearrange them if her research reveals a new system of classification. Instead, she seems to epitomize how openness and easy moves over the earth lead to lack of direction and involvement. Ulf Hannerz, who has sketched a clear portrait of this cosmopolitan face, contrasts it to that of the local, and finds in it a possibility for positive direction in a more genuine stance: "A more genuine cosmopolitanism is first of all an orientation, a willingness to engage with the Other. It is an intellectual and asethetic stance of openness toward divergent cultural experiences, a search for contrasts rather than uniformity."[3] But how are identifications of otherness reached? From where and with whom might lines of divergence be traced?

One might engage with another or others, but the Other has no identifiable face. Engagement implies a sense of shared possibilities and projects. Like beauty itself, it is a kind of promise. It implies particular kinds of eyes and complicities; it requires shared worlds. And for all projects, interests of many kinds are fundamental. These define what can be considered creative or worth fighting for. They determine how we are involved with others and what exactly makes us interesting to them. To explore even the definitions we use to structure here and anywhere, us and the Other, requires some work on interest in ways that even Søren Kierkegaard, for all of his mistrust of the aesthetic, intimated when he wrote, "The category of the interesting is (moreover), a borderline one, it marks the boundary between the aesthetic and the ethical. For that reason in our inquiry we must be constantly glancing over into the territory of ethics, while to give our inquiries weight the problem must be grasped with genuine aesthetic feeling."[4]

Might interest be located on borders between aspects of experience or at the edges of societies? Might newness be a lure or a sign of deeply interesting reflections that come together to propose truer understandings of beauty and virtue? Working through beauties and their different faces shows how beauty is interesting not because it necessarily produces a special aesthetic emotion or territory but because it is so intimately involved in issues of value of all kinds.[5] We cannot look from beauty to ethics because determining that divide would itself place us in a particular world. We can, however, follow a variety of ways of making and valuing beauties toward a new and interesting sense of virtue and of place. Getting beyond the in-between of beauty as light or as thickly veiled interest leads us to take up and follow the two-step as it designs the worlds we think we know. People do weave many threads of meaning with words that move toward ever greater lightness. Talk often contrasts the particular to the universal, and many claims to modernity rest on how they explain the way freedom is a movement away from faces. But to use such stories to imagine we can identify any particular face or type as the key to new ways of walking is misleading. It is instead in the dynamic sidesteps we take from one world or another that motives for newness might be found. It is in a dynamic mimesis that creativity can emerge rather than in a process of progressive illumination. It is in the play of different versions, some of which might appear from afar, that we might actually ponder sources of the new as claims to freedom. Recognizing this through ethnography implies that "thickening" description or a "plunge into" a single, deeply significant world is not sufficient to explain that people in so many places are today living with a shared body. It is with a tightening of the threads of the nets that moved me from one salon that I was able to move with it in all of its strangeness. I could then feel where the edges of my nets were frayed, where different versions played on what looked to be the same world. These in turn led me to notice how beauty's nets sometimes snagged on falling foreign objects, or failed to capture certain faces due to lack of interest.

The nets of all worlds weave conceptions of shame into evaluations of excellence. They develop categories and projects that promise to take us in certain directions, toward certain ideals that involve us in evaluations much finer than some image of how we appear to just any other eyes. In this sense, the styles we select or their interpretation are at once a declaration and a request for protection, a variation on the hijab. Our way of wearing what looks like similarity can indicate what we fear and to whom we might turn for solace, encouragement, and excitement. Which are the eyes we hope to challenge? What kind of judgments do we overtly ignore? Making up each and every face involves processes that reaffirm or challenge the eyes that are authoritative and radiant, powerful or right. To favor one set world is not necessarily to adopt an identifiable cut or style, but to interpret these in terms of one or another set of eyes. And so aesthetic treatments and the value of our looks are intimately linked not just across geographical spaces, from city to city, but to how we can imagine who we are in these worlds and where we might go. Freedom is not the result of a simple unveiling but of gaining technical mastery and knowing how to attract and work with partners whose faces take on distinct shades in various worlds. Worlds of elite networks around persons, of modern maps of equalizing rationality and the face-to-face spaces of patriarchal sights were everywhere evident to me as I traveled through triangles of beauty. These were perhaps not the only worlds to be found, but they seemed to me to be the clearest that have, as yet, been possible to describe.

Description of these worlds and the stakes of their crossings is my way of mastering the moves between grounds that Hourriya or Leila might hope to achieve by provoking or playing with eyes with diverse versions of en-lightenment. Because eyes' intelligence cannot be reduced to issues of optics, to account for it here suggests new combinations, new sites for exploring how the ability to play with and in several worlds gives one a chance to work on the order of these worlds. For certain worlds can dominate the versions we see as correct at a point in time. To think about how shame and beauty work with the eyes of each world and the movements from one to another makes us alert to the way faces work on this world order. It helps us to understand why knowing the ways of one world might render one quick and apt at learning other ways of moving. But it also explains why mastery can sometimes set us in our ways or blind us to emerging arrangements. It suggests that we might not think only about foreignness and centers but about how eccentricities and alterations work themselves from the fine points out.

Like Mauss's parisienne, the ethnographer must learn to walk with the shared, en-lightened body, through movies, through stories, through ways of learning to walk down city streets. He or she must remain supple enough to dance in many directions, yet strong enough to take a stand. This is often difficult because the very sense of mastery we develop as scholars tends to develop certain gestures; it sets our work in terms of tempos that facilitate particular motions. In thought, as in action, fully mastering a discipline can hinder one's ability to mime, make fun, and innovate. Like a prima donna moving from ballet to tango, excellence in one world can imply a disposition to learn easily, but it can also imply refusing to alter patterns of motion one accomplishes with such ease and perfection. Just like women who want to walk in a single world because that is the world they want to generalize and believe in, the stubborn body of the scholar can be caught in an unwillingness to relate thought to the moving ground it stands on. The moves between the worlds are for him or her, as for Hourriya, the challenge and the possibility that linked comparisons provide. For, given this approach, taking a stand is a matter not of set principle or opinion but of ongoing process. It is a way of moving through worlds always on to others in ways that cannot be predicted.

Work between worlds can be exhilarating and threatening because it relies on what is held in common to suggest new ways of attributing value and determining how we collect, move, or see. The process of linking might begin with something shared, of a complicity wrought of a discourse that touches us all. Perhaps a vague connection to shared stories or recipes is enough to move us to get to work, to imagine a set of force fields. But to work through things in ways that contribute to an understanding of how new stands are possible, and where, one needs to think too of how the process is not just one of generalities but of producing versions on one's own. To produce versions implies issues of access, of partaking, of being drawn by movements of people, things, or ideas. This implies not only seeking new perspectives, but recognizing that to speak in terms of perspective is already to assume a shared plane of sight.

Hourriya, Jamal, and Isabelle showed me how likeness can play on what we think is near and far, how this is what gives form to the lands we can know. They did not take shape in a world of their own but led me to think that understanding emerging modes of walking and of potential ways of living or of conflict involves noticing faces and their different eyes. This requires not collecting and generalizing but patiently moving from shared pictures, ideas, tales, to follow how these are differently understood in order to dance through a given place. This place, not equatable with an already given field, might be tied together by flows of things, of songs or books. But from those initial connections, more focused faces can be derived. It is in the context of the worlds thus recognized that the ethnographer must work, contribute in some way to charting possible moves, inflecting how we might think about choice and infinity and making our place in the world.

Hierarchies of worlds and the passages among them are a part of what makes a city or an individual story unique. But to grasp this uniqueness we must abandon the urge to immediately identify a place with a way of walking. We must not too readily disappear but fix our eyes to meet those of many others in mirrors, in magazines, or walking down the street. We must observe how what is interesting might very well involve issues of judging and naming beauties. But this implies reworking our ideas of the genuine in ways that, though releasing the heavy, do not disappear like a butterfly hunter into the unbounded space of charting the evolution of a given species. It involves trying to find our balance without seeking to locate truth in the representative eye or a single, given goal. In other words, it requires rethinking not simply scholarly comparisons but the way we think of the relationship between the cosmos and the polis and the way representative eyes might guide the stitching together of partially shared nets into a single garment. Nets woven perhaps of talk and sharing certain myths of gazes meeting, but yet distinctly different in the voices they allow to tell the stories or the shades of meaning they invoke to convince us of their legitimacy. Being attentive to how difference works to create sameness, we come to see how cosmopolitans and foreigners are always being shaped in our midst. For these figures are figments of the tale of opening that guides us and misleads us and pushes us toward what look like the edges of beauty. They lure us to spaces where there is no jumping off but instead of playing on the eyes of the world to produce lighthearted gravity.

Hourriya invites us to take steps that might lead us to experience a new gravity wrought of motion and of many-colored lights. With words that dwell on notions of closeness, play on privileged gazes, or pretend to offer us infinity, she dances from world to world attracting partners who follow the paths she traces through passages that are often narrow and tight and difficult to enter. Her moves and the way she talks about them might provoke you to consider those intelligent eyes that have formed you as they have me. Then, perhaps, you might trace other regions and alternative points of rest than those I have described. You might form projects for walking out and around freedoms that Hourriya cannot yet imagine. And you might do all of this not to disappear and fly toward an ultimate lightness, but because of the faces you assume in worlds that are both anywhere and somewhere, worlds formed by faces whose eyes can be worked on with intelligence to make a difference.

NOTES

INTRODUCTION
Unless otherwise specified, all translations are mine.

1 Jürgen Habermas, *The Structural Transformation of the Public Sphere: An Inquiry into a Category of Bourgeois Society,* trans. Thomas Burger with Frederick Lawrence (1962; Cambridge, MA: MIT Press, 1991).

2 There are, however, some books that deal with hairdressing, barbers, and the history of beauty salons. I address these throughout the study as well as draw on the growing literature on fashion, body techniques, and ideas of beauty.

3 The book that resulted from this research was *Picturing Casablanca: Portraits of Power in a Modern City* (Berkeley: University of California Press, 1994). In that work, I noticed how studying the exclusion of certain types of faces from images of the nation can teach us how power is produced in a contemporary monarchy. There, as here, I established the site of my study by "following" pictures and stories as they created Casablanca and its public spaces in consonance with modern media technologies. I noted that mass images often require bridging states and thus encourage the development of research in sites that are distant but linked by currents of trade, media, and migration. But though I recognized that patterned procedures of assembly need to be described, I merely noted that we ought to identify the regularities of their embodiment. The present study works from what was then left undone.

4 I first wrote about beauty salons after an eventful visit to have my hair cut in Casablanca in 1990. I published an article based on that experience and my visits to the local hammam in a special section of the *Cahiers de l'Orient* that Yves Gonzalez-Quijano and I prepared the following year. See "Les Salons de beauté au Maroc," *Les Cahiers de l'Orient,* no. 20 (spring 1991): 227–40. I expanded this project in Susan Ossman, ed., *Miroirs maghrébins: Itinéraires de soi et paysages de rencontre* (Paris: CNRS Editions, 1998).

5 Arjun Appadurai first suggested that following the circulation of things could be a good way to come to terms with changes being wrought by globalization. Yet, even his recent developments of this idea in terms of a variety of "flows"

and "scapes" don't quite tell us how to enter into these movements ourselves. As George Marcus notes, "Powerful conceptual visions of multi-sited spaces for ethnographic research that have been especially influential in anthropology, such as Haraway's construct of the cyborg and Appadurai's idea of the global cultural economy with its variety of "scapes," do not also function as guides for designing the research that would exemplify and fulfill such visions. This requires a more literal discussion of the methodological issues, such as how to construct the multi-sited space through which the ethnographer traverses": *Ethnography through Thick and Thin* (Princeton, NJ: Princeton University Press, 1999), 89.

This study makes linked comparisons in an attempt to work through some of the problems and promises of the very notion of the field or the site. Developing research out of salons not only offers a grounded point of departure but includes the very notion of the global in the object of study. This helps in becoming more explicit about the connections that do or do not make a difference. Instead of simply referring to vague weavings, interconnectedness, or assuming that media, beauty, and so on necessarily constitute an independent field of activity, working from such a shared space obliges the researcher to note the strength, meaning, and *nature* of the links he or she follows. This approach allows the emergence of regions of study that are patterned by the times of these exchanges and concretized not only in individual bodies but in spaces of sociability. This project is thus not about relationships between given fields, but rather about how spaces of sociability and imagination work on the constitution of possible fields. For further discussion of Marcus's article, see Paul Rabinow, *French DNA: Trouble in Purgatory* (Chicago: University of Chicago Press, 1999), 169–71.

6 I lived in Morocco from 1988 until 1996, with frequent trips to Paris, a city I have regularly visited or lived in for twenty years. My work in Cairo, on the other hand, was carried out in two research trips in 1995 and 1996. Surely such differences, not to mention the enormous diversity of historical and ethnographic work on each city, affected the lines of my research.

7 Gupta and Ferguson note, "If one begins with the premise that spaces have always been hierarchically interconnected, instead of naturally disconnected, then cultural and social change becomes not a matter of cultural contact and articulation but one of rethinking difference *through* connections": in *Culture, Power, Place: Explorations in Critical Anthropology*, ed. Akhil Gupta and James Ferguson (Durham, NC: Duke University Press, 1997), 35.

8 For more on movement and ethnography, see my introduction to *Mimesis: Imiter, représenter, circuler*, special issue of *Hermès* 22 (1998): 9–15.

1. ANYWHERE BODIES AND FARAWAY EYES

1 Richard Friedland and Dierdre Boden, eds., *NoWhere: Space, Time and Modernity* (Berkeley, University of California Press, 1994).

2 One thing worth noting here is that what Susan Gubar says as a critique of much

current feminist theory bears a direct relationship to the way that women I met in the course of my study tended to speak about "modern" lives and bodies. For better or worse, many of the "postmodern" tropes with which she takes issue in the work of scholars such as Butler, Haraway, and Spivak can easily be related to this everyday talk. This is not to say that Gubar does not voice some legitimate anxiety about the "light" quality of much of current feminist scholarship (or academic work more generally). However, I think it is essential to notice the intensities and pervasiveness of this quality not only among literary scholars, but in the way people make sense of their life experiences, which, both in their movement and the words available to speak about them, do often "float," or, to use another favorite image in contemporary writing, fragment. See Susan Gubar, "What Ails Feminist Criticism," *Critical Inquiry* 24, no. 4 (summer 1998).

3 BCBG means *bon chic bon genre*, a style that might very roughly correspond to the American "preppie" style of the 1980s. See François de Negroni, "Le BCBG et les usages de masse de la distinction," *Parure, pudeur, étiquette: Communications*, no. 46 (1987): 315–19.

4 On the "fashion system," see Roland Barthes, *Le system de la mode* (Paris: Le Seuil, 1967); translated by Matthew Ward and Richard Howard as *The Fashion System* (Berkeley: University of California Press, 1990). Also see Ellen Leopold, "The Manufacture of the Fashion System," in *Chic Thrills: A Fashion Reader*, ed. Juliet Ash and Elizabeth Wilson (Berkeley: University of California Press, 1992), 101–17. For a different perspective, see Gilles Lipovetsky, *L'empire de l'éphémère: La mode et son destin dans les sociétés modernes* (Paris: Gallimard, 1987); translated by Catherine Porter as *The Empire of Fashion: Dressing Modern Democracy* (Princeton, NJ: Princeton University Press, 1994).

Studies of fashion diffusion have tended to be debated in terms of theories of the "trickle up" or "trickle down" of particular models. Consult Diana Crane, "Diffusion Models and Fashion: A Reassessment," *Annals of the American Academy of Political and Social Science*, 566 (November 1999): 13–24.

5 On brands, see Rosemary J. Coombes, "The Demonic Place of the 'Not There': Trademark Rumors in the Post-Industrial Imaginary," in *Culture, Power, and Place: Explorations in Critical Anthropology*, ed. Akhil Gupta and James Ferguson (Durham, NC: Duke University Press, 1997), 249–76. Also see Andréa Semprini, *La marque* (Paris: Presses Universitaires de France, 1995); Roy Wagner, "If You Have the Advertisement You Don't Need the Product," in *Rhetorics of Self-Making*, ed. Deborah Battaglia (Berkeley: University of California Press, 1995), 59–76.

6 We might do well to listen to Inderpal Grewal and Caren Kaplan remark that "U.S. feminists often have to be reminded that all peoples of the world are not solely constructed by the trinity of race-sex-class; for that matter, other categories also enter into the issues of subject formation both within and outside the borders of the United States, requiring more nuanced and complex theories of social relations": Introduction to *Scattered Hegemonies. Postmodernism and Transna-*

tional Feminist Practices, ed. Inderpal Grewal and Caren Kaplan (Minneapolis: University of Minnesota Press, 1994), 19.

Some of the ways I first thought about this project were inspired by the idea of developing the description not just of "others" but of models from alternative spaces that might be used in what are usually the central places whose experiences have led to what we seek in order to generalize social theory. Here, however, the worlds I describe are not comprehensible in terms of "first" and "third," or Eastern and Western as will quickly become apparent. The ways that I use many of the French texts that are now familiar to English-speaking audiences perhaps offer a clue to readers as to how the paths of this fieldwork have influenced how I read as well as how I interpret what I experience in salons or record in interviews. Before ever setting foot in Casablanca in 1983, my paths toward that place were marked by reading magazines from the 1960s and 1970s like *Souffles* and *Lamalif.* It was through articles written by Moroccan writers that I read the work of Roland Barthes, who taught in Rabat in the early 1970s. Many of those whose articles I was reading, and who have now become my friends, attended his lectures. To travel out of Casablanca, especially if I want to bring you, my English-reading reader, along with me, involves remembering this influence or that of Paul Pascon on fieldwork in Morocco over the past half century. Pascon is not widely known outside of the Maghreb. He played a special part in developing a tradition of fieldwork in Morocco because of his role as a teacher and researcher at the Institut Agronomique. To the best of my knowledge, his only work published in English is *Capitalism and Agriculture in the Haouz of Marrakesh* (London: Kegan Paul, 1986). For more on my ideas about ethnography, see Susan Ossman, "Parcours et partages: Pérégrination sur le savoir pratique des anthropologues," in *Parcours d'Intellectuels Maghrebins,* ed. Aïssa Kadri (Paris: Karthala, 1999), 355–64.

7 *Pose* is an upscale magazine in English. Other women's magazines in Egypt include *Nisf el Dounia* (Half of the world), *Hawa* (Eve), *Kull le nas* (Everyone), *Hurreyati* (My liberty), *Majalati* (My magazine), *Sayedat Anissati* (Mrs. and Misses). Also see *Al Ahram's* Thursday section on beauty and Friday section on women and children, as well as regular columns on women and beauty in *Al-Akhbar Al-wafd, Akhbar al yum, Al Jumhuriyya, al Mesaa,* and *Sayedati* (which often features Egyptian stars, although it is produced in London with Saudi financing).

8 *Femmes Marocaines* is produced in Casablanca and sells for 14 dirhams, about $1.40.

9 The magazine produced by the hairdressing franchise Buigine is distributed free of charge in every salon. Many salons also leave a stack of magazines just outside their doors to make it easy for anyone, not just customers, to pick up a copy. The poem by Baudelaire that carries us through this spread is the first part of "L'invitation au voyage" in *Oeuvres Complets* (Paris: Robert Laffont, 1980), 39–40. It is a poem with which most people who have gone through French high school would be familiar. Here is a portion of the original, and Arthur Symons's very free 1926

translation in *Baudelaire: Prose and Poetry*, trans. Arthur Symons (New York: A. and C. Boni, 1926), 157. (Of course, many other translations have since been published; any bookstore or university library has them on hand.)

L'invitation au voyage

Mon enfant, ma soeur,
Songe à la douceur
D'aller là-bas vivre ensemble!
Aimer à loisir
Aimer et mourir
Au pays qui te ressemble!
Les soleils mouillés
De ces ciels brouillés
Pour mon esprit ont les charmes
Si mystérieux
De tes traîtres yeux,
Brillant à travers leurs larmes.

. . . .

My child and my star,
Let us wander afar,
None can resist her,
In the desire of living together;
—To live there at leisure,
To die there for pleasure
Under this wonderful weather!
The suns that have sunken
From these skies drunken
For my spirit have charms and have fears.
Like the mysteries that rise
From your treacherous eyes
That dazzle me over their tears.

. . . .

10   Khadija Bnoussina, "Approche socio-semiotique du tatouage," *Actes du colloque Le Corps et l'image de l'autre*, 20–23 February 1989, *Revue de la faculté des lettres et des sciences humaines de Marrakech*, no. 5 (1989): 61.

It is noteworthy that it is not the fact of indelible marks that is at issue, but rather, the reasons motivating them. "Permanent" eye and lip liner have become quite common treatments. Plastic surgery and tattoos are gaining popularity among those who can manage to get together the often large sums needed to undergo such operations. For details on cosmetic surgery in Egypt, including standard prices for treatments there, see Hadia Mostafa, "In Search of Beauty," *Egypt*

Today vol. 16, no. 11 (November 1995): 64–70. Many other articles, books, and films have taken tattoos as their subject. For a bibliography and some comments on the circulation of skin inscription, see Marc Blanchard, "Post-Bourgeois Tattoo: Reflections on Skin Writing in Late Capitalist Societies," in *Visualizing Theory: Selected Essays from V.A.R. 1900–1994* (London: Routledge, 1994), 285–300.

11 The *minitel* is a small computer terminal that was widely distributed in France in the late 1980s. The Internet has now rendered the minitel partially obsolete, although it continues to provide easy access to phone numbers and train schedules, as well as addresses for pornography and amorous exchange. Such sites are referred to as the *minitel rose* (literally, the pink minitel).

12 Adefettah Kilito, *La Querelle des images* (Casablanca: Eddif, 1995), 115–66; my translation.

13 Amira Sonbol, "Changing Perceptions of Feminine Beauty in Islamic Society," in *Ideals of Feminine Beauty: Philosophical, Social and Cultural Dimensions*, ed. Karen A. Callaghan (Westport, CT: Greenwood Press, 1994), 60. Safia K. Mohsen's interviews with working middle-class women in Cairo are also revealing on this score. For instance, H.M. explains that her husband thinks men are like gods in their homes. One of the strongest images she uses to get across the idea that he is old-fashioned in his ideas about marital relations and women is that of the lively laughing woman versus the woman who remains, unmoving: "Of course, I have friends my own age and people I work with and like, but I do not entertain them at home. He would not see them. He thinks my friends are frivolous and lack maturity because they laugh and joke and are human. To him the ideal wife is a fat, sluggish cow with ten children and who does not have any existence apart from his, a full-time wife like those of most of his friends": Safia K. Mohsen, "New Images, Old Reflections: Working Middle-Class Women in Egypt," in *Women and the Family in the Middle East: New Voices of Change,* ed. Elizabeth Warnock Fernea (Austin: University of Texas Press, 1985), 65.

14 "Léa," performed by Louise Attaque, lyrics by Gaëtan Roussel, www.multimania.; com/motaboy/lea.html, 1 July 2000.

15 Susan Bordo, *Unbearable Weight: Feminism, Western Culture and the Body* (Berkeley: University of California Press, 1993), 168. Also see K. Gara, "Différences sexuelles dans les perceptions et préférences relatives aux modèles corporels féminins: recherche exploratrice auprès d'étudiants maghrébins," *Les Cahiers internationaux de psychologie sociale,* no. 25 (March 1995): 44–52. Gara shows that many male students from North Africa prefer slightly "rounder" women than their European counterparts. But although the ideal might still be slightly heavier than in Western Europe, one need only consult the many diet formulas in women's magazines or listen to programs on beauty on the radio or how women speak about their mother's weight to get a sense of the changes that have taken place in recent decades.

For a very different perspective on fleshy containment in other contexts, see Caroline Walker Bynum, *Holy Feast and Holy Fast: The Religious Significance of Food to Medieval Women* (Berkeley: University of California Press, 1987).

16 Philippe Perrot, "Pour une généologie de l'austérité des apparences," *Communications*, no. 46 (1987): 163–64.

17 Sonbol, "Changing Perceptions."

18 For some ideas on the history of the concept of light as truth, see Hans Blumenberg, "Light as a Metaphor for Truth: At the Preliminary Stage of Philosophical Concept Formation," 1957, trans. Joel Anderson, in *Modernity and the Hegemony of Vision*, ed. D. M. Levin (Berkeley: University of California Press, 1993), 30–62.

19 See Malcolm Gladwell, "True Colors: Hair Dye and the Hidden History of Postwar America," *The New Yorker*, 22 March 1999, 70–81. Also see Grant McCracken's amusing approach to big hair and blondeness: *Big Hair: A Journey into the Transformation of Self* (London: Indigo, 1997), 81–112.

20 Baudelaire, *Oeuvres Complets*, 19–20; "The Head of Hair," in *Flowers of Evil*, trans. Geoffrey Wagner (Norfolk, CT: New Dimensions, 1946), n.p.

21 Myriam Saadi, "Quand les cheveux parle," *Opinion des jeunes*, 2 February 1993 (1 Ramadan), 6.

22 Negotiation and the market have been frequent metaphors in research for anthropologists, especially in the Arab world. See, for instance, Laurence Rosen, *Bargaining for Reality: The Construction of Social Relations in a Muslim Community* (Chicago: University of Chicago Press, 1984). On the role of markets in changing taste and fashion, see Amina Aouchar's study of how the *triq es sultan* trade route affected the garments in a rural region of eastern Morocco: "Pratiques vestimentaires et mutations sociales en Haute Moulouya," in Ossman, ed., *Miroirs*, 57–76. In her study of contemporary markets in central Morocco, Deborah Kapchan notes how market women determine what kinds of items are available to the middle classes in the central part of the country: *Gender on the Market: Moroccan Women and the Revoicing of Tradition* (Philadelphia: University of Pennsylvania Press, 1996). Negotiation is an important part of what goes on at the market beyond, but we must also keep in mind Weiner's caution that certain things are not negotiable. This has important political and personal as well as economic consequences. See Annette Weiner, *Inalienable Possessions: The Paradox of Keeping While Giving* (Berkeley: University of California Press, 1992).

2. BACKGROUND BODIES

1 Cited in Jean-Marie Apostolidès, "Impudique Aurélie," *Communications*, no. 46 (1987): 206.

2 It is interesting that working from the perspective of North Africa, Pagnol's films seem to take on a renewed import. Thus, for example, in her recently published memoirs, Germaine Tillion also brings up the "heroic" stance of his films: *Il était une fois l'ethnographie* (Paris: Éditions du Seuil, 2000). I cannot help tying Tillion's comments on the heroic struggle in Pagnol's cinema to General Lyautey's earlier enchantment with what he saw as the intact "aristocracy" of Moroccan cities and his own adoption of what he saw as that style. These and other notes on chivalry and heroism might, as Tillion often tries to show in her academic writ-

ing, speak of a pan-Mediterranean honor code. But they might also be seen as essential moments in the development of a very modern use of time in the service of a dandy's style. See Daniel Rivet, *Lyautey et l'institution du Protectorat francais* (Paris: L'Harmatan, 1988).

3   Apostiledès, "Impudique Aurélie," 204–8.

4   Ibid.

5   Mauss published "Les techniques du corps" in the *Journal de Psychologie* in 1935. Here I cite Marcel Mauss, "Les techniques du corps," *Sociologie et anthropologie* (1985): 368.

6   Here, Mauss relies on the distinction between parisiennes and provinciales to develop his argument. In the other instances cited in his article, however, he speaks of national or ethnic groups as wholes.

7   Valerie Steele notes that the grissette actually had to sew from 9 in the morning to 11 at night, with only an occasional Sunday off; she was very poorly paid for her efforts. Many girls occasionally engaged in prostitution to survive. This led to the development of the image of the grisette as a typically parisienne woman (she is poor but pays attention to what she wears). Steele also writes of how, "in the early part of the nineteenth century, we find a noticeable romanticization of the poor grisette: she is of easy virtue, but with a heart of gold. Later in the century, there is lore of an emphasis on her supposedly mercenary lascivious character": *Paris Fashion: A Cultural History* (1988; London: Berg Publishers, 1988), 69.

8   Steele, *Paris Fashion*, 75.

9   See Ellen Furlough, "Selling the American Way in Interwar France: *Prix Uniques* and the Salons des arts ménagers," *Journal of Social History* (spring 1993): 491–519. Furlough's work offers a great deal of information on department stores and the "Americanization" of consumer culture in France. In the context of the present study, it is interesting to note that by 1935 the dime store Prisunic, which is owned by the Galleries Lafayette group, already had established three stores in North Africa. The Casablanca store was destroyed to make way for a Hyatt Regency Hotel in the early 1970s. See Jean-Louis Cohen and Monique Elib, *Casablanca Mythes et figures d'une aventure urbaine* (Paris: Hazan, 1998), 440. On parisienne vendors and shoppers, see Jennifer Jones, "Coquettes and Grisettes: Women Buying and Selling in Ancien Régime Paris," in *The Sex of Things: Gender and Consumption in Historical Perspective,* ed. V. deGrazia with E. Furlough (Berkeley: University of California Press, 1996).

10   This too is something that evolves early in the nineteenth century. In Zola's *Au bonheur des dames*, for example, we read of how Denise arrives from her small-town life in Normandy with her younger brothers. When she finds work in a department store she is given a silk dress to wear. But her employer does not provide shoes. The distress of the heroine grows as her cheap shoes cut into her feet, gradually falling apart as she struggles to provide for herself and her two younger brothers: Emile Zola, *Au Bonheur des Dames* (Paris: 1883; Pocket, 1998). Also see Marshall Berman's analysis of "The Modernism of Underdevelopment,"

particularly the section entitled "Wars and Shoes: The Young Dostoyevsky," in *All That Is Solid Melts into Air: The Experience of Modernity* (New York: Penguin, 1988), 206–12. For comparisons with the Middle East, see Elizabeth Thompson, *Colonial Citizens: Republican Rights, Paternal Privilege, and Gender in French Syria and Lebanon* (New York: Columbia University Press, 2000), 171–210.

11 So there is a sense in which conferring an urban identity includes a judgment about the individual's or group's willingness and ability to adopt certain new body techniques.

12 Guiliana Bruno works with the relationship of street to film in her study of the films of Elvira Nottari in Naples: *Streetwalking on a Ruined Map* (Princeton, NJ: Princeton University Press, 1993).

13 Marshal Berman notes how circulation is organized to provide certain vistas ("The Modernism of Underdevelopment"). For more on how Casablanca was planned to give form to certain powers, see Paul Rabinow, *French Modern: Norms and Forms of the Social Environment* (Cambridge, MA: MIT Press, 1989).

14 de Certeau distinguishes between *espace* (space) and *lieu* (place). He defines a space as an order where elements are distributed in terms of relations of coexistence. This means that things are set side by side. Space is set by positions and tends to indicate stability. A place, on the other hand, is a practiced space: not the line on a map but people walking through it transforming it into something else. Space refers to things taking up space; place is determined by the actions of historical subjects. See Michel de Certeau, *L'invention du quotidien: Arts de faire*, 2d ed. (Paris: Gallimard, 1990), 172–74; English translation 117–18.

Two studies that analyze how such deambulations are represented and recounted in different places in Morocco are Mohamed Boughali, *La représentation de l'espace chez le marocain illetré* (Paris: Anthropos, 1974), and Stefania Pandolpho, *Impasse of the Angels: Scenes from a Moroccan Space of Memory* (Chicago: University of Chicago Press, 1997).

15 Again, I rely on Apostiledès's remarkable essay, "Impudique Aurélie," 215–18.

16 Nicholas Green, "Looking at the Landscape: Class Formation and the Visual," in *The Anthropology of Landscape: Perspectives on Place and Space*, ed. Eric Hirsch and Michael O'Hanlon (Oxford: Oxford University Press, 1995), 31–42.

17 Production of this fashion, as of art, has always thrived because of its ability to center an international milieux both in design and production. Thus, I think it is important to qualify statements of "fact," such as "If Paris is hegemonic, it is no longer the Paris designed exclusively by the French. Indeed French fashion, itself emblematic of French nationhood, is created by Germans, Italians, Japanese, and North and West Africans, among many others." See Dorinne Kondo, *About Face: Performing Race in Fashion and Theater* (London: Routledge, 1997), 59.

Fashion has long been a profoundly cosmopolitan activity in Paris. If it has served at times as a symbol of the nation, it has done so with incredible ambivalence. Jack Lang's promotion of fashion as a national art when he was minister of culture had an effect on how fashion is presented in museums, on television, and in the press in the 1980s. Remarks like Kondo's are perhaps a tribute to his success in this respect.

18 See Richard Kuisel, *Seducing the French: The Dilemma of Americanization* (Berkeley: University of California Press, 1993).

19 To get a look at how this was strikingly expressed in hair and clothing styles, see, for example, the late nineteenth- and early twentieth-century photographs published by Jacques Borgé and Nicolas Viasnoff, *Archives du Maroc* (Milan: Éditions Michèle Trinckvel, 1995). See especially the photo on p. 127, where we can see not only the stylishly bobbed hair of a military wife, but the way she smoothes her husband's hair for the snapshot.

20 Fatima Mernissi, *Dreams of Trespass: Tales of a Haram Girhood* (Reading, MA.: Addison Wesley, 1994), 118–28.

21 Céza Nabaraouy, "Le développement de la culture physique en egypte," *L'Egyptienne*, no. 49 (1929): 3.

22 I address this issue in another way in chapter 5. It is important to notice, though, the extent to which movement away from a set background presents the danger of being called vice. See my "Savior se montrer: Modèles, modes et salons de coiffure à Casablanca," in Ossman, ed., *Miroirs Maghrébins*.

23 Women were first allowed to vote in France in 1945; men were legally designated as "head of the household" until 1985.

24 These moves out have been the subject of extensive debate about the notion of public space and its relations to the state. For issues of state and Islam, see the essays in Deniz Kandiyoti, ed. *Women, Islam, and the State* (Philadelphia: Temple University Press, 1991).

25 Jeanne Marques, "La femme marocaine," *L'Egyptienne*, no. 119 (January 1936): 13. Note, though, that although "Oriental" authors influenced Moroccan discussions, the Moroccan Constitution of 1908 stipulated that girls had a right to primary education. See Aïcha Belarabi, *Le Salaire de Madame* (Casablanca: Le Fennec, 1993), 20–23.

26 Virginia Danielson, "Artists and Entrepreneurs: Female Singers in Cairo during the 1920s," in *Women in Middle Eastern History: Shifting Boundaries in Sea and Gender*, ed. N.R. Keddie and B. Baron (New Haven: Yale University Press, 1991), 299. Also see Danielson's *The Voice of Egypt: Umm Kulthum, Arabic Song and Egyptian Society in the Twentieth Century* (Chicago: University of Chicago Press, 1997). For more recent developments on cinema and song, see Walter Armbrust, *Mass Culture and Modernism in Egypt* (Cambridge, England: Cambridge University Press, 1996), and on the publishing industry, see Yves Gonzalez-Quijano, *Les Gens du Livre: Edition et champ intellectuel dans l'Egypte républicaine* (Paris: CNRS éditions, 1998).

27 Mauss, "Les techniques du corps," 195 (trans. p. 75).

28 "Little maids" is the expression used to refer to children who work as maids in urban families. Often, they are "sold" by their country families and brought up by

the city people they work for. In 1988, when Touriya Hadraoui published an article on the subject called "Ces petites qui travaillent pour nous," *Kalima* (November 1988): 16–19, it caused quite a bit of controversy. Since then, many articles on the issue have appeared in the Moroccan press, but the practice itself has far from disappeared. On the figure of the maid in Morocco in general, see chapter 8 of Kapchan's *Gender on the Market*, 212–34. The situation of the little maids might be related to the long history of social categories, domestic labor, and slavery in Morocco. See Mohammed Ennaji, *Soldats, domestiques et concubines: L'esclavage au Maroc au XIXième siècle* (Casablanca: Editions Eddif, 1994).

29 Marques, "*La femme marocaine*," 13.

30 Mauss, "Les techniques du corps."

31 In the context of a discussion with Richard Beardsworth, Jean-François Lyotard remarks on the importance of Freud's treatment of the "remainder":

> Simply put, it designates that there is a remainder [*qu'il y a du reste*] and that it is not true that discourse can get to the end of this remainder, can as it were, get the better of it. From this perspective, there is, within this Freudian problematic, no question of negotiation. In this sense, Freud is for me the name of what is intractable [*intraitable*] in terms of litigation. This intractable points to a sort of region of resistance, a presence, to be found also within discourse, that blocks the philosophical project that is, let us say, incarnated by Hegel: a process of memorization, a return upon the self, a coming to the self for the self and what is in itself that is "total" and that has as its objective, in philosophical terms, what we call "absolute knowledge."

See Richard Beardsworth, "Freud, Energy, Chance: A Conversation with Jean-François Lyotard," *Tekhnema: Journal of Philosophy and Technology, Energy and Chance*, no. 5 (1999): 11–12. We need not follow Lyotard's analysis of libidinal economy to notice the extent to which remainders are often expressed in terms of the body (as in Marques). Many accounts of social life have taken the *suq* or the market as their preferred space, focusing on negotiations. Such an emphasis might obscure some of the ways in which talking things out or altering discourses might not be enough to "get to the end" of the power of remainders.

32 Mamoun Fandy's work on clothing as politics in Egypt is of particular interest because he uses clothing to question dualistic East/West and center/periphery versions of the state and society. His examination of "cross-dressing," contrasts Cairenes and southern Egyptians, explaining the diverse "disguises" that southern migrants use to facilitate their movement through Cairene streets and bureaucracy. He notes, for instance, that many young male rural migrants adopt the Saudi *jallabia* instead of Western clothing because they prefer to "pass" as Saudis rather than be associated with the prevalent image of the poor, ignorant Southerner. His perspective reacts to "recognizing the ways the Western self and sense of identity continue to be formed through an opposition to the non-

Western other," not so much because he rejects a reappraisal of "anthropology's origin and center" (or, for him, that of political science), but because his view of the "local" is particularly attuned to how arguments about homogeneous societies are produced not only by anthropologists but by nation-states. See Mamoun Fandy, "Political Science without Clothes: the Politics of Dress or Contesting the Spatiality of the State in Egypt," *Arab Studies Quarterly* 20, no. 2 (spring 1998): 87–103.

It is perhaps telling that whereas the urban/rural contrast was so important to Ibn Khaldun's analysis of Maghrebian history, recent studies of Moroccan cities note how such terms figure in discourses but do not give them as primary a role as in Egypt. Indeed, in the course of my research on television in Morocco, I found that the contrast of elite to popular was expressed in terms of viewing habits. Thus, for example, sociologists and educated friends alike expressed their good taste by the fact that they never watched Egyptian serials. Men in general tended to perceive these shows as "feminine," and educated women said they were for the *bonnes* (maids). Only "serious" Egyptian art, represented by classic films or the songs of Umm Khalthum, were deemed worthwhile by educated city dwellers (Ossman, *Picturing Casablanca*, 128).

33 Suzanne Voilquin, *Souvenirs d'une fille du peuple on La Sainte-Simonienne en Egypte 1834–1836* (Paris: Chez E. Sauzt, 1866), 295. For accounts of a hammam in Marrekech in the 1930s, see Leonora Peets, *Women of Marrakech* (Durham, NC: Duke University Press, 1988), 50–60.

34 Voilquin, *Souvenirs*, 298.

35 For a description of a hammam in an "ethnological experience in Morocco," see Hélène Martin, "Quelques espaces de vie quotidienne et d'interactions verbales comme lieux d'ouverture: Une expérience ethnologique au Maroc," *Recherches et Travaux en Anthropologie*, Université de Laussane, Institut d'anthropologie et de sociologie, no. 10 (1998). A Tunisian film inspired by a boy's youth, with scenes from the hammam, *Halfaouine* by Ferid Boughedir, is available in North Africa, Europe, and North America.

36 Some scholars work from this perspective, for example, Malek Chebel, *Le Corps dans la tradition au Maghreb* (Paris: Presses Universitaires de France, 1984). This book presents "the" Maghrebian body. It divides this body in terms of a series of themes, such as "tears," "the stomach," "the breasts," and "sterility," which are then defined with reference to literature of various periods, adages, and interpretations of historical process. In fact, this is a good example of the kind of dismemberment of the body that I suggest is an important but recent move. Chebel dissects a body that we can never see but that might guide certain manners of operating on the body politic.

For some ideas on how hairdressers might themselves use ideas from around the world about religion, bodies, and meditation to characterize different kinds of hair and styles, see Lichel Odoul and Rémy Portrait, *1997 Cheveau, parle-moi de moi: Le Cheveu, fil de l'âme* (Paris: Éditions Dervy, 1997).

37 Kilito, *La Querelle*, 115.

38 Omar Carlier, "Le hammam maghrébin, héritage séculaire et acculturation à la modernité (xixe–xxe siècles)," in Ossman, ed., *Miroirs*, 163.

39 Although this is often the case, do take a look at Justin McGuinness's account of Casablancan history and architecture in *Footprint Morocco Handbook,* 2d ed. (Bath, England: Footprint Handbooks, 1999), 168–77.

40 Although many tourists and some Moroccans see the national female dress, the jellaba, as dating from antiquity, it is in fact a recent piece of clothing for women. It was, a bit like trousers in Europe, a male garment that has been taken up by some women in this century (Aouchar, "Pratiques vestimentaires").

41 Carlier, "Le hammam," 159.

42 Hannah Davis Taieb, Rabia Bekkar, Jean-Claude David, eds., *Espace Public, Parole publique au Maghreb et au Machrek* (Lyon: Maison de l'Orient/L'Harmattan, 1997); and Diane Singerman, *Avenues of Participation* (Princeton, NJ: Princeton University Press, 1996).

43 Philippe Perrot, *Le Travail des apparences: Le corps féminin* xviiie–xixe siècle (Paris: Le Seuil, 1984).

44 The extent to which the hammam, for example, has spread to France and even to North America is directly related to the emergence of athletic clubs. See my introduction to the edited book on the relationship between sociability and the media (Ossman, *Miroirs*), and the essays of Habib Belaïd on the history of sport in Tunisia, "Le phénomène sportif dans la Tunisie coloniale: l'exemple du football et de la boxe entre les deux guerres," and Hadj Miliani's on martial arts, "La Salle de sport: espace de sociabilité," about the socialization of young men, and para-military training in contemporary Algeria in that same volume. Look too at how Susan Slyomovics analyzes the "displacement" of the spa, jacuzzis, and steam baths in the United States as representing "the American desire for a European presence mistakenly understood as absence" in "The Body in Water: Women in American Spa Culture," in *Bodylore,* ed. Katharine Young (Knoxville: University of Tennessee Press, 1993), 35–56.

45 Although a precise number of beauty salons for any of these cities is difficult to establish, in 1998 the Yellow Pages in Casablanca advertised 103, but a separate rubric for "beauty institutes" also lists additional salons and repeats the names of several shops. Advertising in the Yellow Pages means that one is trying to reach clients who have phones; this was far from being the case for all households in Casablanca until the past couple of years with the development of the cellular phone. Advertisements are also printed in magazines and in leaflets, but all of these types of publicity are necessary only for salons that draw their clientele from a large area. Neighborhood salons do not seek such a clientele; they need not advertise to draw their clients.

According to *Cairo Today*, there were twenty-thousand Egyptian hairdressers in 1992 (May 1992 13, no. 5, 97).

46 Some preliminary work on the subject was conducted by Sandrine Faivre and Franck Gallet in "La représentation spatiale et symbolique du salon de coiffure

africaine dans le quartier de la goutte d'or" (Mémoire de maitrise, Université Paris X, 1996). It would be interesting to study the beauty exchanges among Paris, West Africa, and the United States in this context.

47   In spite of the fact that there are no statistics on frequency of consumer visits to salons in Casablanca, the figures we do possess indicate an incredible rise in the purchase of beauty products and perfumes in recent decades. A study done by the BMCE (Banque Marocain du Commerce Extérieur) showed that in 1967, Moroccan expenditure on cosmetics and perfumes totaled 7 million dirhams; in 1977, it was up 58 percent to 48 million. (This includes perfumes, lotions, suntan oils, shampoos, toothpaste, and soaps.) The majority of the materials used to make these products were imported, primarily from France (58 percent) and Italy (12 percent). See "L'industrie de la parfumerie et des cosmétiques," *L'Opinion*, 25 July 1978, 7. The 1984 report of the Direction of Statistiques notes the huge increase in the amount people in Morocco spent for hygiene and beauty in prior decades, but because such figures take the household as their unit of analysis, it is impossible to know who is spending this money on what kind of products. The interviews I conducted showed that most young working women in each of the cities spend a considerable percentage of their income on their looks.

48   There are many ways of wearing the veil (hijab), but it is perhaps in Egypt that the largest spectrum of styles is apparent. Indeed, there is no absolute frontier between muhajibat style and those proposed by international fashion. For a study of fashion magazines and an analysis of the "limits" of what might be worn by women in Cairo, see Jean-Noël Ferrié, "La petite robe ou le dépassement des limites dans un régime de civilité", in Ossman, *Mimesis: Imiter, représenter, circuler,* special issue of *Hermès* 22 (1998): 111–20.

49   Gunter Gebauer and Christof Wulf, *Mimesis: Culture, Art, Society,* trans. Don Reneau (Berkeley: University of California Press, 1994), 318.

50   Girard's classic study is *La Violence et le sacré* (Paris: Grasset, 1972).

51   Scenes of instruction might include several routes to knowledge. For a glimpse at how a science museum provides different ways of imparting understanding, see Roger Silverstone, "Les espaces de la performance: Musées, sciences et rhétoriques de l'objet," *Mimesis,* 175–88.

52   Amazigh Kateb, "Ombre Elle," *Algeria*, Gnawa Diffusion G.D.O. Records, Laknal, Grenoble, 1997.

53   It would seem that the salon, like the hammam, can become a place in which to imagine what Marc Schade Poulsen has called a "disinterested meeting with femininity." Schade Poulsen explains how, in a context in which women are confined, difficult to meet, out of reach except in the legal context of marriage and its obligations, the lyrics of Algerian Raï music offer a dream of disinterest. We might think of how the situation changes when women can walk the streets, or when they establish places to go from which men are excluded: "Le raï et ses espaces de rencontres musicales," in Ossman, *Miroirs,* 205–16.

3. SOCIETY, SALONS, AND SIGNIFICANCE

1 Derek Gregory, for instance, refers to this definition of society to discuss Anthony Giddens's contribution to theories of space in social science. I will have occasion to mention this study again in the next chapter. Suffice it to say here that the moves I make from spaces of what some call the "lifeworld" is not a priori set in distinction to some kind of system. This does not indicate that there is no routinization (to employ Giddens's vocabulary). See Derek Gregory, "Presences and Absences: Time-Space Relations and Structuration Theory," in *Social Theory of Modern Societies: Anthony Giddens and His Critics*, ed. David Held and John B. Thompson (Cambridge, England: Cambridge University Press, 1989), 185–214.

2 Witold Rybczynski, *Home: A Short History of an Idea* (London: Penguin Books, 1987), 88.

3 Ibid., 88–99.

4 In this they differed from the coffeehouse or café. Jürgen Habermas based his analysis on such specialization: *The Structural Transformation of the Public Sphere*, 45.

5 Margot Badran, *Feminists, Islam, and Nation: Gender and the Making of Modern Egypt* (Princeton, NJ: Princeton University Press, 1995), 15.

6 Ibid., 56.

7 On the development of the salon in homes and businesses in the Middle East and the Maghreb, see H. D. Taïeb, J. C. David, and R. Bekkar, eds., *Espaces Publics, Paroles Publiques au Maghreb et au Machrek* (Lyon, France: L'Harmattan, Maison de l'Orient Méditerranéen, 1997), 15–82.

8 See, for instance, Hassan Rachik, "Roumi et beldi: Réflexions sur la perception de l'occidental à travers une dichtomie locale," *Egypte Monde Arabe: Droit, économie, société*, nos. 30–31 (1997): 293–301. This theme is also developed in the context of exchanges between the Maghreb and France in three case studies in Rabia Bekkar, Nadir Boumaza, and Daniel Pinson, eds., *Familles maghrébines en France* (Paris: L'épreuve de la ville, Presses universitaires de France, 1999).

9 Omar Carlier, "Le Café maure: Sociabilité masculine et effervescence cityoenne (Algérie XVII–XXe siècles), *Annales ESC*, no. 4 (July–August 1990): 975–1003. Also see Abderrahmane Lakhsassi and Abdelahad Sebti, *Al shay ila al atay: Al ʿada wal tarikh* (From "shay" to tea: Practice and History), (Rabat, Morocco: Presse de la faculté de lettres et des sciences humaines de Rabat, Université Mohammed V, 1999).

10 On urban planning, see Rabinow, *French Modern*, and for more on how cafés offer vistas of passersby, see my *Picturing Casablanca*, 45–47.

11 On saloons and bars in the United States, see Madelon Powers, *Faces along the Bar: Lore and Order in the Workingman's Saloon, 1870–1920* (Chicago: University of Chicago Press, 1998).

12 W. Scott Haine, *The World of the Paris Café: Sociability among the French Working Class, 1789–1914* (Baltimore: Johns Hopkins University Press, 1996).

13 On salons, surrealism, and walking, consult Susan Rubin Suleiman, "Between the

Street and the Salon: The Dilemma of Surrealist Politics in the 1930's," in *Visualizing Theory: Selected Essays from V.A.R. 1990–1994*, ed. L. Taylor (London: Routledge, 1994), 143–58.

14 This is something that both Haine and Powers discuss at length in the context of the working-class café owner's relation to his clients. Powers does not see this same tendency in the bourgeois cafés on the boulevards. It would be tempting to develop the comparison in terms of a historical study of such "therapeutic" talk, but I cannot do this in the context of the present project. I do, however, develop distinctions among different kinds of contemporary salons based on different ways of relating to the coiffeur and other clients.

15 We might relate such learning back to what was going on in bourgeois or artistic salons as well. See Catherine Bidou-Zachariasen, especially the chapter "Le travail du salon" (87–110), in *Proust Sociologue: De la maison aristocratique au salon bourgeois* (Paris: Descartes and Cie, 1997). The importance of learning remains central in salons today. See Michaëla Bobasch, "Femmes cherchent coiffeurs talentueux à petits prix," *Le Monde*, 23 October 1998, 29.

16 Steven Zdatny, "Fashion and the Class Struggle: The Case of *Coiffure*," *Social History* 18, no. 1 (1993), 55.

17 We should keep in mind the extent to which the "new woman" was a global movement, even if it was not universal. For a fascinating example of how bobbed hair, foot binding, and politics intermingled in Chinese politics of the period, see Lung-kee Sun, "The Politics of Hair and the Issue of the Bob in Modern China," *Fashion Theory* 1, no. 4 (1997): 353–56. On the United States, consult Simone Davis's recent analysis and bibliography in *Living Up to the Ads: Gender Fictions in the 1920s* (Durham, NC: Duke University Press, 2000).

18 The clubs that were a mainstay of bourgeois life in Morocco as well as in other French colonies sometimes persist up to the present. For example, the prestigious C.A.F. Club in Casablanca continues to draw European and Moroccan elites as members. Other clubs, including many started by corporations or government departments, also flourish as places where well-to-do men and women can meet away from "the street." A similar system of clubs operates in Cairo. For photographs of clubs and swimming pools in Casablanca, see Cohen and Elib, *Casablanca Mythes*, 410–13.

19 Much further work could be done on the history of salons in each of the cities in this study. The accounts I give here are based on interviews and the perusal of family photographs, the possession of which was already an indication of the family's status in the 1940s and 1950s. To get a glimpse of hairstyle in the rural areas of southern Morocco, see the photographs that Mireille Morin-Barde took between 1950 and 1952 in her *Coiffures féminines du Maroc* (Aix-en-Provence: Edisud, 1997).

20 On the way the headscarf was popularized "from the top," see Ossman, *Picturing Casablanca*, 23, n. 3.

21 Habermas, *The Structural Transformation of the Public Sphere*, 36, 37.

22 Don Herzog, "The Trouble with Hairdressers," *Representations*, no. 53 (winter 1996): 21–43. For a recent account of interactions in a male-dominated salon, see Yves Winkin, "Conversations de salon (de coiffure): Une première exploration des possibilités d'une ethnographie de la communication en Wallonie," in *Langages et collectivités: Le cas du Québec*, ed. K. M. Klinkenberg, D. Racelle-Latin, and G. Connoly (Montréal: Leméac, 1981).

23 Michael Schudson brings this up with respect to theories of the role of proximate conversation in debates on democracy. He draws attention to the way conversations are permeated by ideas and references from the mass media. See, for example, "Why Conversation Is Not the Soul of Democracy," *Critical Studies of Mass Communication* 14, no. 4 (December 1997): 297–309.

24 Seyla Benhabib, *Situating the Self: Gender, Community and Postmodernism in Contemporary Ethics* (Oxford: Polity Press, 1992), 152. On the "generalized other," see 148–77.

25 Steven Shapin, *A Social History of Truth: Civility and Science in Seventeenth Century England* (Chicago: University of Chicago Press, 1994), 184.

26 Herzog, "The Trouble with Hairdressers," 21–43.

27 See Ossman, *Picturing Casablanca*, 75.

28 Lila Abu-Loghud, *Veiled Sentiments: Honor and Poetry in a Bedouin Society* (Berkeley: University of California Press, 1986), 108; italics mine. Also see Lila Abu-Loghud, *Writing Women's Worlds: Bedouin Stories* (Berkeley: University of California Press, 1993), 205–42.

29 Soumaya Naamane-Gessous, *Au-delà de toute pudeur* (Casablanca: Editions Eddif, 1984), 5, 6.

30 Bernard Williams, *Shame and Necessity* (Berkeley: University of California Press, 1993), 84, 82. However, Williams also suggests that we must base our discussions of ethics in the West on a reinterpretation of Greek heritage. This is obviously a problematic position, especially as he contrasts his approach to that of anthropologists based on this "connection" of Ancient Greece with European philosophical and political traditions. This ignores the many developments of Greek thought and their links to the geographic area in which I conducted the research for this book. In addition, contrary to his ideas about it, anthropology is not simply a matter of looking for differences per se, but also explaining these, which means also thinking in terms of similarity and comparison, explicitly or implicitly.

31 Some people I spoke with in Casablanca also made a point of how beauty salons were a place where petty crime and vice were enabled by a certain lack of ethics. Many cited examples of salons as sites of clandestine exchanges: prostitution rings, the sale of drugs, or simply beauty products or clothing imported without being declared to customs officials.

32 The term "mixed" refers here to male/female, but we might keep in mind the ways it has been used to speak of religious, racial, or national entities being brought together in a variety of contexts.

33 For more on virility and femininity in other contexts, see Abellah Hammoudi's

analysis of political power and charisma in terms of a schema involving periods of "feminization" on the part of the son and disciple: *Master and Disciple: The Cultural Foundations of Moroccan Authoritarianism* (Chicago: University of Chicago Press, 1997), 138–41. A series of essays on virility and Islam are presented by Fethi Benslama and Nadia Tazi in "La virilité en islam," *Intersignes*, nos. 11–12 (spring 1998).

34   Hoda Hoodfar, *Between Marriage and the Market: Intimate Politics and Survival in Cairo* (Berkeley: University of California Press, 1997), 130. On women working in Cairo, also consult Andrea B. Rugh, "Women and Work: Strategies and Choices in a Lower-Class Quarter of Cairo," in Fernea, ed., *Women and the Family in the Middle East*, 273–88.

35   Hoodfar, *Between Marriage and the Market*, 103–40.

36   Alsdair MacIntyre, cited in Paul Rabinow, *Essays on the Anthropology of Reason* (Princeton, NJ: Princeton University Press, 1996), 6. Because Rabinow is playing off Bourdieu's "disinterest" in this essay, he emphasizes ethical rather than political aims. But we should not forget that excellences also have a role in establishing prestige, power, and authority. See, for instance, discussions on *padeia* and *adab* as they relate to power in Peter Brown, "Late Antiquity and Islam: Parallels and Contrasts," in *Moral Conduct and Authority: The Place of 'adab' in South Asian Islam*, ed. Barbara Metcalf (Berkeley: University of California Press, 1984), 23–37. See also Michel Foucault's development of the idea of mastery over self and ability to lead others in *Histoire de la sexualité: Le souci de soi* (Paris: Gallimard, 1984); *The Care of the Self* (New York: Penguin 1986).

37   Rabinow, "Science as a Practice: Ethos, Logos, Pathos," in *Essays on the Anthropology of Reason*, 7.

38   Cited in Françoise Vernant Frontisi-Ducrous and Jean-Pierre Vernant, *Dans l'oeil du miroir* (Paris: Odile Jacob, 1997), 63.

39   Ibid., 243.

40   Ibid.

41   David C. Lindburg, *Theories of Vision from Al-Kindi to Kepler* (Chicago: University of Chicago Press, 1976).

42   Of course, modern sociology has developed by opposing the magical to the rational. But for some comments on alternative histories of our modernities, see Bruno Latour's now well-known *Nous n'avons jamais été modernes: Essai d'anthropologie symetrique* (Paris: La découverte, 1997); translated by Catherine Porter as *We Have Never Been Modern* (Cambridge, MA: Harvard University Press, 1993), and the recent study by John Durham Peters, *Speaking in the Air: A History of the Idea of Communication* (Chicago: University of Chicago Press, 1999).

43   Richard Rorty, *Philosophy and the Mirror of Nature* (Princeton, NJ: Princeton University Press, 1978), 12.

44   In Paris, male hairdressers dominated the most expensive salons and haut coiffure from the start. Zdatny writes, "In 1896, according to the Ministry of Commerce,

women [coiffeuses] comprised only 8.6 per cent of the hairdressers in Paris, though they made up 15 per cent of the shop owners. In 1936, by comparison, 44 per cent of the workforce in *coiffure* was female, as were 45 per cent of the shop owners. Throughout the country the percent of women active in the profession rose from 10.3 per cent in 1906 to 19.7 per cent in 1926 and 36 per cent in 1936" ("Fashion and the Class Struggle, 11). He goes on to note that women who worked in the *salons pour dames* were generally the highest paid, yet, they remained excluded from trade organizations and the circle of haute coiffure (56).

45 Thus, male hairdressers in Casablanca tend to be associated with a specific kind of salon where women are styled in "individualized" or "artistic" ways. I will address this type of salon in detail in chapter 4.

46 Excerpts from an interview recorded and published by Bouchra Lahbabi, "Enquête dans les salons branchés: Le coiffeur confident de ces dames," *L'Economiste*, 5 January 1995, 54.

47 Such ideas are not foreign to how the "mirror stage" has been conceptualized in modern psychoanalysis. Martin Jay presents some interesting comparisons between Lacan's *stade du miroir* and ideas like Merleau-Ponty's *autoscopie*: "The external perception of a self was responsible, among other things, for an ideal, uniform notion of space, which is assumed to be the same wherever the image of the child appears. It also has profound affective implications, which purely cognitive psychology fails to explain": "Sartre, Merleau-Ponty, and the Search for a New Ontology of Sight," in *Modernity and the Hegemony of Vision,* ed. D. M. Levis (Berkeley: University of California Press, 1993), 173. For further notes on the history of the mirror stage and some suggestive points about the spacialized self and reification in Lacan (but also Sartre), see Jay's *Downcast Eyes: The Denigration of Vision in Twentieth Century French Thought* (Berkeley: University of California Press, 1994), 341–53, and Véronique Nahoum, "La belle femme ou le stade du miroir en histoire," *Communications* 31 (1979): 22–32.

48 So the mirror is involved in a process of thought that includes a complex set of present-absent actors or imaginations. The ways they intervene need not be modeled on conversation nor thought of only as a set of models on which to mold selves. They can include such visual picturings, but the light of the mirror might also introduce echoes of absent voices.

49 Gebauer and Wulf, *Mimesis,* 3.

50 Thus, although a certain sensitivity to interaction is implied in thinking about how salons produce beauties, the approach developed here works with a variety of others, some of them absent, and a variety of patterns that are not merely a matter of framing but entail detailing several distinct worlds.

4. STYLING DISTINCTIONS

1   Dierdre Boden and Harvey L. Motloch, "The Compulsion of Proximity" in Friedland and Boden, *NoWhere,* 257–86.

2   Steven Shapin, for instance, writes:

> So one story about the modern condition points to anonymity and system-
> trust in abstract capacities, while the other identifies persisting patterns of
> traditional familiarity and trust in known persons. The first captures some-
> thing important about our lived experience as we move away from the famil-
> iar place of work, family and neighborhood; the second reminds us of the
> texture of relations within familiar places. One can then characterize the late
> modern condition through the serial applicability of both stories. There are
> now so many settings through which we move, so many institutions with
> which our lives bring us in contact, and so few of these evidently offer us the
> warrants of familiarity. The very elaboration of unfamiliar places, however,
> seems to blind us to the residual significance of face to face interaction. (*A
> Social History of Truth*, 415–16)

This balancing act between intimacy and anonymity has indeed been at the heart
of many of our ideas about what contemporary "society" is all about. I wonder,
though, whether we really are confronted with unfamiliar things so very often.
Anonymity and familiarity can be linked, and very strange things take place in the
most intimate face-to-face encounters. I address the kinds of relationships that
salons work with to suggest that they are familiar for a variety of reasons, all of
which do not imply the same idea of the anonymous or the face-to-face.

3   I use the term "neighborhood" in the vague way that people tend to speak about
these salons. It was because people in Casablanca, particularly women, spoke
about space in terms of who "could" go where that I began to work with the three
salons I describe in this chapter. The proximate salon as I describe it here might
not actually be in a specific, named quarter of the city, although it often is. Mobility and its lack, as expressed in "where one can go," made me attentive to the ways
that circulation of body, name, or assets over land, news, or stock markets were
important. For creating the "where" relates to how one arrives at that "place" (see
chapter 2, n. 14).

4   Hoodfar, *Between Marriage and the Market*, 185.

5   On ideas about the reliability of witnesses, see Rosen, *Bargaining for Reality*, 124–
26. On law and women's rights in Morocco, consult Moulay Rachid Abderazak,
La Femme et la loi au Maroc (Casablanca: United Nations/Fennec, 1991).

6   In French, this idea of "surface" can be expressed in everyday conversation.

7   In his study of marriage in urban Morocco, Mostafa Aboumalek notes the extent
to which people tend to be "homosocial" in their marriage choices. In rural areas,
this often means marrying within one's ethnic group. In cities, however, issues of
profession and education are prominent. It is revealing that whereas workers and
artisans tend to meet their future spouse either through family relations or a
known intermediary, professionals and managers tend to be much more likely to
meet their future spouse "by chance." He also remarks that in women of this
educated and working group, there is even less expectation of "formalism" (i.e., a

tendency to work via intermediaries) than among men. Further study of where such "chance" encounters can take place is surely necessary, as is the way in which these are articulated with the step of introducing the chosen partner to the world of the family and neighbors. See Mostafa Aboumalek, *Qui épouse qui: Le mariage en milieu urbain* (Casablanca: Afrique Orient, 1994), 196.

8 Jean Tiberi, originally the mayor of the fifth district of Paris, then became the mayor of the whole city. During the period of my research, he was accused of having had the town hall pay his wife, Xavière, to act as a consultant and produce a report. Xavière did write a report—a very short and ill-written one—that put her in the center of controversy about corruption in town hall. One particularly amusing article by Judith Perrignon was published by the newspaper *Libération* following Xavière's case being thrown out of court due to procedural problems. In "And Déssange Created Xavière," *Libération*, 6 January 2000, 14, we get a blow-by-blow account of how the mayor's wife's old-fashioned bourgeois bun was transformed by Jacques Déssange. The hairdresser, who was "brave" enough to set his scissors to Xavière's hair, later suggested that he was about to "position himself as an image consultant."

9 *Entourer* means to circle, to enclose; your "entourage" is composed of people who "circle" around you.

10 Fatima Mernissi suggests that such a place is perhaps necessary to how one learns through observation. Growing in cocoonlike warmth might be necessary to sprout wings strong enough to carry you out to discover other worlds:

> Aunt Habiba said that anyone could develop wings. It was only a matter of concentration. The wings need not be visible like the birds': invisible ones were just as good, and the earlier you started focusing on the flight, the better. But when I begged her to be more explicit, she became impatient and warned me that some wonderful things could not be taught. "You just keep alert, so as to capture the sizzling silk of the winged dream," she said. But she also indicated that there were two prerequisites to growing wings: "the first is to feel encircled and the second is to believe that you can break the circle. . . . A third condition, as far as you are concerned, my dear, is that you stop bombarding people with questions. Observing is a good way to learn, too." (*Dreams of Trespass: Tales of a Haram Girlhood*, 5)

11 Salon work, even in fast salons, does not correspond completely to the routinization of the fast food world. See Robin Leidner, *Fast Food, Fast Talk: Service Work and the Routinization of Everyday Life* (Berkeley: University of California Press, 1993).

12 Lahbabi, "Enquête dans les salons branchés," 54.

13 I am referring to Martin Heidegger's essay by that title, in which he discusses science and its specialization, but also the "modern world picture." For him, "The fundamental event of the modern age is the conquest of the world as picture. The word 'picture' (*Bild*) now means the structure image (*Gebild*) that is the creature

of man's producing which represents and sets before. In such producing man contends for the position in which he can be that particular being who gives measure and draws up the guidelines for everything that is." Such ideas have been crucial to many recent analyses of the nature of power and its relationship to sight. In the next chapter I take note of how Heidegger's development of these ideas in terms of "worldviews" has not, however, been as convincing to many recent analysts as has the idea that sight has something important to do with modern forms of power: Martin Heidegger, "The Age of the World Picture," trans. William Lovitt, in *The Question Concerning Technology and Other Essays*, (1938; New York: Harper and Row, 1977), 134.

14 Lindberg, *Theories of Vision*, 19. "The Burning Mirror" is the title of one of the works of Al-Kindi, whose work on optics was supported by three califs in ninth-century Baghdad (18).

15 Danielson, "Artists and Entrepreneurs," 303.

16 *Le Quotidienne*, no. 568 (10–16 April 1998): 21–22.

17 "La Coiffure marocaine au firmament," *Le Matin du Sahara et du Maghreb Magazine*, 24–30 August 1992, 20. Of course, just having one's work written up in the paper can set one up as a "radiant" center. For a fascinating personal account of how television can produce fame, see Joel Gordon, "Becoming the Image: Worlds of Gold, Talk Television, and Ramadan Nights on the Little Screen," *Visual Anthropology*, vol. 10, nos. 2–4 (1998), 247–63.

18 When a Franck Provost salon was recently set up in Casablanca, the grand opening celebration was marked by the presence of Provost himself. (Thanks to the owners of the shop for an invitation, which I unfortunately was unable to accept.) This also reminds us of the process by which bleached or dyed hair retains something of what it was "before" while demonstrating that the process is an act of artistry.

19 On the idea of the symbolic center, see Clifford Geertz, "Centers, Kings and Charisma: Reflections on the Symbolics of Power," in *Local Knowledge: Further Essays in Interpretive Anthropology* (New York: Basic Books, 1983), 121–46. For a recent reconsideration of charisma and kings in the Moroccan context, see Hammoudi, *Master and Disciple*, 82–85.

20 Weddings are the typical time for splurging. Mervat Atallah runs one of the most complete upscale salons in Cairo. She also offers advice on beauty in the *Al Ahram* daily newspaper. See, for instance, "Jamalek fi lila le 'amr" (Your beauty on the night of your life), *Al Ahram*, 26 October 1995, 26.

21 Quoted in Badran, *Feminists, Islam, and Nation*, 38.

22 Certeau, *L'invention du quotidiene*, 147 (English trans., 95).

23 Nelson Goodman, *Ways of Worldmaking* (Indianapolis: Hackett Publishing, 1978), 11. Thinking about versions in different worlds is not like working through approaches that imply diverse spheres, such as, for instance, Weber's three kinds of charisma. See H. H. Gerth and C. Wright Mills, *From Max Weber: Essays in Sociology* (New York: Oxford University Press, 1977), 294–96.

There is an inkling of what I am getting at in Marc Augé's description of "world" as the means by which meanings pass in a world where the "new frontiers are no longer mixed up with old borders of the social and cultural." However, Augé's account remains very general and he ends up suggesting that worlds are similar to fields of activity (e.g., "sport" or "medicine," "worker's world" or "peasant world"). For him, one belongs to a world, but this does not mean that one shares the same values as others in that world. I am suggesting that it is precisely the ways of attributing value that are at stake in world making. See Marc Augé, *Pour une anthropologie des mondes contemporaines* (Paris: Flamarrion, 1994), 129.

24 One example of an ethnographic approach that helps us think about face, power, and ethnicity in bodily terms is Dorinne Kondo's work on fashion, *About Face*.

25 Many have followed Weber in seeing modernity as a separating out of "spheres of value." The worlds I am working through here might help or hinder such a development, but they are not a priori confined by these terms. They are not domaine-specific a priori.

26 This includes how one masters these moves by practice and valuing particular kinds of excellence. One intriguing text that works with ideas of excellence in terms of specific worlds is Luc Boltanski and Laurent Thévenot's collaborative account of justification, *De la justification: Les économies de la grandeur* (Paris: Gallimard, 1991). Their analysis of the way judgment conflicts between worlds is thought-provoking (265). However, it seems to me that the worlds they contrast (e.g., domestic and commercial) are not related to given historical settings. They offer no sense of "place" from which to move out of the unstated situation that has produced the worlds they evoke. For a discussion of this work, see Jean-Noël Ferrié, "La traversée des mondes," *Mimesis: Imiter, représenter, circuler*, special issue of *Hermès* 22 (1998): 35–40.

5. FORMS AND PASSAGES

1 A good deal of attention has been paid to the globalizing policies of multinational and midsize businesses, as well as the work of the media in the dissemination of cultural practices and norms throughout the world. But little attention has been given to how small businesses such as salons, restaurants, and cafés play a part in this process. Although increasingly, studies of these places of sociability are being conducted, they are often conceived within a logic of "locality." One recent work that addresses issues of artisanal work in France is Susan Terrio, *Crafting the Culture and History of French Chocolate* (Berkeley: University of California Press, 2000).

2 This is neither an "event" nor a habit, but it might take on the characteristics of either of these, we don't yet know—neither does Jamal.

3 These comments, quoted by Barbara Letham Ibrahim, show not only that women in Egypt are working more and more outside the home but that once they are wage earners they develop a special link to each other and compare themselves to

housewives. See Barbara Letham Ibrahim, "Cairo's Factory Women," in Fernea, ed., *Women and the Family in the Middle East*, 299.

4   Compare to Evelyn Early's "Fatima: A Life History of an Egyptian Woman from Bulaq," in Fernea, ed. *Women and the Family in the Middle East*, 76–83. Also see Early's longer study of the Bulaq neighborhood, *Playing with an Egg and a Stone: Baladi Women of Cairo* (Cairo: American University of Cairo, 1993).

5   Michael Oakeschott, *Experience and Its Modes* (1933; Cambridge, England: Cambridge University Press, 1995), 309.

6   Goodman, *Ways of Worldmaking*, 31.

7   For another view of women and beaches, see Walter Armbrust, "Bourgeois Leisure and Egyptian Media Fantasies," in *New Media in the Muslim World: The Emerging Public Sphere*, ed. D. Eickelman and J. Anderson (Bloomington, IN: Indiana University Press, 1999), 106–32.

8   Thinking of versions makes us think again of the way the term might operate in terms of witness: Whose version is correct? Can they all be true? For thoughts on possible worlds and versions developed in terms of historical causality, see Geoffrey Hawthorne, *Plausible Worlds* (Cambridge, England: Cambridge University Press, 1991).

9   On frames, see Hubert Damish's detailed and insightful comments in *L'origine de la perspective* (Paris: Flammarion, 1987); translated by John Goodman as *The Origin of Perspective* (Cambridge, MA: MIT Press, 1995). Damish suggests that we should not be too hasty in characterizing the subject of perspective. He remarks that this subject, "which is said to be 'dominant' because it's established in a position of mastery, this subject holds only by a thread, however tightly stretched this might be." His discussion of this point in the context of his study of the Urbino perspectives is beyond the scope of the present project. Nonetheless, the way he notes how the line (rather than the point) of perspective draws the viewer into the painting, this line that is "indistinguishable from the labyrinth in which it traps the subject" (English trans., 389), reminds me of how the nets of the butterfly hunter draw him or her on to ever further conquests set in terms of how these nets are strung. I cannot help but relate this "labyrinth" to the idea that culture might be conceived in terms of "webs of meaning."

10   Goodman, *Ways of Worldmaking*, 6.

11   This might suggest that although the idea of self-narrative as giving direction to life might work well in some worlds, its nature and its very continuity might not carry it through to all worlds. Indeed, to move through a world certainly includes the ability to address such narratological questions as well as the kind of bodily techniques I foreground here. Cf. Anthony Giddens, *Modernity and Self Identity* (Oxford: Polity Press, 1991).

12   Samuel Ijsseling, *Mimesis* (Kampen, the Netherlands: Kok Pharos, 1997), 34. Also see my introduction, in *Mimesis*, 9–15.

13   Ijsseling, *Mimesis*, 76. Of course, we might remember that Mauss associated imitation with prestige. Michael Taussig addresses such prestige as well as how it

creates a complex relationship of colonizer to colonized in his *Mimesis and Alterity: A Particular History of the Senses* (London: Routledge, 1993). I have addressed this work and some of the debates among Taussig, Martin Jay, and Paul Stoller that ensued after its publication in "Anthropologie et mimesis chez Michael Taussig," in Ossman, ed., *Mimesis*, 57–62.

14 So Mauss's ideas about the prestigious model might encourage us to think about how prestige is differently developed and evaluated.

15 Thus, we might expand the kind of analysis Taussig describes in situations of colonial "first contact" not to those "second contact" reproductions of the White Man as other, but in terms of how patterns of prestige can include colonial forms in many diverse arguments on style and power (*Mimesis and Alterity*).

16 Abderrahmane Moussaoui, "Le Libas al sunnî: Les raisons sacrées d'un habit profane," in Ossman, ed., *Miroirs*, 77–86.

17 This is one of the points that Françoise Gaspard and Farhad Khosrokhavar address in interviews with young women who wear the hijab in *Le Foulard et la République* (Paris: La Découverte, 1995).

18 Michel Rocard, cited in *Le Monde*, 30 November 1989, 14.

19 Hassan II, on *L'heure de Verité* (The hour of truth), French national television channel "Antenne 2," December 17, 1989.

20 Georg Simmel, "Fashion" (1904), *American Journal of Sociology* 62, no. 6 (May 1957): 543.

21 Pierre Bourdieu, *Le sens Pratique* (Paris: Les éditions de minuit, 1980), 101; cited in James Faubion, ed., *Rethinking the Subject: An Anthology of Contemporary European Social Thought* (Boulder, CO: Westview Press, 1995), 39.

22 Of course, this is precisely what interests Bourdieu in his work on taste and distinction. See his *La Distinction: Critique sociale du jugement* (Paris: Éditions de minuit, 1979).

23 Voices from the margins seem to have been especially loud and varied in the past decade. Homi Bhabha's influential work, for instance, suggests, "Differences in culture and power are constituted through the social conditions of enunciation: the temporal caesura, which is also the historically transformative moment, when a lagged space opens up in-between the intersubjective reality of signs . . . deprived of subjectivity and the historical development of the subject in the order or social symbols." Rather than dwelling on the "position of relative strength" of the often middle-class migrants (or writers) to critique Bhabha, it might be more significant to think about why the marginalities he imagines seem to be particularly productive of narrative and, at the same time, limited by this centering on narration. See Homi K. Bhabha, *The Location of Culture* (London: Routledge, 1994), 242.

Debates on these representations and their relationship to sociological conceptions of marginality in French do not follow the lines of those produced in London or New York, but they are nonetheless sometimes quite passionate. See, for example, the controversy between Kmar Bendana and Fanny Colonna concerning Fanny Colonna with Zakya Daoud, eds., *Etre Marginal au Maghreb* (Paris: CNRS éditions, 1993) in *Correspondances: Bulletin de l'IRMC*, Tunis, nos. 11 (1993) and 18 (1994).

24 James Faubion, "Anthropology and Social Theory," in Bryan Turner, *Blackwell Companion to Social Theory*, 2d ed. (Oxford: Blackwell, 2000), 260.

6. BEAUTY'S EDGE

1 Clifford Geertz, "Common Sense as a Cultural System," in *Local Knowledge: Further Essays in Interpretive Anthropology* (New York: Basic Books, 1983), 88.

2 Bhabha, *The Location of Culture*, 227.

3 Ulf Hannerz, "Cosmopolitans and Locals in World Culture," in *Global Culture: Nationalism, Globalization and Modernity*, ed. M. Featherstone (London: Sage, 1990), 239.

4 Søren Kierkegaard, *Fear and Trembling,* trans. and introduction by Alstair Hanny (London: Penguin, 1985), 110.

5 This might bring to mind Elaine Scarry's comments about how we look at beautiful faces. But she follows the usual two-step of such debates: that this might lead us to some absolute recognition of the beautiful does not detract from the importance of noticing the way someone followed inspires the one who pursues. But the question of vulnerability cannot be posed in a strictly individual sense, nor can it be convincingly argued that following beauties necessarily implies some kind of meeting of souls or glimpses of a series of beautiful things. The idea of beauty as revealing justice draws us to think not of how beauties are made but how they appear, all of a piece to each of us, their symmetry guiding us. Scarry is surely right to focus on showing that "interest" is not the point of beauty, but because her approach is fundamentally individual and idealist, she too easily refutes the "historicist" idea of diverse ideas of beauty as the only alternative to the kind of pastel approach she poses. See Elaine Scarry, *On Beauty and Being Just* (Princeton, NJ: Princeton University Press, 1999), 70.

BAINS DOUCHES: Public baths in France.

BALADY (BELDI): Like *ʿroubi*; countrified.

BCBG: *Bon chic bon genre:* an often pejorative reference to a conservative, conformist style of dress.

BEURETTE: Feminine form of *beur*, a word that inverses the syllables of *arabe* in the manner of the popular *verlain* slang of French suburbs. The term refers to youths of Maghrebian origin in France and is now commonly used in standard French.

CIRCULATION: Traffic.

COIFFEUR: Hairdresser.

COIFFURE: Hair style.

COPIE CONFORME: A copy of a document that has been certified by a town official as to its being a precise replica of the original.

DRAGUE: Literally "to dredge"; to flirt.

DRARI: Young men.

ĠSALLA: Literally, the "washer": she rubs down women in the hammam.

HAJA (masc. haj): Literally, one who has made the pilgrimage to Mecca; a term of respect.

HALQA ʿLIA: Literally, "high hairdressing"; a translation from the French *haute coiffure*.

HAMMAM: Steam bath; sometimes referred to as a Turkish bath.

HELWA: A sugar and lemon juice mixture used to remove body hair.

HEMM: The blues.

HIJAB: Any of several styles of head covering. It is often worn to show a woman's religiosity and/or modesty. Particular versions, from color-

ful scarves to heavy black drapes, indicate ethnic, political, and religious affiliations. The root *hjb* implies ideas of protection.

HSHUMA: Shame.

JALLABIYA: A long cotton tunic worn by men in Egypt and the Arabian
Peninsula.

JELLABA: A long robe with a hood, originally worn by men but now
commonly worn by Moroccan women. It can be made of wool, heavy
cotton, or synthetic fabrics.

JNUN (plural of JEEN): Genies.

KHOL: Black eyeliner.

KHULKHAL: Bracelets, anklets.

MEDINA: Literally, "city," the term used to indicate the old parts of Moroccan cities as opposed to the newer sections first built during the
French Protectorate.

MESKEEN (fem: MESKEENA): Poor.

MISSION CIVILISATRICE: The doctrine that saw it as France's mission to
bring universal culture and science to less-developed nations she
colonized.

MODE (LA): Fashion.

MUHAJIBA: A woman who adopts the hijab.

PARISIENNE: A stylish, urbane woman, usually an inhabitant of Paris.

PAS DE BOURRÉ: The "drunk's step"; a basic two-step.

SIYYED EL BNAT: To hunt or fish for girls; to flirt.

SUQ: Market.

TELECOMMANDE: T.V. remote control.

TTARZ: Embroidery.

WESHMA: Tattoos.

'IN: Eye, source.

'ROUBI (fem: 'roubiyya): From the Arabic speaking countryside near
Casablanca or simply "countrified."

SELECTED BIBLIOGRAPHY

Abu-Lughod, Lila, ed. *Remaking Women: Feminism and Modernity in the Middle East.* Princeton, NJ: Princeton University Press, 1998.

Affergan, Francis. *La pluralité des mondes: Vers une autre anthropologie.* Paris: Albin Michel, 1997.

Ahmed, Leila. *Women and Gender in Islam: Historical Roots of a Modern Debate.* New Haven: Yale University Press, 1993.

Apostolidès, Jean-Marie. "Impudique Aurélie." *Communications*, no. 46 (1987), Paris, Le Seuil.

Appadurai, Arjun. *Modernity at Large: Cultural Dimensions of Globalization.* Minneapolis: University of Minnesota Press, 1996.

Armbrust, Walter. *Mass Culture and Modernism in Egypt.* Cambridge, England: Cambridge University Press, 1996.

——, ed. *Mass Mediations: New Approaches to Popular Culture in the Middle East and Beyond.* Berkeley: University of California Press, 2000.

Ash, Juliet, and Elizabeth Wilson, eds. *Chic Thrills: A Fashion Reader.* Berkeley: University of California Press, 1992.

Augé, Marc. *Pour une anthropologie des mondes contemporaines.* Paris: Flammarion, 1994.

Badran, Margot. *Feminists, Islam, and Nation: Gender and the Making of Modern Egypt.* Princeton, NJ: Princeton University Press, 1995.

Bahbah, Homi. *The Location of Culture.* London: Routledge, 1995.

Baron, Beth, and Nikki Keddie, eds. *Women in Middle Eastern History: Shifting Boundaries in Sex and Gender.* New Haven: Yale University Press, 1991.

Barthes, Roland. *Le system de la mode.* Paris: Le Seuil, 1967. Translated by Matthew Ward and Richard Howard as *The Fashion System.* Berkeley: University of California Press, 1990.

Battaglia, Deborah, ed. *Rhetorics of Self-Making.* Berkeley: University of California Press, 1995.

Baudelaire, Charles. *Oeuvres complètes.* Paris: Robert Laffont, 1980.

Baudrillard, Jean. *De la séduction.* Paris: Éditions Galilée, 1979.

——. *Simulacre et Simulations.* Paris: Gallillé, 1981. Translated by Paul Foss, Paul Patton, and Philip Beitch as *Simulations.* New York: Semiotext(e): 1983.

Beaugé, Gilbert, and Jean-François Clément, eds. *L'image dans le Monde Arabe.* Paris: Presses du CNRS, 1995.

Benhabib, Seyla. *Situating the Self: Gender, Community and Postmodernism in Contemporary Ethics.* Oxford: Polity Press, 1992.

Benjamin, Walter. *Illuminations: Essays and Reflections.* Edited and with an introduction by Hannah Arendt. New York: Schocken, 1969.

Berman, Marshall. *All That Is Solid Melts into Air: The Experience of Modernity.* 1982. New York: Penguin, 1988.

Boltansi, Luc, and Laurent Thévenot. *De la justification.* Paris: Gallimard, 1991.

Bordo, Susan. *Unbearable Weight: Feminism, Western Culture and the Body.* Berkeley: University of California Press, 1993.

Bourdieu, Pierre. *La Distinction: Critique sociale du jugement.* Paris: Éditions de minuit, 1979. Translated by Richard Nice as *Distinction: A Social Critique of the Judgement of Taste.* London: Routledge and Kegan Paul, 1984.

——. *Le sens Pratique.* Paris: Éditions de minuit, 1980.

Brown, Peter. *The Body and Society: Men, Women and Sexual Renunciation in Early Christianity.* New York: Columbia University Press, 1988.

Callaghan, Karen A., ed. *Ideals of Feminine Beauty: Philosophical, Social and Cultural Dimensions.* Westport, CT: Greenwood Press, 1994.

Certeau, Michel de. *L'invention du quotidien: Arts de faire.* 1980. Paris: Gallimard, 1990. Translated by Steven F. Randall as *The Practice of Everyday Life.* Berkeley: University of California Press, 1984.

Cohen, Jean-Louis, and Monique Elib. *Casablanca: Mythes et figures d'une aventure urbaine.* Paris: Hazan, 1998.

Communications: Parure, pudeur, étiquette, no. 46 (1987), Le Seuil, Paris.

Cox, Rupert. *The Zen Arts: An Anthropological Study of the Culture of Aesthetic Form in Japan.* Richmand, England: Curzon Press, 2000.

Damish, Hubert. *L'origine de la perspective.* Paris: Flammarion, 1987. Translated by John Goodman as *The Origin of Perspective.* Cambridge, MA: MIT Press, 1995.

Danieleson, Virginia. *The Voice of Egypt: Umm Kalthoum, Arabic Song and Egyptian Society in the Twentieth Century.* Chicago: University of Chicago Press, 1997.

Davis Taïëb, H., R. Bekkar, J.C. David, eds. *Espace Public, Parole Publique au Maghreb et au Machrek.* Paris: Maison de l'Orient/L'Harmattan, 1997.

de Grazia, V., with E. Furlough, eds. *The Sex of Things: Gender and Consumption in Historical Perspective.* Berkeley: University of California Press, 1996.

Dewey, John. *Art as Experience.* New York: Paragon Books, 1934.

Eagleton, Terry. *The Ideology of the Aesthetic.* London: Basil Blackwell, 1990.

Early, Evelyn. *Baladi Women of Cairo: Playing with an Egg and a Stone.* Boulder, CO: Lynn Reinner Publishers, 1993.

Eickelman, Dale, and Jon Anderson, eds. *New Media in the Muslim World: The Emerging Public Sphere.* Bloomington: Indiana University Press, 1999.

El Aoufi, Nourreddine. *La Société Civil au Maroc: Approches.* Rabat: Signes du Présent, Smer, 1992.

Fandy, Mamoun. "Political Science without Clothes: The Politics of Dress or Contesting the Spatiality of the State of Egypt." *Arab Studies Quarterly* 20, no. 2 (spring 1998): 87–103.

Fashion Theory. Special ed. 1, no 4 (December 1997).

Finkelstein, Joanne. *The Fashioned Self.* Philadelphia: Temple University Press, 1991.

Foucault, Michel. *L'archéologie du savoir.* Paris: Gallimard, 1969.

——. *Histoire de la sexualité.* 3 vols. Paris: Gallimard, 1984. Translated by Robert Hurley as *The History of Sexuality,* vol. 1. New York: Vintage, 1990; *The Use of Pleasure,* vol. 2. New York: Penguin, 1985; *The Care of the Self,* vol. 3. New York: Penguin 1986.

——. *Surveiller et Punir.* Paris: Gallimard, 1975.

Friedland, Richard, and Dierdre Boden, eds. *NoWhere: Space, Time and Modernity.* Berkeley: University of California Press, 1994.

Frontisi-Ducrous, Françoise, and Jean-Pierre Vernant. *Dans l'oeil du miroir.* Paris: Odile Jacob, 1997.

Gaspard, Françoise, and Farhad Khosrokhavar. *Le Foulard et la République.* Paris: La Découverte, 1995.

Gebauer, Gunter, and Christof Wulf. *Mimesis: Culture, Art, Society.* Translated by Don Reneau. Berkeley: University of California Press, 1994.

——. "Mimesis-Poiesis-Autopoiesis." *Paragrana, Internationale Zeitschrift für Historische Anthropologie,* vol. 4, no. 2, 1995.

Geertz, Clifford. *Local Knowledge: Further Essays in Interpretive Anthropology.* New York: Basic Books, 1983.

Giddens, Anthony. *Modernity and Self-Identify: Self and Society in the Late Modern Age.* Oxford: Polity Press, 1991.

Gonzalez-Quijano, Yves. *Les Gens du Livre: Edition et champ intellectuel dans l'Egypte républicaine.* Paris: CNRS éditions, 1998.

Gonzalez-Quijano, Yves, with Susan Ossman. "Nouvelles Cultures dans le Monde arabe." *Les Cahiers de l'Orient,* no. 20 (spring 1991).

Goodman, Nelson. *Ways of Worldmaking.* Indianapolis: Hackett, 1978.

Grewal, Inderpal, and Caren Kaplan, eds. *Scattered Hegemonies: Postmodernity and Transnational Feminist Practices.* Minneapolis: University of Minnesota Press, 1997.

Grosz, Elizabeth. *Volatile Bodies: Toward a Corporeal Feminism.* Bloomington: Indiana University Press, 1994.

Gupta. A., and J. Ferguson, eds. *Anthropological Locations.* Berkeley: University of California Press, 1997.

——, eds. *Culture, Power, Place: Explorations in Critical Anthropology.* Durham, NC: 1997.

Habermas, Jürgen. *The Structural Transformation of the Public Sphere: An Inquiry into a Category of Bourgeois Society.* 1962. Trans. Thomas Burger with Frederick Lawrence. Cambridge, MA: MIT Press, 1991.

—— The Theory of Communicative Action. Vol. 1, Reason and the Rationalization of Society. Boston: Beacon, 1984.

Haine, W. Scott. The World of the Paris Café: Sociability among the French Working Class, 1789–1914. Baltimore: Johns Hopkins University Press, 1996.

Harvey, David. Justice, Nature and the Geography of Difference. Oxford: Blackwell, 1996.

Hawthorne, Geoffrey. Plausible Worlds. Cambridge, England: Cambridge University Press, 1991.

Hebdige, Dick. Hiding in the Light. London: Routledge, 1989.

Heidegger, Martin. The Question Concerning Technology and Other Essays. Translated by William Lovitt. New York: Harper, 1977.

Held, David, and John B. Thompson, eds. Social Theory of Modern Societies: Anthony Giddens and His Critics. Cambridge, England: Cambridge University Press, 1989.

Herzog, Don. "The Trouble with Hairdressers." Representations, no. 53 (winter 1996): 21–43.

Hirsch, Eric, and Michael O'Hanlon. The Anthropology of Landscape: Perspectives on Place and Space. Oxford: Clarendon Press, 1995.

Hoodfar, Homa. Between Marriage and the Market: Intimate Politics and Survival in Cairo. Berkeley: University of California Press, 1997.

Ijsseling, Samuel. Mimesis. 1990. Kampen, Netherlands: Kok Pharos, 1997.

Jackson, Michael. Minima Ethnographica: Intersubjectivity and the Anthropological Project. Chicago: University of Chicago Press, 1998.

Jay, Martin. Downcast Eyes: The Denigration of Vision in Twentieth Century French Thought. Berkeley: University of California Press, 1994.

Kapchan, Deborah. Gender on the Market: Moroccan Women and the Revoicing of Tradition. Philadelphia: University of Pennsylvania Press, 1996.

Kierkegaard, Søren. Fear and Trembling. Translated and with an introduction by Alstair Hanny. London: Penguin, 1985.

Kilito, Adefettah. La Querelle des images. Casablanca: Eddif, 1995.

Kondo, Dorinne. About Face: Performing Race in Fashion and Theater. London: Routledge, 1997.

Lacan, Jacques. Ecrits I. Paris: Editions du Seuil, 1966.

Lakoff, Robin Tolmach. Face Value: The Politics of Beauty. Boston: Routledge and Kegan Paul, 1984.

Latour, Bruno. Nous n'avons jamais été modernes: Essai d'anthropologie symetrique. Paris: La décourte, 1997. Translated by Catherine Porter as We Have Never Been Modern. Cambridge, MA: Harvard University Press, 1993.

Leidner, Robin. Fast Food, Fast Talk: Service Work and the Routinization of Everyday Life. Berkeley: University of California Press, 1993.

Levin, D. M., ed. Modernity and the Hegemony of Vision. Berkeley: University of California Press, 1993.

Lindburg, David C. Theories of Vision from Al-Kindi to Kepler. Chicago: University of Chicago Press, 1976.

Lipovetsky, Gilles. *L'empire de l'éphémère: La mode et son destin dans les sociétés modernes.* Paris: Gallimard, 1987. Translated by Catherine Porter as *The Empire of Fashion: Dressing Modern Democracy.* Princeton, NJ: Princeton University Press, 1994.

MacIntyre, Alsdair. *After Virtue.* Notre Dame, IN: University of Notre Dame Press, 1981.

Malkki, Liisa. *Purity and Exile: Violence, Memory, and National Cosmology among Hutu Refugees in Tanzania.* Chicago: University of Chicago Press, 1995.

Marcus, George. *Ethnography through Thick and Thin.* Princeton, NJ: Princeton University Press, 1999.

Mauss, Marcel. *Sociologie et anthropologie.* 1950. Paris: Quadridge, PUF, 1985.

———. "Body Technics." Translated by Ben Brewster. *Economy and Society* 2, no. 1, 1973.

McCracken, Grant. *Big Hair: A Journey into the Transformation of Self.* London: Indigo: 1997.

Merleau-Ponty, Maurice. *Le visible et l'invisible.* Paris: Gallimard, 1964.

Mernissi, Fatima. *Dreams of Trespass: Tales of a Haram Girlhood.* Reading, MA: Addison Wesley, 1994.

Miller, Daniel. *Modernity: An Ethnographic Approach. Dualism and Mass Consumption in Trinidad.* Oxford: Berg Publishers, 1994.

Morin-Barde, Mireille. *Coiffures féminines du Maroc.* Aix-en-Provence, France: Edisud, 1997.

Mulvey, Laura. *Visual and Other Pleasures: Theories of Representation and Difference.* Bloomington: University of Indiana Press, 1989.

Naamane-Gessous, Soumaya. *Au-delà de toute pudeur.* Casablanca: Editions EDDIF, 1984.

Nabokov, Vladimir. *The Gift.* 1952. Translated by Michael Scammell with the collaboration of the author. New York: Vintage International, 1991.

Oakeschott, Michael. *Experience and Its Modes.* 1933. Cambridge, England: Cambridge University Press, 1995.

Ossman, Susan. *Picturing Casablanca: Portraits of Power in a Modern City.* Berkeley: University of California Press, 1994.

———, ed. *Mimesis: Imiter, représenter, circuler. Hermès* 22 (September 1998), CNRS Editions.

———, ed. *Miroirs maghrébins: Itinéraires de soi et paysages de rencontre.* Paris: CNRS Editions, 1998.

Pandolfo, Stefania. *Impasse of the Angels.* Chicago: University of Chicago Press, 1998.

Perrot, Philippe. *La Travail des apparences: Le corps féminin XVIIIe—XIXe siècle.* Paris: Le Seuil, 1984.

Rabinow, Paul. *Essays on the Anthropology of Reason.* Princeton, NJ: Princeton University Press, 1996.

———. *French DNA: Trouble in Purgatory.* Chicago: University of Chicago Press, 1999.

———. *French Modern: Norms and Forms of the Social Environment.* Cambridge, MA: MIT Press, 1989.

Raymond, André. *Le Caire.* Paris: Fayard, 1993.

Rorty, Richard. *Philosophy and the Mirror of Nature.* Princeton, NJ: Princeton University Press, 1979.

Rosen, Laurence. *Bargaining for Reality: The Construction of Social Relations in a Muslim Community.* Chicago: University of Chicago Press, 1984.

Rugh, Deborah. *Reveal and Conceal: Dress in Contemporary Egypt.* Syracuse, NY: Syracuse University Press, 1986.

Rybczynski, Witold. *Home: A Short History of an Idea.* London: Penguin, 1987.

Sennett, Richard. *The Conscience of the Eye: The Design and Social Life of Cities.* New York: Alfred A. Knopf, 1991.

Seremetakis, Nadia, ed. *The Senses Still: Perception and Memory as Material Culture in Modernity.* Chicago: University of Chicago Press, 1996.

Shapin, Steven. *A Social History of Truth: Civility and Science in Seventeenth Century England.* Chicago: University of Chicago Press, 1994.

Singerman, Diane. *Avenues of Participation.* Princeton, NJ: Princeton University Press, 1996.

Slyomovics, Susan. *The Object of Memory: Arab and Jew Narrate the Palestinian Village.* Philadelphia: University of Pennsylvania Press, 1998.

Steele, Valerie. *Paris Fashion: A Cultural History.* 1988. London: Berg, 1998.

Taylor, Lucien, ed. *Visualizing Theory: Selected Essays from V.A.R. 1990–1994.* London: Routledge, 1994.

Taussig, Michael. *Mimesis and Alterity: A Particular History of the Senses.* London: Routledge, 1993.

Williams, Bernard. *Shame and Necessity.* Berkeley: University of California Press, 1993.

Zdatny, Steven. "Fashion and the Class Struggle: The Case of *Coiffure.*" *Social History* 18, no. 1 (1993): 53–72.

——, ed. *Hairstyles and Fashion: A Hairdresser's History of Paris, 1910–1920.* Oxford: Berg Press, 1999.

Zola, Emile. *Au Bonheur des Dames.* Paris: Pocket, 1998. Translated by Kristin Ross as *The Ladies' Paradise.* Berkeley: University of California Press, 1992.

INDEX

Aboumalek, Mostafa, 182–83 n.7
Abu-Loghud, Lila, 77
Advertising, 16–17, 24–25, 27, 51, 125–26
African salons, 55
Al-Kindi, Abu Yusuf Yaqub, 125
Al-Tunsi, Bayram, 20
Americanization, 35–36
Ancien régime, 64–65
Anywhere bodies, 74; advertising and, 24–25, 27; forgetting and, 27–28; heaviness and, 16–23; hybridization, 8–9; images of orient, 6–7; imitation, 13–14; as lacking quality, 20–22; new orientalism, 7–16; seasons of fashion, 5–6. *See also* En-lightening
Apostiledès, Jean-Marie, 34
Appadurai, Arjun, 163–64 n.5
Architecture, 64, 68–69
Artistry, special salons, 123–24, 127, 138
Athletic clubs, 53–54, 175 n.44
Audiovisual media, 41
Augé, Marc, 185 n.23
Authenticity, 14, 26–29, 48
Avant-garde, 37, 172 n.19

Background bodies, 25–27, 63, 97–98, 131–32, 148; displacement of, 52–55; Moroccan women, 38–39, 44, 48; rural/urban contrast, 35–40, 56–57; ways of walking, 30, 32, 36–39; as

whole/real, 45–52. *See also* Epics of opening
Badran, Margot, 129
Barbershop, 74, 76, 79–80
Barber stalls, 86
Baroque, 22
Barthes, Roland, 166 n.6
Baths. *See* Hammam
Baudelaire, Charles, 11, 25–26, 166–67 n.9
BCBG (bon chic bon genre), 5, 165 n.3
Beautician-client pairs, 92–96; fast salons, 114, 118–20; at special salons, 122–23
Beauticians, 80–81; communication with, 92–96; gaze of, 93–94; hierarchy, 115, 117; listening skills, 118, 119; male, 89–91, 180–81 n.44; management of, 116–17; medical imagery and, 116–17, 118; owners/operators, 82–84, 90, 115; as remainders, 84–85; reputation, 111, 123–24; skill, 80–85; socioeconomic backgrounds, 82–85; specialists, 28, 112
Beauty: learning, 31–32; local cultures and, 3, 97–98, 100; new orientals and, 7–16
Beauty salons: Cairo, 90–91, 109–10; Casablanca, 2, 23–24, 70–71, 80–81, 90, 175 n.45; comfort and conversation, 71–80; comparison with hammam, 49–50; decor, 71–72, 111–12, 114, 133;

Beauty salons (*cont.*)
experience and, 71–72; and fast salons, 90, 93, 112–20; mixed-sex, 55, 79–80, 89–90, 114–15, 179 n.32; as objects of study, 1–2; Paris, 90, 106–7; as protected spaces, 100–101, 110, 112, 139, 141; routines, 62–63, 72, 135–38; salon pour dames, 69–70; as space of danger for men, 63, 79, 89, 104; special salons, 121–29, 137–38, 143; tools, 66, 67. *See also* Proximate salons

Belles dames, 20, 76–77, 79, 149
Benhabib, Seyla, 75, 131
Beurettes, 55
Bhabha, Homi, 156–57, 187 n.23
Bnoussina, Khadija, 12
Boden, Dierdre, 100
Bodies, 174 n.36; body sizes and, 19–20, 168 n.15; hammam as site of, 46–47; male, 76–77; social, 50–51. *See also* Anywhere bodies; Background bodies; En-lightening; Heaviness; Lightness
Bodily technique, 40–45, 82, 84, 113
Bohemians, 149
Bon chic bon genre (BCBG), 5, 165 n.3
Bordellos, 76, 79–80
Bordo, Susan, 21–22
Boulaq, 133–35
Boundaries, 143–44
Bourdieu, Pierre, 57, 151–52
Bourgeoisie, 64, 69
Boyle, Robert, 76
Brands, 6, 141; tattoos (*weshma*), 12–13, 167–68 n.10
Buiguine, 11–12, 166 n.9
Bureaucrats, 77
Butterfly imagry, 38, 99–101, 154

Cafés, 68–69, 79, 178 n.14
Cairo, 2–3, 68; beauty salons, 90–91, 109–10; hammam, 45, 47–48, 50, 52
Camille Aubin salons, 114
Carlier, Omar, 47, 50, 68

Casablanca: beauty salons, 2, 23–24, 70–71, 80–81, 90, 175 n.45; cafés, 68–69; hammam, 48, 50, 53–55; political discussions, 74–75; ways of walking, 36–37

Categorization, 6–7, 165 n.6
Catholic Church, 17
Certeau, Michel de, 129–30, 171 n.14
Chevelure, La (Baudelaire), 25–26
Child workers, 43, 172–73 n.28
Cities, new, 70
Citizens, 63, 87
Civility, 73, 76–77
Classicism, 22
Class issues, 56–57, 69
Claudel, Camille, 37
Closure, 60–62, 87
Clothing, 15–18, 173–74 n.32; heavy garments, 17–18; jellaba, 48, 56–57, 173 n.32; unwearable, 11, 14. *See also* Hijab
Clubs, 69, 178 n.18
Coffee houses, 68
Coiffure, 70, 181 n.44
Colonization, 68, 186–87 n.13, 187 n.15
Comfort, 71–80
Common concerns, 75–76, 89
Communication, 50–51, 71–80; with beautician, 92–96; cafés, 79, 178 n.14; common concerns, 75–76, 89; density of talk, 50–51, 79, 101–3; en-lightening and, 78–79; Greek Forum, 87–88; in mixed-sex salons, 55, 79, 89; political, 73–75; and spaces for talk, 51–52
Community: fraternity and, 75–76
Comparisons, linked, 2–4, 130, 160–62, 163–64 n.5
Competition, 58, 138, 143
Constraints, 36–39, 103, 136, 176 n.53; hammam and, 46, 51; mirrors and, 87–88; on movement between worlds, 144–49; shame, 77–78, 107–8
Continuity, 49–52
Contradictions, 23, 139–40

Franck Provost salons, 184 n.18
Fraternity, 75–77
Freedom, 159
French Enlightenment, 77
Frontisi-Ducroux, Françoise, 87
Furlough, Ellen, 170 n.9

Gaultier, Jean Paul, 13
Gaze, 11, 24, 34, 37, 69, 118; of beauticians, 93–94; of father, 136–37, 141–42, 145–49; of husbands, 105–6, 140–42; mirrors and, 85–96; proximate salons and, 104–5, 108–10; shame and, 77–78, 99, 111–12; skill and, 81–82
Gebauer, Gustave, 57, 95–96
Geertz, Clifford, 154
Generalization, 155–56, 160
Gessous, Soumaya Naamane, 77–78
Giddens, Anthony, 177 n.1
Girard, René, 57
Globalization, 5–6, 50–51, 163–64 n.5, 185 n.1
'gl (reason), 77–78
Gnawa Diffusion, 60–62, 79
Goodman, Nelson, 130–31, 139–40, 142
Greek thought, 86–88, 179 n.30
Gregory, Derek, 177 n.1
Grewal, Inderpal, 165 n.6
Grisette, 33, 170 n.7
Gubar, Susan, 164–65 n.2
Guerlain, 121

Habermas, Jürgen, 73–74
Habitus, 41–42, 84, 129, 151
Hair, 11, 13, 24–26; menus, 112–13, 117–18, 126–27
Hairdressers, 54–55, 71–72, 74; male, 54, 89–91, 180–81 n.44, 181 n.45
Hammam (baths), 37, 45–52, 175 n.44; Cairo, 45, 47–48, 50, 52; Casablanca, 48, 50, 53–55; continuity and, 49–52; displacement of, 52–55; men in, 19, 46–47, 52; Paris, 52–53

Hannerz, Ulf, 157–58
Hasham. *See* Shame
Hassan II, 148–49
Hawanim, 20
Heaviness, x, 15–23, 40, 120, 154–55, 162; forgetting, 27–28, 97; light images of, 22–23; tradition as, 17–19. *See also* En-lightening; Lightness
Hegel, G. W. F., 151
Heidegger, Martin, 183–84 n.13
Herzog, Don, 73–74, 76
Hierarchy, 115, 117, 128, 142, 161, 164 n.7
Hijab: as fashion, 23, 56, 176 n.48; muhajibat, 55–57, 91, 109–10, 115; reveiling, 90–91; unveiling, 15–17, 39, 71; veil crises, 56, 147–49
History, 14–15, 46–48, 150
Homogenization, 72
Honor, 103–5, 137
Hoodfar, Homa, 82, 103
Hospitality, 68
Hshouma, 77–78
Husbands, gaze of, 105–6, 140–42
Hybridization, 8–9
Hygiene, 17–18, 47–48, 53, 72

Ideals, 73–75
Identity, 146
Ijsseling, Samuel, 144
Imitation, 13–14, 44, 143–44, 149. *See also* Mimesis
Independence, 38
Individualism, 77
Information, 73, 105, 124; fashion publications, 7–11
Instruction, 57–58, 176 n.53. *See also* Learning
Intelligent eyes, 75–76, 99, 112, 130, 160, 162
Interests, 158–59, 188 n.5
"Invitation au voyage, L'" (Baudelaire), 11, 166–67 n.9

Models, 9, 24–25, 55, 58–59
Modernity, 11–13, 44, 47, 77, 106, 185 n.24; literature of, 1–2; parisienne and, 32–33; philosophy, 75, 91
Mohsen, Safia K., 168 n.13
Moral landscape, 130–31
Moral self, 75
Moroccan salon, 68
Morocco: as backward, 38–39, 44, 48; literary salons, 68. *See also* Casablanca
Mosque of Paris, 52–53
Motoloch, Harvey L., 100
Movement, 134–35; reputation and, 136–37; staying put, 136–44; through social worlds, 1, 58–59, 144–49; ways of walking, 30, 32, 36–39, 96, 138
Muhajibat, 55–57, 91, 109–10, 115

Nabaraouy, Céza, 38
Names, special salons and, 121–27, 138
Narcissus, 87
Natural products, 26–28
Negotiation, 169 n.22, 173 n.31
Neighborhood, 182 n.3; honor and, 103–4; Paris, 106–7
Neighborhood salons. *See* Proximate salons
Nelly, 8–9, 29
Newness, 149–53, 156–59
New woman, 70, 178 n.17
Nonsense, 138–39, 153
Nostalgia, 19, 47, 52, 157

Oakeschott, Michael, 138–39
Observation, 183 n.10
Odalisque, 46
Oikos, 87–88
Ombre Elle (Gnawa Diffusion), 60–62
Opening. *See* Epics of opening
Opinion, L', 26
Optics, 88
Oral transmission, 44
Orientalism, 6–7, 46; distant places, 25–26; modernity and, 11–12; new orientals, 7–16
Other, 6–7, 76, 78, 152, 165–66 n.6; mirrors and, 87, 95–96; newness and, 156–58

Pagnol, Marcel, 31–32, 35, 169–70 n.2
Paris, 2–3, 33, 35, 69, 171–72 n.17, 183 n.8; athletic clubs, 53–54, 175 n. 44; beauty salons, 90, 106–7; hammam in, 52–53; versions of, 24–25
Parisiennes, 32–33, 55, 160, 170 nn. 7, 10
Pascon, Paul, 166 n.6
Passions, discipline of, 21–22
Perrot, Philippe, 23
Personalism, 77
Perspective, 186 n.9
Philosophy, 75, 91
Physiology of the Parisienne, 33
Picturing Casablanca: Portraits of Power in a Modern City (Ossman), 163 n.3
Plutarch, 85
Point of view, 95–96
Political clubs, 69, 178 n.18
Political communication, 73–75
Politics of disappearance, 21–23
Pompadour, Madame de, 64, 65
Pose, 7–9, 166 n.7
Postmodernism, 165 n.2
Power, 95–96, 125, 144–49
Powers, Madelon, 178 n.14
Practice, 82, 84–85, 95
Prestige, 144, 186–87 n.13
Privacy, 64–65
Privatization of experience, 75
Production: of newness, 149–53; of styles, 98–99, 128–29, 139
Products, 70, 74, 127–28, 176 n.47; makeup, 27–28, 59, 140; natural, 26–28
Pro-Mod, 114
Protected spaces, 100–101, 110, 112, 139, 141, 159
Protectorate, 146

Susan Ossman is Associate Professor at the American University of Paris and Visiting Professor at Georgetown University. She is the author of *Picturing Casablanca: Portraits of Power in a Modern City* (University of California Press, 1994) and editor of *Miroirs maghrébins. Intinéraires de soi et paysages de rencontre* (CNRS Editions, 1998) and *Mimesis: Imiter, représenter, circuler* (Hermès/CNRS, 1998).

Library of Congress Cataloging-in-Publication Data

Ossman, Susan.

Three faces of beauty : Casablanca, Paris, Cairo / Susan Ossman.

p. cm.   Includes bibliographical references and index.

ISBN 0-8223-2881-x (cloth : alk. paper)

ISBN 0-8223-2896-8 (pbk. : alk. paper)

1. Beauty, Personal—Cross-cultural studies.

2. Fashion—Social aspects—Cross-cultural studies.

3. Beauty shops—Cross-cultural studies. I. Title.

GT499 .O77 2002   391.6—dc21   2001047513